Global Power Shift

Comparative Analysis and Perspectives

Ample empirical evidence points to recent power shifts in multiple areas of international relations taking place between industrialized countries and emerging powers, and between states and non-state actors. Yet there is a dearth of theoretical interpretation and synthesis of these findings, and a growing need for coherent approaches to understand and measure the transformation. This edited series aims to bring together scholars from all major world regions as well as different disciplines in order to discuss and possibly blend their different approaches and provide new frameworks for the understanding of global affairs and the governance of global power shifts.

For further volumes:
http://www.springer.com/series/10201

Sandra Heep

China in Global Finance

Domestic Financial Repression and International Financial Power

Springer

Sandra Heep
Freiburg University
Institute of Chinese Studies
Freiburg
Germany

ISBN 978-3-319-02465-3 ISBN 978-3-319-02466-0 (eBook)
DOI 10.1007/978-3-319-02466-0
Springer Cham Heidelberg New York Dordrecht London

Library of Congress Control Number: 2014930573

Printed on acid-free paper

Springer is part of Springer Science+Business Media (www.springer.com)

Acknowledgements

First and foremost, I would like to express my gratitude to Sebastian Heilmann for his permanent support and motivation, his inspiring ideas and critical feedback. However, above all, I would like to thank him for having encouraged me to delve into the world of finance. I would also like to thank Hanns Maull for his support of this project from its very beginning. Besides, I am grateful to the Scholarship Foundation of Rhineland-Palatinate (Stipendienstiftung Rheinland-Pfalz) for having funded the first 2 years of this project. I would also like to express my gratitude to the Krupp Foundation (Alfried Krupp von Bohlen und Halbach-Stiftung) whose generous financial support made my research stay at the Chinese Academy of Social Sciences possible. During my time as a visiting scholar in Beijing, I enjoyed the generous help of Zhang Ming who shared his insights and introduced me to a number of knowledgeable individuals. Interview partners, many of whom wished to remain unnamed, helped me gain a deeper understanding of the political economy of China's financial system. In place of all of them, I would like to express my gratitude to Vivek Arora of the International Monetary Fund for his kind support. Back in Germany, I benefited from the hospitality of the German Institute for International and Security Affairs (Stiftung Wissenschaft und Politik) that hosted me as a visiting scholar. During my time at the Institute, I gained many insights into Japan's political economy from Hanns Günther Hilpert to whom I am very grateful for his support. I would also like to thank my colleague Marcus Conlé who repeatedly challenged my assumptions from an economist's point of view and thus helped me to refine my thoughts.

Contents

1 Introduction 1

2 Financial Power and the Developmental State 7
2.1 Conceptualizing the Developmental State 7
2.2 China as a Developmental State? 12
2.3 A Typology of Financial Power 15
2.3.1 Conceptualizing Financial Power 15
2.3.2 Relational, Structural and Institutional Financial Power 16
2.3.3 Manipulative and Non-manipulative Financial Power 18
2.3.4 Objectives of Financial Power 19
2.3.5 Summary: Types of Financial Power 20
2.3.6 Relational Financial Power 20
2.3.7 Institutional Financial Power 21
2.3.8 Structural Financial Power 22
2.4 Preview of the Argument 25

3 Financial Repression and Structural Financial Power 27
3.1 Liberalizing Japan's Financial Markets 28
3.1.1 The Political Economy of Japan's Postwar Financial System 28
3.1.2 The Impact of the Growing Government Deficit 29
3.1.3 Structural Changes and Foreign Pressure to Liberalize 31
3.2 The Political Economy of China's Financial System 34
3.2.1 Turning Shanghai into an International Financial Center . . . 34
3.2.2 China's System of Financial Repression 37
3.2.3 China's Bond Markets 41
3.2.4 China's Equity Markets 44
3.2.5 China's Approach to Capital Controls 46
3.2.6 Financial Repression and Structural Financial Power 50
3.3 Financial Repression and Liberalization Pressures 52

4 Financial Repression and Currency Internationalization 55
4.1 Determinants of Currency Internationalization 56
4.1.1 Aspects of Currency Internationalization 56
4.1.2 Economic Determinants of Currency Internationalization . . . 56
4.1.3 Political Determinants of Currency Internationalization 57
4.1.4 Internationalization of 'Negotiated Currencies' 58
4.2 Japan's Failure to Internationalize the Yen 59
4.2.1 Foreign Exchange Controls in the Early Postwar Years 60
4.2.2 The Effects of the Yen-Dollar Agreement 60
4.2.3 Currency Internationalization in the Wake of the Plaza Agreement 62
4.2.4 Changing Attitudes Following the Asian Financial Crisis . . . 63
4.3 China's Approach to Currency Internationalization 65
4.3.1 China's Criticism of US 'Monetary Hegemony' 65
4.3.2 Motives for the Internationalization of the Renminbi 67
4.3.3 Assessing the Renminbi's Potential to Internationalize 69
4.3.4 Policy Measures Promoting the Renminbi's Internationalization 74
4.3.5 Experimenting with Controlled Currency Internationalization 77
4.4 Wholesale Rejection Versus Controlled Internationalization 78

5 Financial Repression and Relational Financial Power 81
5.1 Japan as a Creditor 82
5.1.1 Japan's Emergence as a Creditor 82
5.1.2 State Control over Japan's Capital Flows 84
5.1.3 Japan's Vulnerability to Its Major Debtor 84
5.2 Investing China's Foreign Exchange Reserves 85
5.2.1 Functions of Foreign Exchange Reserves 86
5.2.2 China's Foreign Exchange Reserves 88
5.2.3 Debating China's Creditor Status 90
5.2.4 Investment Agencies 93
5.2.5 China's Relational Financial Power 98
5.3 Financial Repression and the Power of Creditors 104

6 Developmental States in the Bretton Woods Institutions 107
6.1 Structures of Power in the IMF and the World Bank 108
6.1.1 Voting Shares 108
6.1.2 Provision of Funds 110
6.1.3 Staff and Management 111
6.2 Japan's Challenge to the Washington Consensus 112
6.2.1 Fighting for a Larger Voting Share 112
6.2.2 Challenging the World Bank 114
6.2.3 Japan's Asian Monetary Fund Proposal 118

6.3 China on the Rise in the Bretton Woods Institutions? 119
6.3.1 China's Voting Power in the Bretton Woods Institutions . . . 119
6.3.2 China's Financial Contributions to the Bretton Woods Institutions 123
6.3.3 China's Representation Among Staff and Management 126
6.3.4 A Beijing Consensus? 129
6.4 Financial Repression and Institutional Financial Power 132

7 Conclusion 135

Interviews 139

References 141

List of Figures

Fig. 2.1	Types of financial power	21
Fig. 3.1	Chinese exports of goods and services (percentage of GDP)	36
Fig. 3.2	Chinese exports of goods and services (annual percentage growth)	36
Fig. 3.3	Distribution of assets in China's financial sector	39
Fig. 3.4	Distribution of assets in China's banking sector	40
Fig. 3.5	Chinese corporate financing	40
Fig. 3.6	Bond issuance volume by major issuers	43
Fig. 4.1	Chinese GDP in comparison	70
Fig. 4.2	Chinese per capita GDP in comparison	71
Fig. 4.3	Chinese total trade in comparison	72
Fig. 4.4	Chinese CPI inflation	72
Fig. 5.1	China's international investment position	86
Fig. 5.2	China's foreign exchange reserves	89
Fig. 5.3	China's twin surplus	89
Fig. 5.4	Chinese holdings of US securities	97
Fig. 5.5	Chinese holdings of US securities in percent of Chinese reserves	98
Fig. 5.6	China's excess reserves in comparative perspective	100

List of Tables

Table 2.1 Aspects, mechanisms and sources of financial power 26
Table 4.1 Selected swap agreements involving the renminbi 75
Table 5.1 China's international investment position 87
Table 6.1 Voting power in the IMF 123
Table 6.2 Voting power in the World Bank 124
Table 6.3 Contributions to the NAB 126
Table 6.4 Contributions to IDA16 127

Abbreviations

ABC	Agricultural Bank of China
ASEAN	Association of Southeast Asian Nations
BIS	Bank for International Settlements
BOC	Bank of China
BOJ	Bank of Japan
BRIC	Brazil, Russia, India, China
CBRC	China Banking Regulatory Commission
CCB	China Construction Bank
CCP	Chinese Communist Party
CDB	China Development Bank
CIC	China Investment Corporation
CNH	Chinese Yuan traded in Hong Kong
CNY	Chinese Yuan
CSRC	China Securities Regulatory Commission
DTC	Developing Countries and Countries with Economies in Transition
EU	European Union
FDI	Foreign Direct Investment
FILP	Fiscal Investment and Loan Plan
G20	Group of Twenty
GAB	General Arrangements to Borrow
GDP	Gross Domestic Product
GNP	Gross National Product
HKMA	Hong Kong Monetary Authority
IBRD	International Bank for Reconstruction and Development
ICBC	Industrial and Commercial Bank of China
IDA	International Development Association
IMF	International Monetary Fund
JPY	Japanese Yuan
MITI	Ministry of International Trade and Industry
MOF	Ministry of Finance
MOFCOM	Ministry of Commerce

NAB	New Arrangements to Borrow
NAFMII	National Association of Financial Market Institutional Investors
NDRC	National Development and Reform Commission
NPL	Non-Performing Loan
OECD	Organisation for Economic Co-operation and Development
OECF	Overseas Economic Cooperation Fund
PBOC	People's Bank of China
QDII	Qualified Domestic Institutional Investor
QFII	Qualified Foreign Institutional Investor
RQFII	Renminbi Qualified Foreign Institutional Investor
SAFE	State Administration of Foreign Exchange
SASAC	State-Owned Assets Supervision and Administration Commission
SDR	Special Drawing Rights
SOE	State-Owned Enterprise
TIC	Treasury International Capital System

Chapter 1
Introduction

In the years since the outbreak of the global financial crisis, the international financial architecture has undergone fundamental changes. Costly bank bail-outs, massive stimulus programs and growing welfare expenses resulting from the economic slump caused by the crisis have put tremendous strains on government budgets in the developed world, thus making many western countries ever more dependent on external financing. At the same time, a number of capital-rich emerging market countries have attracted attention not only as increasingly important engines of global economic growth, but also as international creditors expected to come to the rescue of the ailing western world. Against the backdrop of these developments, reforms of the governing structures of the International Monetary Fund and the World Bank have given emerging market countries a bigger say in the world's most important international financial institutions, thus bolstering their ability to put their mark on the global financial system. With the dollar's international attractiveness suffering from America's enormous government deficit and its inflationary monetary policy and the euro teetering on the edge of collapse, a window of opportunity has opened up for new players to launch a currency offensive and improve the international standing of their domestic money. Similarly, a regulatory backlash against the financial services industry in the developed world has provided rising economic powerhouses with the chance to push their financial markets towards greater international importance.

China has in recent years come into the picture as the most important emerging player in international finance. The country first stepped into the limelight in 2007 when it established a sovereign wealth fund in order to increase the return on part of its enormous foreign exchange reserves by diversifying away from the US dollar and investing in riskier asset classes, thereby drawing attention to the fact that China was becoming one of the world's biggest creditor nations. While the western world initially displayed a hostile attitude towards China's growing importance as an international investor due to fears that it might bolster China's political clout, the country became increasingly attractive as a creditor in the eyes of many western leaders in the face of ever more dismal public finances. With its tremendous financial resources and its economy sustaining its growth momentum while large

S. Heep, *China in Global Finance*, Global Power Shift,
DOI 10.1007/978-3-319-02466-0_1, © Springer International Publishing Switzerland 2014

parts of the developed world found themselves on the brink of recession, China was well placed to push for a bigger voting share in the IMF and the World Bank. Only 3 years into the crisis, China's leaders thus succeeded at securing the number 3 position for their country in both institutions. Also in reaction to the global financial crisis, China in 2009 began to introduce measures aimed at internationalizing its currency in an effort to try and decrease its dependence on the US dollar. In line with this policy, the Chinese government at the same time announced its intention to turn Shanghai into a global financial center by 2020.

China's growing prominence in the international financial architecture is highly reminiscent of Japan's rise in global finance in the 1980s. Just as China's growing financial clout, Japan's rising financial power mainly resulted from its emergence as one of the world's leading creditor countries (Chin and Helleiner 2008: 88). Due to Japan's increasingly important role as a provider of funds, many analysts were convinced that the country had replaced the United States as the world's leading financial power (e.g. Gilpin 1987). However, at the same time, others drew attention to the purely domestic role of Japan's currency and its underdeveloped financial markets that severely constrained the country's financial clout (e.g. Strange 1990).

Even though the question of the extent of Japan's financial power was high on the academic research agenda, no attempt was made to explain how Japan's political economy influenced the country's financial power potential or, in other words, why Japan's political economy was conducive to the acquisition of some aspects of financial power while it was a hindrance to others. Similarly, no attempt has so far been made to examine the implications of the basic features of China's political economy for its ability to acquire power in international finance.

Against the backdrop of China's increasingly proactive international financial policies, numerous studies on China's growing financial clout have been conducted in recent years. However, the majority of these studies have been constricted to the analysis of individual sources of China's increasing financial power, such as the country's creditor status or the internationalization of its currency. For this reason, these studies have failed to provide a systematic assessment of China's financial power potential.[1] Moreover, they have generally not been informed by a theoretical account of the concept of financial power and have thus fallen short of contributing to our understanding of the different types, mechanisms and sources of power in international finance.[2] On the other hand, the theoretical study of financial power has strongly focused on the United States and hence implicitly on the ways in which

[1] For analyses of China's growing foreign exchange reserves and its creditor status see Ma and Zhou (2009), Zhang and He (2009), Wang (2007b), Fung et al. (2007). For analyses of the internationalization of the renminbi see McCauley (2011), Yu and Gao (2011), Subacchi (2010), Dobson and Masson (2009), Murphy and Yuan (2009).

[2] Notable exceptions to this rule have been studies by Gregory Chin and Eric Helleiner (2008) and Daniel Drezner (2009). The former has inspired this work both in terms of its approach to the subject of China's financial power via a comparison with the case of Japan and the application of Susan Strange's (1988) differentiation between structural and relational power.

financial power may develop within the framework of a neoliberal political economy.[3] Yet the ways in which financial power may be acquired by more interventionist states that do not fit into the neoliberal category have so far remained largely unexamined in this strand of literature.

In view of these research gaps, this book brings the model of the developmental state into the study of financial power in an attempt to deepen our understanding of the relationship between a state's basic politico-economic structures and its ability to acquire power in international finance. By comparing China's present role in global finance with Japan's position in the 1980s, it highlights the implications of the defining features of the developmental state for its ability to acquire financial power. At the same time, however, it draws attention to the crucial differences between the Chinese and the Japanese version of the developmental state and examines how these have affected the countries' financial power potential.

Drawing on Chalmers Johnson's (1982) seminal conceptualization of the developmental state as well as a contemporary interpretation of the crucial features of the developmental states of Japan, South Korea and Taiwan by Arthur Kroeber (2011), this book holds that developmental states pursue comprehensive industrial strategies aimed at securing rapid economic growth and technological autonomy in order to enhance the nation's international competitiveness. Referring to the work of John Zysman (1983), it highlights the dependence of the developmental state on a financial system that allows it to control the allocation of financial resources in line with its industrial policy objectives. It thus holds that developmental states maintain systems of financial repression characterized by the prevalence of bank loans over securities, administratively set interest rates and strict capital controls to ensure the availability of national savings for domestic investment. Due to the centrality of a system of financial repression to the developmental state's political economy, it pleads for a minimalist definition of the developmental state according to which the developmental state pursues comprehensive industrial strategies to enhance the nation's international competitiveness by controlling the allocation of financial resources in a financial system characterized by a high national saving rate.

In line with this definition, this book argues that despite the differences between China's political economy and the political economy of the developmental states of Japan, South Korea and Taiwan, China should be considered a developmental state since the Chinese party-state heavily relies on its control over the financial system to pursue its comprehensive industrial policy objectives. At the same time, however, the book takes account of the most crucial differences between the political economies of China and the traditional East Asian developmental states by introducing a distinction between classic developmental states that pursue the above mentioned goals as ends in themselves and instrumental developmental states that only embrace these objectives with the ultimate goal of securing the ruling elites' grip on power.

[3] See for example the collection of essays in Andrews (2006a).

With regard to the concept of financial power, this book draws on the insights of the leading scholars of the subject to establish a typology of financial power in the context of interstate relations. Subscribing to a definition of financial power as a state's ability to influence the behavior of other states through its financial relations with them, it refers to the work of Susan Strange (1988) and Eric Helleiner (2006) in its distinction between relational and structural financial power that it complements with the category of institutional financial power. It understands relational financial power as a state's ability to influence the behavior of other states directly by applying financial pressure or providing financial incentives. Structural financial power, on the other hand, is considered a state's ability to influence other states indirectly through the structure of the international financial system. Last but not least, institutional financial power is understood as a state's ability to influence other states indirectly through the decisions of international financial institutions concerning the provision of credit and the conditions upon which this provision relies. In line with the work of Strange (1990) and Helleiner (1989, 1992), it holds that relational financial power mainly derives from a state's creditor status. Structural financial power, on the other hand, is understood to be mainly based on the international pulling power of a state's financial markets and the function of its currency as an international store of value, while institutional financial power is considered to derive from a state's voting share, its contribution of funds and its representation among the staff and management of the International Monetary Fund and the World Bank.

Bringing the model of the developmental state into the literature on financial power, this book argues that the political economy of the developmental state inhibits the acquisition of structural financial power since its system of financial repression is not compatible with the development of financial markets that are capable of attracting international investors on a significant scale. For the same reason, the developmental state is not in a position to acquire structural financial power by establishing its currency as an international store of value since this aspect of currency internationalization requires the very development of financial markets that is not compatible with a system of financial repression. However, since the developmental state's system of financial repression allows it to withstand currency appreciation pressures, it provides it with the power to maintain current account surpluses, an aspect of structural financial power that has so far been neglected in the literature due to its focus on the financial power of neoliberal political economies.

Closely related to the latter point is the fact that developmental states typically embark on export-led growth strategies since their systems of financial repression are not compatible with a focus on consumption. The political economy of the developmental state is thus also highly conducive to the acquisition of relational financial power since export-led growth strategies result in current account surpluses that turn the developmental state into a net creditor. Due to their strong creditor positions, developmental states are not as dependent on the acquisition of institutional financial power as neoliberal states whose relational financial power tends to be much more limited since they frequently run current account deficits and fail to muster significant degrees of control over their financial systems. The developmental state's relational financial power thus renders the acquisition of institutional financial power largely dispensable since the exercise of both relational and institutional financial power may be directed at the same objectives.

Against the backdrop of the theoretical framework developed in Chapter 2, Chapter 3 analyzes the political economy of the financial systems of the Japanese and the Chinese developmental state. It shows that China's state-ownership of the dominant financial institutions has provided it with a significantly higher degree of control over the country's political economy and has made it much more immune to liberalization pressures than its Japanese counterpart.

Chapter 4 looks into the determinants of currency internationalization and examines the differences between the Japanese and the Chinese approaches to the internationalization of their domestic money. It points out that the Japanese authorities were heavily opposed to the yen's internationalization since they feared that it would undermine the country's system of financial repression. It then analyzes China's strategy of promoting the renminbi's role as an international medium of exchange while at the same time maintaining the country's capital controls, arguing that a long-standing tradition of policy experimentation and strong nationalistic feelings have encouraged China's authorities to choose this unorthodox approach even though they should be expected to try and prevent a global role of the renminbi on the very same grounds that their Japanese counterparts opposed the internationalization of the yen.

Chapter 5 explains why the political economy of the Japanese and the Chinese developmental state resulted in a focus on the generation of growth through the export sector and thus turned the countries into net creditor states. Moreover, it analyzes the relational financial power deriving from this creditor status and draws attention to China's state-ownership of the dominant financial institutions that has provided it with a particularly high degree of control over the country's capital outflows and thus bolstered its relational financial power.

Chapter 6 focuses on the policies of the Japanese and the Chinese developmental state towards the Bretton Woods institutions. It argues that China has not yet developed an ambition for ideological leadership similar to the one of the Japanese developmental state in the 1980s since its leaders are too concerned with maintaining growth and stability in a country that on account of its low per-capita GDP still has to be considered a developing country.

The analysis of Japan's financial system and its international financial policies focuses on the developments between the early 1970s, when liberalization pressures began to threaten the country's developmental political economy, to the late 1990s, when the Asian Financial Crisis prompted Japan to assume a more active role in the international financial system. The analysis of China's financial system and its international financial policies concentrates on the developments between 2007, when China established its sovereign wealth fund, and mid-2013, when a cut had to be made to finish this project.

While the analysis of Japan's political economy is solely based on a review of the existing scholarly literature, the analysis of China's political economy and its international financial policies heavily draws on primary sources such as speeches given by Chinese government officials, reports and statistics provided by Chinese government agencies as well as Chinese and English media reports.[4] A deeper understanding of China's international financial policies could be gained during a research fellowship at the Chinese Academy of Social Sciences in Beijing from October 2008 to March 2009 and a brief period of field research in the Chinese capital from October to November 2010, during which 45 interviews with 31 Chinese and foreign journalists, researchers, government officials, banking staff and representatives of international organizations and business associations were conducted.

In addition to deepening our understanding of the relationship between financial repression and financial power, this book aims to make a contribution to a number of related research areas. For one, it aims to shed light on the domestic factors that have shaped China's increasingly proactive international financial policies in recent years. Secondly, it aims to enhance our understanding of the Chinese political economy by putting it in comparative perspective, an endeavor that due to the assumed uniqueness of the Chinese politico-economic system only has a very limited number of examples to follow (Kennedy 2011). Thirdly, it aims to increase our insight into the economic and political implications of financial repression and to draw attention to the importance of financial repression to the maintenance of authoritarian regimes. Last but not least, it aims to reinvigorate the model of the developmental state as a category that is highly useful to the study of China as an emerging economic powerhouse that refuses to follow some of the main tenets of neoliberalism. At a time that is witnessing growing distrust towards the economic consensus that has long dominated the western world, it thus attempts to make a modest contribution to the understanding of alternative politico-economic models that may come to put their mark on the global political economy of the present century.

[4] All quotations from Chinese sources have been translated by the author.

Chapter 2
Financial Power and the Developmental State

This chapter develops the theoretical framework that will guide the empirical analysis. To this end, it first characterizes the political economy of the developmental state. In a second step, it examines if China falls into the category of the developmental state. It then introduces the concept of the instrumental developmental state to account for the crucial differences between China's political economy and the political economy of the classic developmental states of Japan, South Korea and Taiwan. In a third step, it develops a typology of financial power and provides an overview of the implications of the political economy of the developmental state for its financial power potential.

2.1 Conceptualizing the Developmental State

The classic conceptualization of the developmental state was put forward in Chalmers Johnson's (1982) seminal analysis of the foundations of Japan's economic success in the postwar era, *MITI and the Japanese Miracle*.[1] Johnson (1982: 19) famously distinguished between regulatory or market-rational and developmental or plan-rational states, arguing that the regulatory state "concerns itself with the forms and procedures [. . .] of economic competition," while the developmental state "will give greatest precedence to industrial policy, that is, to a concern with the structure of domestic industry and with promoting the structure that enhances the nation's international competitiveness." Depicting the pursuit of industrial policy as the defining feature of the developmental state, Johnson (1982: 24–25) argued that the developmental state's industrialization efforts were driven by a nationalistic desire to catch up with the advanced industrialized nations. On the basis of Johnson's work, the model of the developmental state came to play a key role in

[1] Two decades earlier Alexander Gerschenkron (1962) had developed similar ideas.

S. Heep, *China in Global Finance*, Global Power Shift,
DOI 10.1007/978-3-319-02466-0_2,

academic attempts to explain the highly successful industrialization process of East Asian nations after the Second World War.

Even though Johnson's model seemed in danger to slide into obscurity in the 2000s, a number of authors have in recent years invoked the idea of the developmental state in studies of China's political economy, thus aiming to put China's development experience in a comparative perspective (Kroeber 2011; Beeson 2009; Nee et al. 2007; Baek 2005; Tsai and Cook 2005). In his comparison of China's political economy since the beginning of economic reforms in the late 1970s with the political economies of the classic East Asian developmental states of Japan, South Korea and Taiwan, Arthur Kroeber (2011) has provided a lucid and comprehensive overview of the most important features of the political economy of the developmental state. Partly drawing on the work of Gordon White and Robert Wade (1988), Kroeber (2011: 45–46) argues that the classic developmental states were characterized by a set of features concerning the conditions, goals, mechanisms and outcomes of development.

According to Kroeber, the crucial conditions upon which developmental states rely are a high national saving rate, a high level of education, equitable land distribution, an effective bureaucracy and ethnic homogeneity. He argues that the developmental states' goals of "rapid economic growth through comprehensive industrial development" (Kroeber 2011: 45) and technological autonomy are pursued on the basis of the state's control over financial resources, market prices for goods that have no strategic importance, private ownership of industrial companies, promotion of exports and discouragement of foreign direct investment and imports of consumption goods. Last but not least, he claims that the catch-up strategies of developmental states usually result in high economic growth, comprehensive industrialization, trade surpluses, underdeveloped service industries and inefficient financial systems (Kroeber 2011: 45–46).

While this comprehensive list of characteristics certainly provides an illuminating picture of the classic developmental states, not all the features mentioned by Kroeber should be considered equally important. According to Johnson's model, the defining feature of the developmental state is the pursuit of industrial policy aimed at enhancing the nation's international competitiveness. On the other hand, the state's ability to engage in industrial policy making crucially relies on its control of a domestic financial system characterized by a high national saving rate that allows it to determine the allocation of financial resources in line with its policy objectives. Even though the other features that Kroeber considers defining of the developmental state certainly did play a role in the industrialization of Japan, South Korea and Taiwan, we should be careful to avoid the model's conceptual overstretch if we want to ensure its applicability to the analysis of the development experiences of other countries. In this book, we therefore subscribe to a minimalist definition of the developmental state according to which the developmental state pursues comprehensive industrial strategies to enhance the nation's international competitiveness by controlling the allocation of financial resources in a financial system characterized by a high national saving rate.

The centrality of the structure of the financial system to the characteristics of a state's political economy in general and the political economy of the developmental state in particular has been widely acknowledged. As Theda Skocpol (quoted after Woo-Cumings 1999: 11) has pointed out,

> [t]he answers to [questions about financial resources] provide the best possible general insight into the direct or indirect leverage a state is likely to have for realizing any sort of goal it may pursue. For a state's means of raising and deploying financial resources tell us more than could any other single factor about its existing (and its immediately potential) capacities to create or strengthen state organizations, to employ personnel, to co-opt political support, to subsidize economic enterprises, and to fund social programs.

With regard to the developmental state, Meredith Woo-Cumings (1999: 10) has pointedly argued that "[f]inance is the tie that binds the state to the industrialists." Johnson (1987: 147) has also highlighted the importance of "government reliance on financial and monetary means to guide and control private activities" in the classic developmental states of Japan, South Korea and Taiwan. However, the most comprehensive analysis of the relationship between a state's financial system and its ability to pursue comprehensive industrial strategies has been put forward by Zysman (1983) in his seminal analysis of *Financial Systems and the Politics of Industrial Change*.[2]

In his examination of the links between financial structures and the ability to pursue industrial policies, Zysman distinguishes between three types of financial systems: The first type is a system based on capital markets in which the long-term funding of companies relies on the issuance of securities. In such a system, the main function of banks is to provide short-term lending. Prices are set by the market, and the central bank is almost exclusively concerned with the control of monetary aggregates. In the words of Zysman (1983: 70), "[t]his model places banks, firms, and governments in distinct spheres from which they venture forth to meet as autonomous bargaining partners." This type is exemplified by the financial systems of the US and the UK.

The second type is a credit-based system dominated by government-administered prices. In such a system, capital markets only play a very limited role in the acquisition of corporate funds, yet they allow the government to issue securities for its own funding. The provision of bank credit thus lies at the heart of the system of corporate finance. The government does not only facilitate bank lending and money creation, but also determines important prices to influence economic development. Due to the administrative setting of prices, markets in such a system tend to be in disequilibrium. Administrative interference is thus necessary to establish a balance between borrowers and lenders. According to

[2] Instead of adopting Johnson's (1982) distinction between regulatory and developmental state, Zysman (1983: 75) distinguishes between the government as an economic regulator, an economic administrator and an economic player. According to Zysman (1983: 326, footnote 14), the difference between a player state and a developmental state is that the former may intervene without pursuing a developmental objective. Zysman thus considers the developmental state a subcategory of the player state.

Zysman (1983: 71), "[t]he issue in this system is [thus] not whether government intervenes to affect the allocation of financial resources; the question is who controls the process and how." Hence "the state's entanglement with industry becomes part and parcel of the financial system" and "[t]he borderline between public and private blurs, not simply because of political arrangements, but because of the very structure of the financial markets" (1983: 72). This type is exemplified by the French and the Japanese financial systems.

The third type is also a credit-based system, yet it is dominated by a limited number of financial institutions that are independent of state support and thus characterized by a lesser degree of government interference. In this system, "[g]overnment does not have the apparatus to dictate allocative choices to the financial institutions and consequently it has no independent instruments in the financial system with which to influence companies" (Zysman 1983: 72).[3] Nevertheless, banks "can serve as policy allies for government, on terms negotiated between the government and finance" (Zysman 1983: 22). This type is exemplified by the German financial system.

Having developed this typology of financial systems, Zysman (1983: 76) argues that state control over the allocation of credit "is the single discretion necessary to all state-led industrial strategies" since it allows the state "to enter continuously into the industrial life of private companies and to influence their strategies in the way that a rival or partner would." To avoid misunderstandings, it needs to be emphasized that Zysman does not deny the possibility of industrial policy making relying on mechanisms other than the control over financial resources. A state may resort to a whole range of measures in its conduct of industrial policy making, including the imposition of sectoral trade barriers, the introduction of local-content requirements or the promotion of specific industries through tax incentives. However, such measures require a time-consuming regulation on a case-by-case basis and thus only permit the state to concern itself with a very limited range of issues. On the other hand, the universal applicability characteristic of selective credit allocation allows the state "to exert influence across a range of issues without having to develop regulatory or administrative apparatus for each specific case" (Zysman 1983: 77). In other words, a regulatory state may occasionally engage in industrial policymaking on the basis of mechanisms other than selective credit allocation, while "a state in which the developmental orientation predominates" (Johnson 1982: 17) can only pursue its comprehensive industrial strategy if it is in a position to exercise control over the allocation of financial resources.

Zysman (1983: 76) does not only draw attention to the importance of selective credit allocation in the state's control over private companies, but also points out that "[e]ven with public companies, the financial instruments for selectively

[3] As Zysman (1983: 72) has pointed out, both the second and the third type are associated with late and rapid development, while the first type has usually emerged within the context of earlier industrial growth. According to Zysman (1983: 63), the reason for the association of credit-based systems with rapid and late economic growth is the fact that companies operating in such an environment need to secure large amounts of funds to be able to achieve high growth rates.

allocating credit provide government a refined set of tools to supplement the appointment of management or the imposition of broadly defined government policy directives." Due to the significance of selective credit allocation to the pursuit of industrial policies, he then argues that only a credit-based financial system that is dominated by government-administered prices allows the state to pursue a comprehensive industrial strategy. However, it needs to be pointed out that a state may in principle also be able to pursue industrial policy objectives within the framework of a credit-based system dominated by financial institutions if the ownership structure of these institutions allows the government to influence their lending decisions. On the other hand, it appears highly unlikely that a state that actively influenced the lending decisions of state-owned financial institutions to achieve industrial policy objectives would refrain from administratively controlling interest rates to ensure low costs of funding. It is therefore more important to draw attention to the fact that the features of a credit-based system dominated by government-administered prices can be combined with state-ownership of the dominant financial institutions to establish a fourth type of financial systems that allows for the highest possible degree of state control over the allocation of financial resources. As the following chapters will show, this type is exemplified by the Chinese financial system.

Against the backdrop of this analysis, it becomes evident that the financial systems of developmental states either belong to the second or the fourth type of the financial systems characterized above. In other words, developmental states either rely on a credit-based system dominated by government-administered prices or a credit-based system that combines government-administered prices with state-ownership of the dominant financial institutions to control the allocation of financial resources in their pursuit of industrial policy objectives. In any case, the financial systems of developmental states are characterized by the prevalence of bank loans over securities, state control of interest rates guaranteeing low costs of funding and the maintenance of capital controls that ensure the availability of national savings for domestic investment. Developmental states thus rely on a policy of financial repression to facilitate rapid economic growth and strengthen the nation's international competitiveness.

The concept of financial repression was originally introduced into the economic literature by Ronald McKinnon (1973) and Edward Shaw (1973) to characterize the shallow financial systems of developing countries. Both authors argued that financial repression was a severe obstacle to economic growth. McKinnon (1973: 69) pointed out that financial repression reduces the amount of funds available for investment since the introduction of interest rate ceilings and the resulting low real returns prompt savers to reduce "their holdings of money and near-monies far below what might be considered socially optimal." At the same time, he argued that financial repression limits the number of potential recipients of funds since interest rate ceilings guarantee that funding is only available for completely safe borrowers or is contingent on political connections while the majority of the population "remain financially 'repressed', although they own a significant proportion of the deposits on which the expansion of bank credit to the favored enclaves is based" (McKinnon 1973: 70–71). In the case of the developmental state, the channeling of funds into sectors and companies that are considered strategically important also has the effect of preventing a large number of potential investors from acquiring funds. However, in contrast to the shallow financial systems that are the focus of McKinnon and Shaw's analyses, the financial systems of developmental states are characterized by high saving rates that allow the authorities to provide industry with an ample amount of funds for investment at the expense of consumers who remain financially repressed.

2.2 China as a Developmental State?

The question if China should be considered a developmental state has been given divergent answers in the literature. It is generally agreed that China's political economy has shared some important features with the classic developmental states of Japan, South Korea and Taiwan since the beginning of the reform policies in the late 1970s. Considering administrative resource management a variety of industrial policy, some authors have even argued that the People's Republic of China has been a developmental state ever since its inception in 1949 (Beeson 2009; White 1988). In contrast with this view, Johnson (1982) explicitly excluded communist political economies from the category of developmental states. He characterized communist states as "plan ideological" as opposed to "plan rational" developmental states, arguing that in the former, "state ownership of the means of production, state planning, and bureaucratic goal-setting are not rational means to a developmental goal [but] fundamental values in themselves, not to be challenged by evidence of either inefficiency or ineffectiveness" (Johnson 1982: 18).

However, with the introduction of economic reforms, the Chinese party-state has discarded at least some of its ideological convictions and has instead adopted a more pragmatic approach to development. On the other hand, the Chinese authorities have continued to engage in state planning and to pursue comprehensive industrial strategies in order to enhance the nation's international competitiveness. China has thus displayed crucial features of the developmental state. Chinese policymakers already formulated the developmental goals of achieving rapid economic growth, comprehensive industrialization and technological autonomy in the Four Modernizations program whose official launch in 1978 marked the beginning of the reform period (Kroeber 2011: 46). Fourteen years later, during his famous southern tour, China's then paramount leader Deng Xiaoping underlined the regime's developmental orientation when he argued that "[o]ur country must develop; if we do not develop then we will be bullied. Development is the only hard truth" (quoted after Kroeber 2011: 204, footnote 4).

With regard to state planning and the formulation of comprehensive industrial strategies, Sebastian Heilmann (2011b: 33) has drawn attention to the fact that instead of gradually abandoning strategic planning, China has "reinvigorated its ambitions in long-term, cross-sectoral coordination of economic, social, technological, and environmental development from the mid-1990s through the 2000s." As Heilmann (2011b: 33) has pointed out, Chinese policymakers have designed "multi-year programs with binding and indicative targets in virtually every sector, from space programs and infrastructural construction through human resources and education to health care, cultural life, and tourism." However, Chinese development planning has undergone substantial changes in the last two decades. While planning was originally considered a "substitute for markets", a reform of the planning system in the early 1990s required planners to take domestic and global market developments into consideration and to "plan with and for markets" (Heilmann 2011b: 34). Planning was thus redefined as a key element of economic macro-management along with fiscal and monetary policy aimed at facilitating comprehensive economic coordination.

In its pursuit of comprehensive industrial strategies, the Chinese party-state has crucially relied on its high degree of control over the domestic financial system that combines government-administered prices with state-ownership of the dominant financial institutions. Characterized by extensive financial repression, this system has allowed the authorities to control the allocation of the country's financial resources and to channel them into sectors and companies that are considered strategically important. Also with regard to the role of the financial sector, post-socialist China has thus displayed a crucial feature of the classic developmental states.[4]

However, attention has also been drawn to the features of China's political economy that distinguish the country from the classic developmental states of Japan, Korea and Taiwan. For one, it has been argued that China's economic reforms have not exclusively been promoted to achieve rapid economic growth in order to turn China into a 'rich and powerful country' (fuqiang guo), but have also been considered a means to ensure the Chinese Communist Party's (CCP) continued grip on power and maintain political stability (Breslin 1996).[5] Besides, it has been pointed out that diverging political demands from different factions of the party, the decentralization of economic decision making and the high degree of intra-bureaucratic contestation in China's system of fragmented authoritarianism have "obstructed the formulation of a coherent and effective national economic development strategy" (Breslin 1996: 691) and resulted in a tendency to favor incremental changes over comprehensive reforms.[6]

Even more importantly, it has been highlighted that China differs from the classic East Asian developmental states insofar as its economy is characterized

---

[4] The centrality of the state's control over the financial system to the classification of China as a developmental state has also been emphasized by Baek (2005).

[5] For a detailed analysis of the political priorities of China's reform process see Susan Shirk (1993).

[6] For a similar argumentation see Kroeber (2011: 47), Beeson (2009: 23–24), Tsai and Cook (2005: 50). The term 'fragmented authoritarianism' was coined by Lieberthal and Oksenberg (1988).

by a high degree of state ownership as a legacy of its communist past.[7] As Kroeber (2011: 50) has pointed out, China avoided the path of privatization in contrast to most other postcommunist economies, instead focusing on the deregulation of prices and the creation of competitive markets. In the 1990s, China began to privatize small enterprises without strategic significance. However, the party-state refrained from forsaking its ownership of major state-owned enterprises (SOEs) in strategically important sectors such as finance, infrastructure and resources. Even though there are also numerous private companies that play a crucial role with respect to the creation of employment opportunities, they are of very limited size and are thus in no position to exercise political influence (Kroeber 2011: 50–51).[8]

Do we have to qualify our classification of China as a developmental state in the light of these differences between the Chinese political economy and the political economy of the classic developmental states? Even though the decentralization and fragmentation of China's political system have at times hampered the formulation and implementation of a coherent development strategy, China has taken the art of planning to a new level since the overhaul of its planning system in the early 1990s and should thus be considered a 'plan rational' developmental state. However, an important difference between China and the classic developmental states is the fact that China's development planning has been heavily influenced by the political priority of securing the CCP's grip on power. Not least in order to protect the political interests of the ruling elites, the state-owned sector continues to play a crucial role in China's political economy. The Chinese party-state thus wields a degree of influence over the country's political economy that is much higher than in the classic developmental states since its control of SOE management through the nomenklatura system provides it with additional leverage over their business strategies.[9] Due to the importance of the state-owned sector to the preservation of the CCP's control over the country's political economy, comprehensive privatization is not deemed an option to be considered in the country's development planning. In contrast to the classic developmental states that pursue the goals of securing rapid economic growth, technical autonomy and international competitiveness as ends in themselves, we should thus consider China an *instrumental developmental state* that only embraces these objectives with the ultimate goal of securing the ruling elites' grip on power.

---

[7] A related difference between China's political economy and the political economy of the classic developmental states is the fact that China's development strategy has crucially relied on the promotion of foreign direct investment for the creation of a competitive export sector, whereas the classic developmental states strongly discouraged FDI. While export-oriented business groups in Japan and South Korea greatly benefited from the state's control over the allocation of credit, China's financial system has been geared to support state-owned enterprises that focus on the domestic market (Kroeber 2011: 48, Beeson 2009: 27–28, Baek 2005: 494).

[8] For a similar argumentation see Tsai and Cook (2005: 50–53). For an analysis of the ownership structure of the Chinese economy see OECD (2005). On the process of SOE reform see Heilmann (2011a).

[9] On the Chinese nomenklatura system see Heilmann and Kirchberger (2000).

2.3 A Typology of Financial Power

Against the backdrop of the preceding examination of the most crucial features of the political economy of the developmental state, the following sections analyze the different types, sources and mechanisms of financial power in the context of interstate relations.

2.3.1 *Conceptualizing Financial Power*

For an inquiry into the implications of the political economy of the developmental state for its ability to acquire financial power, a clear definition of the concept of financial power is needed. However, as Benjamin Cohen (2001: 433) has noted, the "meaning of power [. . .] is no better understood in monetary scholarship than it is in the broader IR literature." Even though the concept of financial power is widely used in the international political economy literature, a comprehensive typology of financial power is still lacking. The following sections therefore draw on the insights of the leading scholars of the subject to establish a typology of financial power that will guide the empirical analysis provided in the following chapters.[10]

In line with Cohen (2001: 430), this book holds that the realm of international finance "encompass[es] all the main features of monetary relations between states – the processes and institutions of financial intermediation [. . .] as well as the creation and management of money itself."[11] In other words, it contends that the realm of international finance comprises the processes and institutions of the international allocation of credit as well as the distribution and the value of the currencies in which international transactions are denominated.

With regard to the definition of financial power, Cohen (2001) has pointed out that we need to distinguish between an internal and an external dimension of power. While the internal dimension of power "corresponds to the dictionary definition of power as a capacity for action," the external dimension of power "corresponds to the dictionary definition of power as a capacity to control the behavior of others" (Cohen 2001: 433). In this book, the concept of financial power solely refers to the external dimension of financial power.

According to David Andrews (2006b: 8), external financial power "is manifest when one state's behavior changes because of its monetary relationship with

[10] To be more specific, the aim of this section is to provide a comprehensive typology of the external dimension of financial power in the context of interstate relations.

[11] In his definition of the realm of international finance, Cohen (2001: 430) draws on Strange (1988: 88) who argued that a "financial structure can be defined as the sum of all the arrangements governing the availability of credit plus all the factors determining the terms on which currencies are exchanged for one another."

another state."[12] In line with this understanding, this book subscribes to a definition of financial power as a state's ability to influence the behavior of other states through its financial relations with them.[13] Power is thus specified as financial if the means through which it is exercised and the sources from which it derives are located in the realm of finance, not if the outcomes that it achieves belong to the realm of finance. Put differently, financial power is defined as power *deriving from the realm of finance* as opposed to power *applied to the realm of finance*.

2.3.2 Relational, Structural and Institutional Financial Power

For the development of a typology of international financial power, it is useful to recall Susan Strange's distinction between relational and structural power in the areas of finance, production, security and knowledge that she developed in her writings on the global political economy.[14] Convinced that structural power was becoming increasingly important in the international system, she argued against the widespread belief in American hegemonic decline.[15] In line with conventional definitions of the concept of power, Strange (1988: 24) thought of relational power as "the power of A to get [. . .] B to do something they would not otherwise do." In contrast with relational power, she defined structural power as

> the power to shape and determine the structures of the global political economy within which other states, their political institutions, their economic enterprises and (not least) their scientists and other professional people have to operate [. . .] Structural power, in short, confers the power to decide how things shall be done, the power to shape frameworks within which states relate to each other, relate to people, or relate to corporate enterprises. (1988: 24–25)

Whereas she thought of relational power as being exercised by the application of direct pressure, she considered structural power a more indirect form of power. According to Strange (1988: 31), the possessor of structural power

> is able to change the range of choices open to others, without apparently putting pressure directly on them to take one decision or to make one choice rather than others. Such power is less 'visible'. The range of options open to the others will be extended by giving them opportunities they would not otherwise have had. And it may be restricted by imposing

---

[12] The concepts of financial power and monetary power are used synonymously in the literature.

[13] We prefer the use of the concept of influence rather than change since the exercise of a state's financial power may also prevent another state from changing its behavior.

[14] For Strange's distinction between structural and relational financial power see for example Strange (1982, 1986, 1988, 1990). The following sections have been influenced by Eric Helleiner (2006) who also discusses the relationship between the concepts of structural power proposed by Strange (1988), Guzzini (1993), Cohen (1977) and Kirshner (1995) but arrives at different conclusions.

[15] For the classic definition of hegemonic stability theory see Keohane (1980).

costs or risks upon them larger than they would otherwise have faced, thus making it less easy to make some choices while making it more easy to make others.

Even though Strange's concept of structural power has greatly influenced international relations theory, it cannot be denied that it is highly ambiguous. As Guzzini (1993: 456–457) has pointed out, Strange in fact refers to two different concepts of structural power without explicitly drawing a distinction between them. According to Guzzini's (1993: 457) interpretation, Strange uses the concept of structural power in the sense of a power to shape structures as well as in the sense of a power deriving from "international structures set up in a way that decisions in some countries are systematically tied to and affect actors in the same and other countries." In Guzzini's understanding, the main difference between these forms of structural power is that the first one – indirect institutional power – is exercised with intent, whereas the second one is by definition non-intentional. While the concept of indirect institutional power refers to an actor's ability to manipulate the formal rules and informal customs that govern the global political economy, the concept of non-intentional power refers to an actor's ability to exercise influence deriving from its position within a certain politico-economic structure.[16] However, Guzzini's implicit claim that power deriving from structures can only be exercised in an unintentional way is not convincing. A structurally powerful state's domestic decisions may have repercussions for other states that are not intended. Yet a structurally powerful state may also exploit its position to deliberately influence outcomes in other states in line with its policy preferences.

While Strange used the term 'structural power' to refer to both power deriving from structures and power applied to structures, this book narrows its conceptual scope down in order to avoid ambiguity and solely uses it to refer to power deriving from structures. It can be briefly illustrated how this narrower conception of structural power affects the distinction between structural and relational power in the realm of finance. According to Strange (1982: 81), the ability of the United States to extract wealth from other states is one of the most important aspects of American structural financial power. Since this power derives from the dollar's role as the global core currency in the structure of the international financial system, the ability to extract wealth qualifies as structural financial power according to our definition. Strange (1986: 55) also pointed out that due to the dominant position of American financial markets in the international financial architecture, US financial regulation had important implications for financial regulation in other states. This book considers this ability to shape financial structures as structural financial power not because it is a power applied to financial structures, but because it is a power that derives from the structure of the international financial system. However, the ability to shape international financial regulation might also stem from a state's position as a creditor that allowed it to exercise direct pressure on other states to

[16] As Helleiner (2006: 76) has emphasized, Strange aimed at providing a definition of power that was not limited to the power of one state over another, but also included a state's power to influence nonstate actors and market forces.

change their financial regulation. In this case, this book would consider it as relational financial power. Alternatively, the ability to shape global financial structures might stem from sources that are not located in the realm of finance, but, for example, in the military realm, in which case this book would not consider it as financial power but as military power.

Notions of structural power have also been discussed in the writings of Cohen (1977) and Kirshner (1995). In *Organizing the World's Money*, Cohen (1977: 56) defines "structure power" as "the ability to extract advantage by favorably modifying the interaction situation" and distinguishes it from "process power" understood as "the ability to extract advantage within the existing interaction situation." In other words, Cohen (1977: 56) considers process power "the ability to gain under the prevailing rules of the game, while structure power is the ability to gain by rewriting the rules of the game." Cohen hence understands structural power as power *applied to structures*. On the other hand, Kirshner in *Currency and Coercion* distinguishes between "overt power" (1995: 116) and the power that a state "derives from the rules of the system, or from the 'structural' forms of dependence" (1995: 117). Kirshner thus defines structural power as power *deriving from structures.*

On the basis of the preceding discussion, this book distinguishes between relational financial power as a state's ability to influence the behavior of other states directly by applying financial pressure and structural financial power as a state's ability to influence the behavior of other states indirectly via the structure of the international financial system. In addition to these two types of power, a third type of financial power that can be characterized as a state's ability to influence the behavior of other states indirectly through the policy decisions of international financial institutions will be incorporated into the following analysis.[17]

2.3.3 Manipulative and Non-manipulative Financial Power

As has already been pointed out, structural financial power can either be exercised in a manipulative (or intentional) way or in a non-manipulative (or non-intentional) way. Structural financial power is exercised in a non-manipulative way when financial policy decisions in one state that do not primarily aim at influencing other states have repercussions for these states due to the structure of the international financial system. On the other hand, structural financial power is exercised in a manipulative way when a state exploits its position in the global financial system to deliberately influence outcomes in other states in line with its policy preferences.

[17] This concept of institutional power should not be confused with Guzzini's (1993) concept of indirect institutional power that is defined as power applied to structures. To avoid misunderstandings, it also needs to be pointed out that due to her broader understanding of the concept of structural financial power, Strange (1982) considered a state's ability to influence the behavior of other states indirectly through the policy decisions of international financial institutions as an aspect of structural financial power.

Just as structural financial power, institutional financial power can be exercised in a manipulative as well as a non-manipulative way. Institutional financial power is exercised in a non-manipulative way when a state influences the policy decisions of international financial institutions without aiming to achieve specific policy outcomes in other states. On the other hand, institutional financial power is exercised in a manipulative way when a state influences the policy decisions of international financial institutions for the sake of ensuring specific policy outcomes in other states. In contrast to structural and institutional financial power, relational financial power is by definition exercised in a manipulative way.

Both Cohen (2006) and Andrews (2006b) have discussed distinctions similar to the one between manipulative and non-manipulative financial power. As we have already noted, Cohen distinguishes between an internal dimension of power that corresponds to a state's autonomy and an external dimension of power that corresponds to a state's authority or influence. According to Cohen, autonomy in the realm of finance implies a certain degree of influence since financial relations are inherently reciprocal. However, the influence that is implied by a state's autonomy is nothing but a "contingent aspect of power" whose impacts are "diffuse and undirected" (Cohen 2006: 34). Cohen (2006: 34) thus argues that this passive mode of influence needs to be distinguished from influence in the conventional sense – the active mode of influence that is "targeted at specific countries and applied with self-conscious purpose."

In a similar vein, Andrews (2006b) distinguishes between monetary power and monetary statecraft. While Andrews (2006b: 16) understands monetary power as a state's ability to change the behavior of other states through its financial relations with them, he argues that the concept of monetary statecraft has a more restricted meaning and refers to "the conscious manipulation of monetary relations in order to affect the policies of other states." Whereas Andrews' concept of monetary statecraft corresponds to Cohen's concept of the active mode of monetary influence and the concept of manipulative financial power, his notion of monetary power is a broader term that contains Cohen's concept of monetary autonomy and his concept of monetary influence as well as manipulative financial power and non-manipulative financial power.

2.3.4 Objectives of Financial Power

Having defined financial power as power deriving from the realm of finance as opposed to power applied to the realm of finance, this book distinguishes between a manipulative exercise of financial power that is targeted at financial objectives and a manipulative exercise of financial power that is targeted at non-financial objectives. All types of financial power mentioned above can be either targeted at financial or non-financial objectives. One of the most prominent examples of an exercise of (institutional) financial power targeted at non-financial objectives was the US decision to block the UK's access to the IMF's reserves in order to make

London withdraw its forces from Egypt during the Suez Crisis in 1956 (Andrews 2006b: 7).[18]

2.3.5 Summary: Types of Financial Power

This book understands financial power as a state's ability to influence other states through its financial relations with them. It distinguishes between relational, structural and institutional financial power. Relational financial power is a state's ability to influence other states directly by applying financial pressure. Structural financial power is a state's ability to influence other states indirectly through the structure of the international financial system. Institutional financial power is a state's ability to influence other states indirectly through the policy decisions of international financial institutions. Whereas relational financial power is by definition manipulative, structural financial power as well as institutional financial power can be exercised in a manipulative as well as a non-manipulative way. The manipulative exercise of power, be it relational, structural or institutional, can be targeted at financial as well as non-financial objectives. The following graphic gives an overview of the different types and subtypes of financial power (see Fig. 2.1).

2.3.6 Relational Financial Power

What are the mechanisms through which these types of power are exercised, and what are the sources from which they derive? As has already been explained, relational financial power is a state's ability to influence other states' behavior directly by applying financial pressure. However, the exercise of relational financial power may also rely on the provision of financial incentives. The main mechanisms for the exercise of relational financial power are the provision of credit as far as incentives are concerned and the withdrawal of credit or the refusal to provide credit as well as the dumping of a debtor state's currency in order to manipulate its exchange rate as far as pressure is concerned. A state's creditor status can hence be considered its main source of relational financial power (Helleiner 1989, 1992; Strange 1990). As Helleiner (1989: 345) has pointed out, the variables that determine the degree of a creditor state's relational financial power are the size and the duration of its capital outflows, the degree of state control over these outflows and the creditor state's vulnerability to its major debtors. Besides, it has to be taken into account that the degree of a creditor state's relational financial power is also influenced by the debtor's vulnerability to the creditor that depends on the

[18] Numerous examples of the exercise of financial power targeted at non-financial objectives can be found in Kirshner (1995, 2006).

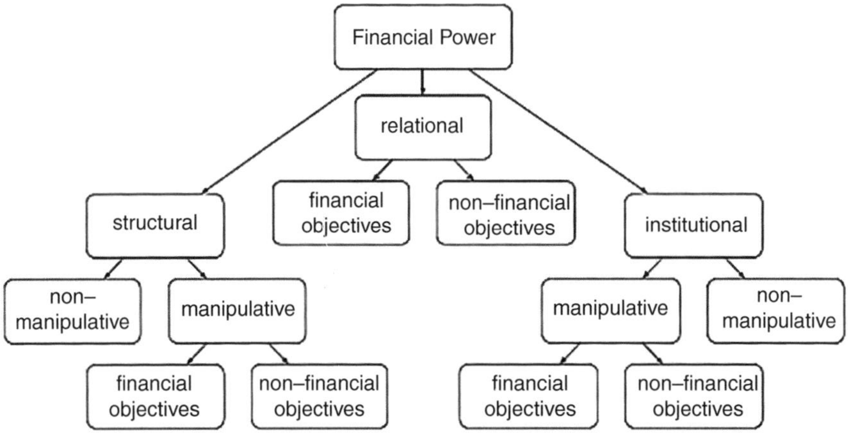

Fig. 2.1 Types of financial power

alternative sources of credit at the debtor's disposal and the nature of the debtor's exchange rate regime (Drezner 2009: 18–20).[19] In order to have relational financial power at its disposal, a state does not necessarily have to be a net creditor. A net debtor that is in the position to provide international credit can also exercise relational financial power. Through the exercise of relational financial power, a state may try to achieve any policy objective it considers important.

2.3.7 Institutional Financial Power

While relational financial power is exercised directly, institutional financial power is exercised indirectly through the policy decisions of international financial institutions. Since the International Monetary Fund and the World Bank are the most important financial institutions in the present international financial architecture, a state's voting share, its contribution of funds and its representation among the staff and management of these institutions are the main sources of its institutional financial power (Woods 2003b). The main mechanism for the exercise of institutional financial power is a state's influence on the provision of credit via these institutions and the conditions on which this provision of credit relies. If a state exercises its institutional financial power in a manipulative way, the objectives of its power exercise usually lie in the realm of economic interests. However, in principle any policy objective may be achieved through the exercise of institutional financial power.

[19] These points will be further explained in Chap. 5.

2.3.8 *Structural Financial Power*

The concept of structural financial power can only be understood on the basis of an examination of its different aspects. This section begins with the analysis of one of the most important aspects of structural financial power that concerns the cost of adjustment to balance of payments disequilibria.

2.3.8.1 Power to Delay Adjustment to Deficits

According to Cohen (2006: 36), who has most prominently discussed this aspect of structural financial power, the continuing cost of adjustment to balance of payments disequilibria "may be defined as the cost of the new payments equilibrium prevailing after all change has occurred."[20] These costs are borne by the deficit state, since for the deficit state the restoration of payments equilibrium requires "a reduction of imports relative to exports" that implies that it will "receive a smaller proportion of the combined output of the two economies" (Cohen 2006: 38). For this reason, deficit states have every incentive to try and postpone the process of adjustment. The longer one deficit country can delay the process of adjustment, "the greater will be the pressure on other deficit countries to bear the burden instead" (Cohen 2006: 42).

According to Cohen (2006: 42–43), the power to delay derives from a state's international liquidity position that allows it to cover deficits in the balance of payments. The main components of a state's international liquidity are its foreign exchange reserves and its external borrowing capacity. The bigger a state's stockpile of reserves, the greater its power to delay. However, since the acquisition of reserves always comes at a price, states usually do not seek a maximum level of reserves, but an optimal level. As reserves are in most cases accumulated as a result of a current account surplus, the costs that are associated with them are a reduction of imports relative to exports.[21]

However, Cohen does not pay attention to the fact that the accumulation of reserves is also associated with sterilization costs that arise because the inflationary impact of reserve accumulation has to be neutralized by the issuance of domestic debt. Since sterilization costs can be a serious hindrance to the accumulation of reserves, a state's ability to acquire foreign exchange reserves is crucially influenced by its ability to control the costs of sterilization. Most important in this

---

[20] Cohen (2006: 46) distinguishes between the power to delay the continuing cost of adjustment and the power to deflect the transitional cost of adjustment, arguing that the power to deflect "derives not from financial variables but [. . .] from more fundamental structural variables that distinguish one national economy from another", namely "the degree of openness and the degree of adaptability of each individual economy." Since the power to deflect does not derive from the realm of finance, its analysis is not included in this book.

[21] Reserves can also be acquired by external borrowing that leads to costs in the form of interest payment.

regard is the authorities' ability to keep interest rates low and mandate domestic financial institutions to purchase sterilization bonds. A state's ability to acquire foreign exchange reserves is thus significantly bolstered by the maintenance of a system of financial repression.

As Cohen (2006: 43–46) has pointed out, a state's external borrowing capacity depends on the international attractiveness of its financial markets and the assessment of its creditworthiness by foreign investors. Like the accumulation of foreign exchange reserves, external borrowing usually comes at a price. In addition to the interest that has to be paid, there is also the risk of a depreciation of the domestic currency against the borrowed currency that would increase the costs of borrowing. However, a different situation arises if the borrower state issues a global currency and is therefore in a position to borrow in its own money. In this case, the borrower state does not only deflect the risk of exchange rate fluctuations to the creditor state. Its interest burden is also decreased by foreigners who hold its money without investing it in financial assets. The issuance of a global currency thus provides the issuing state with the power to extract wealth from other states that enhances its power to delay adjustment to deficits. Moreover, due to the international demand for its domestic money, a state that issues the international core currency will find it easier than any other state to borrow from abroad. Its power to delay is by far greater than the power to delay of a state that has accumulated reserves by running a balance of payments surplus that would allow it to delay the adjustment to external imbalances if its surplus turned into a deficit. Whereas the borrowing capacity of the state that issues the global currency is almost unlimited, reserves will be spent rather quickly and can therefore only function as an insurance against balance of payments shocks, but do not allow a state to run a permanent current account deficit.

2.3.8.2 Power to Delay Adjustment to Surpluses

Cohen's (2006) analysis of the power to delay explicitly refers to the power of deficit states to delay the process of adjustment. He mentions that surplus states may also want to delay the process of adjustment if they fear the transitional costs associated with that process. Yet he emphasizes that the motivation of surplus states to delay the process of adjustment is not as intense as the motivation of deficit countries since the former do not have to worry about the continuing costs of adjustment (Cohen 2006: 42). However, surplus states may have strong incentives to delay the process of adjustment if they want to sustain their surpluses because they rely on an export-led growth strategy. For this reason, the power to delay adjustment to surpluses that may hinder deficit countries from restoring balance of payments equilibrium should be considered an important aspect of structural financial power. The source of this power is a state's ability to maintain a fixed exchange rate regime that allows the authorities to prevent the domestic currency from appreciating, which in turns depends on a state's ability to maintain capital controls and neutralize the inflationary impact of a trade surplus under a fixed exchange rate regime.[22] In other words, the source of the power to delay adjustment to surpluses is the maintenance of a system of financial repression within the context of an international financial architecture dominated by floating exchange rate regimes.

2.3.8.3 Power to Project Macroeconomic Preferences

As Strange (1986) and Helleiner (2006) have argued, structural financial power also includes a state's ability to project its macroeconomic preferences onto other states. The main mechanism of this aspect of structural financial power is a state's ability to attract international capital, which stems not only from the depth and openness of its financial markets, but also from the international status of its currency. With regard to this aspect, Strange (1986: 22) has drawn attention to the fact that "when US domestic monetary policy changed direction, and when interest rates in the United States responded to changes of policy, other states had no choice but to adjust their own interest rates and their domestic policies to such changes, whereas it never happened the other way around." One of Strange's (1986: 55) examples was the US decision to hike interest rates in its fight against inflation in the late 1970s and "the consequent imposition on other countries and on the world economy of interest rates that were both high and volatile." Besides, macroeconomic preferences can also be projected via a currency's function as a monetary anchor, since a state that chooses to adopt a currency peg without being able to effectively enforce capital controls will inevitably import the latter's monetary policy.

2.3.8.4 Power to Shape International Financial Regulation

According to Strange (1986) and Helleiner (2006), the power to shape international financial regulation is another important aspect of structural financial power. The sources of this power are the dominant international position of a state's currency and its financial markets that allow it to influence international regulatory trends via the regulation or deregulation of its domestic financial system. Since the 1970s, the US has exercised this aspect of structural financial power via domestic liberalization measures that prompted other states "to follow the U.S. regulatory lead because of their fear of losing financial business and capital to liberal and deregulated U.S. dollar markets" (Helleiner 2006: 80).

[22] According to the Mundell-Fleming Model, a state cannot simultaneously maintain a fixed exchange rate, an independent monetary policy and free movement of capital. See Mundell (1963) and Fleming (1962).

2.3.8.5 Entrapment

Last but not least, Kirshner (1995) has discussed two important aspects of structural financial power in his analysis of monetary entrapment. Kirshner draws attention to the fact that most states' "primary motivation for leading monetary systems [...] is to reap the benefits of entrapment" (Kirshner 1995: 117) which he defines as the "transformation of interests that results from participation in a currency system" (Kirshner 1995: 118). Membership in a currency system fosters trade and investment links with the dominant state by altering transaction costs via the elimination of costs resulting from exchange rate fluctuations. Besides, participation in a currency system creates a common interest in the value and stability of the dominant state's currency since member states usually come to hold significant amounts of that currency. According to Helleiner (2006: 80–82) we can thus distinguish between two different aspects of the mechanism of entrapment that establish two different aspects of structural financial power: Whereas the issuer of an international currency gains the power to reshape economic geography via the alteration of transaction costs, it gains the power to reconstruct economic interests via the creation of dependencies on the value and stability of its currency. The following table gives an overview of the different types of financial power, their mechanisms and their sources (see Table 2.1).

2.4 Preview of the Argument

On the basis of the preceding conceptualization of the developmental state and the development of a typology of financial power, a preliminary explanation of the implications of the political economy of the developmental state for its ability to acquire financial power can now be provided. Since the developmental state's system of financial repression is not compatible with the development of financial markets capable of attracting international investors on a significant scale, it largely prevents the acquisition of structural financial power deriving from the international pulling power of financial markets. For the same reason, the developmental state is not in a position to develop structural financial power by establishing its domestic currency as an international store of value since this aspect of currency internationalization requires the very development of financial markets that is not compatible with a system of financial repression. However, since the developmental state's system of financial repression allows it to withstand currency appreciation pressures, it provides it with the power to delay the costs of adjustment to balance of payments surpluses. Moreover, since their systems of financial repression are geared to facilitate rapid economic growth through comprehensive industrial development at the expense of consumption, developmental states frequently embark on export-led growth strategies resulting in significant current account surpluses that turn them into net creditors with significant relational financial power. Due to their strong creditor positions, developmental states are thus not as dependent on the

Table 2.1 Aspects, mechanisms and sources of financial power

Aspect/Objective	Mechanisms	Sources
Structural financial power		
Power to delay adjustment to deficits	External borrowing	International currency (store of value)
		International pulling power of financial markets
Power to delay adjustment to surpluses	Maintenance of fixed exchange rate regime	Maintenance of capital controls
		Ability to contain sterilization costs
Power to project macroeconomic preferences	Attraction of portfolio investment	International currency (store of value)
		International pulling power of financial markets
	Provision of monetary anchor	International currency (unit of account)
Power to shape international financial regulation	Regulation of financial markets using core currency	International currency (store of value)
		International pulling power of financial markets
Power to shape economic geography	Alteration of transaction costs	International currency (medium of exchange, unit of account, store of value)
Power to reconstruct economic interests	Creation of a common interest in value and stability of core currency	International currency (store of value)
Relational financial power		
Any policy objective possible	Provision of credit	Creditor status:
	Refusal to provide credit/withdrawal of credit	Size and duration of capital outflows
	Dumping of debtor's currency	State control over capital outflows
		Creditor's vulnerability to debtor
		Debtor's vulnerability to creditor
Institutional financial power		
Any policy objective possible	Influence on provision of credit and its conditionality	Influence in IMF and World Bank:
		Voting share
		Contribution of funds
		Representation among staff and management

Adapted from Helleiner (2006: 84)
Additional Sources: Drezner (2009), Woods (2003b), Helleiner (1989)

acquisition of institutional financial power as neoliberal states whose relational financial power tends to be much more limited. In the following chapters, a detailed account of the political economy of the financial systems of both the Japanese and the Chinese developmental state will be provided that will allow for a more profound explanation of the relationship between the political economy of the developmental state and its financial power potential.

Chapter 3
Financial Repression and Structural Financial Power

As has been explained in Chap. 2, structural financial power is a state's ability to influence the behavior of other states indirectly through the structure of the international financial system. One of the main sources of structural financial power is the international role of a state's financial markets. Since only liberalized financial markets have the potential to attract international investors on a significant scale, this book considers financial system liberalization a precondition for financial market internationalization.[1] To allow for an assessment of China's potential to acquire structural financial power, this chapter examines the political economy of China's system of financial repression and the role that the country's capital markets play within this system.

Section 3.1 examines Japan's postwar financial system and analyzes the pressures that resulted in its gradual liberalization. Section 3.2 looks into China's plan to turn Shanghai into an international financial center and analyzes the motives behind it. It then examines the political economy of China's system of financial repression, analyzes the role of capital markets within this system and sheds light on China's approach to capital controls. Against the backdrop of these analyses, it inquires into the compatibility of China's system of financial repression with the acquisition of structural financial power deriving from the international role of a country's financial markets. Section 3.3 tries to provide an answer to the question if the Chinese party-state is in a better position to maintain its high degree of control over the country's financial system than Japan's authorities were from the end of the 1970s.

[1] On the other hand, internationalization in the sense of an increasing involvement of international actors may contribute to liberalization. For an analysis of the role of international actors in the liberalization of China's financial system see Schlichting (2008).

S. Heep, *China in Global Finance*, Global Power Shift,
DOI 10.1007/978-3-319-02466-0_3,

3.1 Liberalizing Japan's Financial Markets

The following sections provide an overview of the political economy of Japan's postwar financial system and analyze the driving forces behind its gradual liberalization, including the growing government deficit, structural changes within the financial system and foreign pressure to liberalize.

3.1.1 *The Political Economy of Japan's Postwar Financial System*

Japan's postwar financial system was characterized by the overriding importance of bank credit for corporate finance. The stock market only accounted for a tiny proportion of funds raised for industrial development. Moreover, since corporate stocks were mainly held by banks or other companies, the stock market did not facilitate the raising of funds from the household sector. Neither did the bond market provide an alternative for corporate finance since the government limited the supply of funds by fixing interest rates on newly issued bonds at artificially low levels (Zysman 1983: 245). Since interest rates on bank deposits were also capped by the authorities, the household sector was forced "to bear the costs of expansion in the form of artificially low interest rates" (Zysman 1983: 250). Internal competition within the financial sector was inhibited by a highly fragmented system in which commercial banking was strictly separated from investment banking (Laurence 2001: 106).

According to Bernard Eccleston (1986: 66), another crucial feature of the system was the high household saving rate that did not only result from the absence of a welfare system and rising incomes, but was also influenced by a lack of consumer credit and mortgage financing opportunities. In this system, "the state moulded the growth of financial institutions to keep savers and investors separated, thus reserving a key intermediary role for state agencies" (Eccleston 1986: 65). The bulk of household deposits were held in the postal savings system whose role was bolstered by the authorities by granting tax exemption on its interests and by restricting the ability of other financial institutions to collect deposits. The deposits in the postal savings system were channeled through the Fiscal Investment and Loan Plan (FILP) to policy banks such as the Japan Development Bank and the Export-Import Bank that provided companies with financial support in line with industrial policy objectives (Eccleston 1986: 66–67).

However, the allocation of credit via Japan's policy banks only supplemented a more indirect mechanism of selective credit allocation. This mechanism was described in a nutshell by Chalmers Johnson (1982: 203), who took it to be one of the "most distinctive characteristics" of the Japanese industrial system. In Johnson's (1982: 203) words, this mechanism relied on a "pattern of dependencies in which a group of enterprises borrows from a bank well beyond the individual companies' capacity to repay, or often beyond their net worth, and the bank in turn overborrows from the Bank of Japan." With the central bank functioning as "the ultimate guarantor of the system" (Johnson 1982: 203), it was well placed to control the lending decisions of the country's banks even though they were formally independent institutions in private ownership.

As Eccleston (1986: 66–67) has pointed out, this indirect method of allocating credit reconciled the government's seemingly contradictive policies towards the commercial banks. On the one hand, it restricted their ability to collect deposits. Yet on the other hand, it encouraged them to lend aggressively to large companies whose financial support was considered crucial to the country's industrial expansion. By providing the commercial banks with funds through the Bank of Japan, the authorities made sure that the country's deposits could be invested by the policy banks while at the same time enabling the commercial banks to provide funds for industrial development. However, commercial bank borrowing from the central bank was also necessitated by a scarcity of capital that would have hampered the country's industrial development if it had not been for the provision of additional funds by the Bank of Japan (BOJ). It was the dependence of the commercial banks on the central bank resulting from this practice that provided the state with considerable leverage over the banks' lending decisions. Zysman (1983: 249–250) has therefore emphasized that "the notion of administrative guidance [...] rests not on some cultural propensity but rather on the dependence of firms on banks and the dependence of the banks on the government." In light of the state's influence on the allocation of credit, neither the companies' overborrowing nor the banks' overlending threatened the stability of the system since "government concern with the well-being of firms in favored sectors [was] seen as an implicit guarantee of the bank loans made to them" (Zysman 1983: 243).

3.1.2 The Impact of the Growing Government Deficit

First signs of a willingness to reform Japan's financial system could be seen in the years between 1970 and 1972, when the country was for the first time building up large current account surpluses. In the face of this development, the government relaxed regulations on the outflow of capital and allowed Japanese residents to purchase foreign securities. Foreign institutions were given approval to tap Japan's financial markets by issuing bonds in Japan. Yet when the 1973 oil crisis resulted in a sharp deficit in Japan's current account, regulation was tightened again. Nevertheless, the rise in oil prices indirectly contributed to a significant restructuring of Japan's financial system (Emmott 1989: 98).

In the early 1970s, inflationary pressures had begun to threaten Japan's economic growth. The main cause for the surge in inflation was the breakdown of the Bretton Woods system and the closure of the gold window in 1971 that resulted in a massive increase in the volume of money circulating within the world economy. A considerable amount of this new money originated from the United States that was no longer constrained in its monetary policy by a system of fixed exchange rates and had thus embarked on a policy of monetary easing to stimulate domestic demand and to strengthen the competitiveness of its export sector (Leyshon 1994: 123).

Japan's response to this development was to relax its monetary policy in order to slow the rise of the yen against the dollar and thus to protect its export industry. In the words of Makoto Itoh (1990: 163), "the Japanese government and monetary authorities took an intentional policy stance to promote inflation in order to mitigate the 'Nixon shock' to its export industries." However, unforeseen by the authorities, the 1973 oil crisis strongly exacerbated inflationary pressures in the Japanese economy. Since Japan was heavily dependent on imported energy sources, the quadrupling of oil prices severely dampened Japan's economic growth and resulted in a fall of GDP by almost 4 % between 1973 and 1974. In response to this crisis, Japan's authorities embarked on a strategy of deficit financing (Leyshon 1994: 124; Itoh 1990: 164; 168).

Until the mid-1970s, Japan had adhered to strict fiscal orthodoxy by following the doctrines of Joseph Dodge, the banker who had been dispatched to Japan by US President Truman in 1949 in order to help Japan's authorities in their fight against the accelerating inflation in the early postwar years. Dodge had advised the Japanese government to run a balanced budget, and Japan's authorities had been happy to follow his advice, not least because Dodge's recommendations were in line with Japan's economic growth model since they ensured that the country's savings were not diverted from the overriding objective of industrial development (Leyshon 1994: 124).

Yet when they were confronted with the severe economic crisis of the early 1970s, Japan's authorities decided to abandon the path of fiscal austerity. Starting in 1975, Japan's government embarked on a successful deficit-led growth strategy financed by the issuance of government bonds in order to pull the country's economy out of recession. While government indebtedness had amounted to a mere JPY 13 trillion in 1973, the massive stimulus program saw public debt skyrocketing to JPY 23 trillion in 1975 and to JPY 95 trillion in 1980, thus rising from 11 % to 40 % of GNP within only 7 years (Leyshon 1994: 125; Itoh 1990: 171). Japan's authorities thus began to engage in Keynesian demand management "at the very moment that [it] was being abandoned in favour of neoliberalism in North America and Western Europe" (Leyshon 1994: 125). While the latter saw their policy options "within the field of monetary and fiscal policy increasingly constrained by the anti-inflationist sanctioning power of international financial capital", Japan's relatively isolated financial system "provided it with policy avenues that other states were being forced to relinquish" (Leyshon 1994: 125).

The rapid growth in the volume of government bonds had profound consequences for Japan's hitherto highly regulated financial system. With the commercial banks barred from trading securities, the markets struggled to absorb the government's debt. Initially, the BOJ stepped in to purchase the majority of the bonds. However, this solution was not sustainable since it created severe inflationary pressures. With the BOJ's withdrawal from the market, the commercial banks were the only entities capable of purchasing significant amounts of bonds, and they soon found themselves under considerable pressure to do so. Yet since they were prohibited from engaging in securities business, they were not allowed to sell the bonds (Laurence 2001: 118). As Henry Laurence (2001: 118) has emphasized, "the prospect of taking these loss-making bonds onto their books and holding them "under water" indefinitely was particularly unappealing for the banks at a time when the demand for corporate loans was declining sharply." For this reason, the banks required a reform of the financial system that would allow them to deal with the ever growing amount of government debt and to gain a foothold in more profitable areas from which they had hitherto been excluded (Laurence 2001: 118).

In 1978, the MOF granted the banks permission to sell government securities on the open market. Besides, it liberalized the money market to facilitate the funding of the banks' bond purchases and to allow the banks to diversify their portfolios (Laurence 2001: 118). With the liberalization of interest rates in the money market, the system of administratively set interest rates began to erode, since financial institutions could react to low interest rates imposed by the BOJ by moving their funds into other markets (Emmott 1989: 98–99). In an attempt to make the rapidly growing number of government bonds attractive to a large range of investors, the MOF also began to increase interest rates on its bonds, thereby introducing "into Japan what was then the novel idea of competition for funds, which began to tip the balance of interests within Japan's financial markets away from borrowers and towards savers and investors" (Leyshon 1994: 125). With an increasing amount of funds flowing into the market for government bonds, internal pressures for the liberalization of the financial system arose, as financial institutions tried to regain control of the funds that were being used to finance the country's budget deficit. The growing level of disintermediation resulted in a weakening of the financial authorities' control over the allocation of credit and bolstered the role of the market in determining the price of funds available for investment. Besides, financial innovation in the disintermediated section of the financial system resulted in the introduction of derivative financial instruments that further impaired the financial authorities' control over the domestic financial system (Leyshon 1994: 125–126).

3.1.3 *Structural Changes and Foreign Pressure to Liberalize*

The liberalization of Japan's financial system significantly accelerated in the 1980s. US pressure for the internationalization of the yen and the opening up of Japan's financial services sector for American financial institutions resulted in the signing of the Yen-Dollar Agreement in 1984 in whose wake Japan's financial system underwent dramatic changes.[2] Yet the main reason why Japan gave in to the pressure of its most important ally was the fact that the country's policymakers

[2] The motives that drove US pressure will be analyzed in Chap. 4. For a detailed account of the negotiations leading to the Yen-Dollar Agreement see Frankel (1984).

were well aware of the structural changes in the domestic economy that necessitated a liberalization of the financial system. In addition to the growing government debt of the 1970s, two major structural changes resulting from Japan's rapid economic growth put the existing system under pressure: a demand for more diversified financial services following a substantial increase in the wealth of households resulting from economic growth and a greater reliance of companies on internal funding from retained earnings that diminished their dependence on the banks (Laurence 2001: 117). In the words of Michael Moran (1991: 101):

> The simplicities of a state-sponsored, bank-dominated financial structure that had emerged in the post-war era of capital shortage gave way to more complex patterns as economic success generated corporate profits that could be used for investment, and as rising levels of real income swelled the volume of personal savings.

As Bill Emmott (1989: 103) has argued, foreign pressure was useful in this context "because it could be exploited to circumvent domestic opposition to reform: It was an excuse rather than a decisive force."

Japan's commitments in the context of the Yen-Dollar Agreement included improved access for foreign financial firms to the country's financial markets and their permission to deal in government bonds and participate in the trust banking business. Japan also agreed to establish a market for bankers' acceptances and to eliminate controls on foreign exchange trading and "laid down a vague plan for the future liberalization of bank deposit interest rates" (Emmott 1989: 102). However, the most important element of reform was the introduction of easier rules for Japanese and foreign companies concerning the issuance of yen bonds in the Euromarkets, a step that significantly altered Japan's system of corporate finance (Emmott 1989: 102).

In order to secure their control over the allocation of credit, Japan's authorities had been determined to prevent corporate bonds from becoming too competitive with loans and had therefore hampered the development of the bond market by introducing highly restrictive rules about collateral and the approval of issues (Emmott 1989: 108). First signs of an erosion of this system could be seen in the 1970s, when Japanese restrictions concerning the raising of funds overseas were gradually lifted and Japanese companies issued growing amounts of bonds in the Euromarkets. The total amount of funds raised by Japanese companies in overseas markets jumped from JPY 15 billion in 1973 to JPY 1,426 billion in 1982, representing approximately one third of the total funds raised through the issuance of securities by Japanese businesses (Laurence 2001: 121).[3]

With their increasing reliance on internal funding, Japanese companies had begun to feel less dependent on the banks and started to look out for cheaper funding opportunities that could be found abroad. With the liberalization of rules governing the issuance of yen bonds in the Euromarkets, the pace of change thus

[3] As Frances Rosenbluth (1989: 57) has pointed out, the revision of Japan's Foreign Exchange and Foreign Trade Control Law did not indicate a significant turning point since it "formally sanctioned rather than initiated the change in policy."

accelerated significantly (Emmott 1989: 108). From 1984 to 1987, Japanese businesses raised about half of their securities funding on overseas markets (Laurence 2001: 121). However, despite the growing importance of overseas markets, ownership of Japanese securities largely remained in the hand of Japanese savers, since they purchased the bulk of the securities issued by Japanese businesses overseas (Emmott 1989: 109). As Laurence (2001: 122) has highlighted, the "use of exit by Japanese borrowers played a key role in persuading the MOF that Japan's domestic markets had to be liberalized" since its bureaucrats were afraid that the country would lose its financial services industry to more competitive financial centers abroad.

The US pressure exercised on Japan in the negotiations leading to the 1985 Plaza Agreement further accelerated the impact of the Yen-Dollar Agreement on the development of Japan's financial system. As a result of the Plaza Agreement, the value of the yen soared to unexpected levels, increasing from JPY 240 to JPY 170 to the dollar within a period of only 7 months (Leyshon 1994: 130). In an attempt to smooth the rise of the yen in the wake of the Plaza Agreement, the Bank of Japan considerably loosened the country's monetary policy (Helleiner 2000: 234). Besides, in the negotiations leading to the 1987 Louvre Accord, Japan was pressured by the US and the rest of the G7 nations to keep its interest rates below those in other countries in order to stimulate its economy and thereby contribute to a rebalancing of its economic relations with the G7 nations (Leyshon 1994: 131).

In the words of Leyshon (1994: 132), the combination of the liberalization of administrative control over the financial system and the holding down of interest rates "made for a heady and potent brew." An explosion in the creation of credit ensued that flew into increasingly speculative investments and thus significantly changed the nature of Japan's financial markets. While the total volume of funds that was intermediated in Japan amounted to JPY 59 trillion per year on average between 1975 and 1984, it more than doubled to JPY 123 trillion per year between 1985 and 1990. The flood of new money drove up the capitalization of Japan's financial markets and catapulted them into the league of the largest financial markets in the world (Leyshon 1994: 132). At the end of the 1980s, Japan's equity markets accounted for 44 % of world stock market capitalization, while US equity markets only accounted for 30 %. Annual bond market turnover in Tokyo had surpassed that of New York, and even Japan's foreign exchange market had come close to rival New York's in terms of daily turnover (Helleiner 1989: 353).

At the same time, new derivative financial markets developed in Tokyo, "which were used first as hedging instruments against investments in securities, and then as purely speculative investments" (Leyshon 1994: 132). Excessive credit creation and financial innovation allowed Japan's companies to make up for the loss of profits resulting from declining exports by turning "risk management strategies into money-making activities in their own right" (Leyshon 1994: 133). With their traditional industrial clients increasingly turning to alternative sources of funding in the international debt markets, Japan's banks began to look out for new borrowers who could help them maintain their rapid asset growth. At the end of the day, they found themselves funding ever more speculative investments (Leyshon 1994: 133–134).

When the global stock market crash in October 1987 only mildly affected Japan's financial markets and measures taken by the MOF succeeded at stabilizing markets abroad, Japan seemed to have established itself as a leading international financial power (Helleiner 1992: 427). However, the boom in Japan's financial markets came to an abrupt end when the BOJ in 1989 began to tighten monetary policy in an attempt to fight the country's increasing asset price inflation. The most prominent symbol of the bursting of Japan's financial bubble was the fall in the Nikkei index of the Tokyo Stock Exchange by more than one half between 1989 and 1992 (Helleiner 2000: 232). The capitalization of Japan's bond markets declined since higher interest rates made the issuance of new bonds less attractive (Leyshon 1994: 126). Due to falling share prices and property values, the huge capital base of Japan's financial institutions began to erode, forcing them to cut back their overseas activities. With the retreat of Japan's financial institutions from international financial markets, turnover in Japan's foreign exchange markets declined significantly, thereby revealing the extent to which the internationalization of Japan's financial markets had been a result of the overseas activities of the country's financial firms (Helleiner 2000: 233). Against the backdrop of the massive economic crisis resulting from the bursting of the bubble, "the issue of system liberalization was replaced by more immediate problems of damage control" (Laurence 2001: 144).

3.2 The Political Economy of China's Financial System

The following sections focus on the political economy of China's financial system. A brief portrayal of the background of the official plan to turn Shanghai into an international financial center will be followed by an analysis of China's system of financial repression and the role that the country's capital markets and its capital controls play within this system. The section concludes with a reflection on the compatibility of China's financial system with the potential to acquire structural financial power.

3.2.1 Turning Shanghai into an International Financial Center

In March 2009, when the world was still battling against the global financial crisis, China's cabinet announced a plan aimed at transforming Shanghai into an international financial center in line with China's economic strength and the international status of its currency by 2020 (State Council 2009). According to the blueprint, foreign investors will gradually be granted access to Shanghai's financial markets, and foreign companies will be allowed to issue renminbi-denominated bonds and list on the Shanghai stock exchange.

Even though the world was taken by surprise by the announcement of the ambitious goal to establish an international financial center on the Chinese mainland, the city of Shanghai had already been working towards this goal for almost two decades before the central government finally granted its blessing. Historically, Shanghai has played a dominant role in China's financial system. Shanghai has not only developed into the country's major financial center during the reform period, but also prides itself of the fact that it used to be the leading financial center in Asia before the establishment of the communist regime in 1949.

The plan to restore Shanghai's former financial glory goes back to Deng Xiaoping's famous inspection tour of Southern China in 1992 during which he expressed his hope that Shanghai would regain its former status in the international financial system. Later on in the same year the CCP's 14th Congress passed a resolution that called for the transformation of Shanghai into an economic 'dragon head' (longtou) simultaneously playing the role of an international economic, trade and financial center. In the following years, Shanghai's municipal government created several blueprints for the development of an international financial center. However, with the final say over the country's financial system in the hands of policymakers in Beijing, Shanghai's officials were not in a position to deal with the serious obstacles to the city's ambitions. Instead of addressing the crucial issues of liberalization and internationalization of China's financial system, they could only focus on market scale enlargement and infrastructure building (Xu 2009).

Leaving regional aspirations aside, we have to ask ourselves why China's leadership embraced the goal of internationalizing the country's financial markets at the height of a global financial crisis that drew attention to the pitfalls of international financial integration. The answer to this question can be found in the dangers of China's economic growth model that this very crisis brought to light. In the course of its economic reform process, China has embarked on a growth model heavily relying on the export sector. Exports only amounted to 6.6 % of GDP at the beginning of the reform period in 1978, but when the US subprime crisis broke out in 2007, they had risen to 38.4 % of GDP (see Fig. 3.1). With the beginning of the new millennium, Chinese exports began to grow ever more rapidly. From 2000 to 2007, China's annual export growth rate amounted to an average of 24 % (see Fig. 3.2). For these impressive growth rates, Beijing heavily relied on excessive US consumption. Yet when the crisis put a damper on the spending of US households, it became obvious that China's exports would be growing far more slowly in the years to come, thereby jeopardizing Beijing's official goal of maintaining a GDP growth rate of 7.5 % on average in the period from 2006 to 2010 covered by the Eleventh Five-Year Plan (Xinhua 2006).

In the short run, China's policymakers addressed the danger of a significant slowdown of the economy with a massive stimulus program. However, in the long run, it appeared necessary to find a domestic source of productivity growth that could replace the role that exports had played in the first decades of China's reform

Fig. 3.1 Chinese exports of goods and services (percentage of GDP) (Source: World Bank: World Development Indicators)

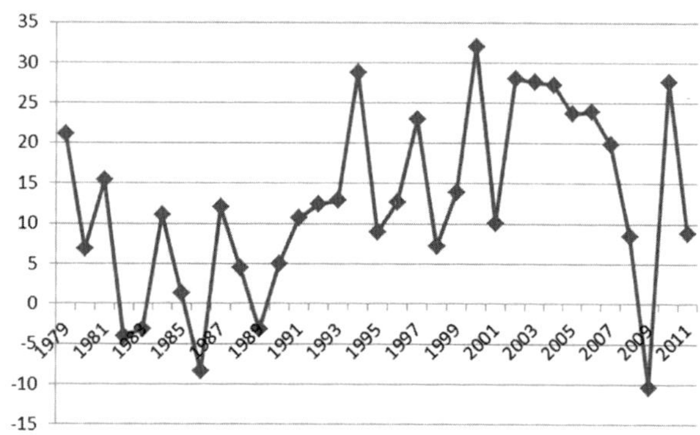

Fig. 3.2 Chinese exports of goods and services (annual percentage growth) (Source: World Bank: World Development Indicators)

period. Arthur Kroeber (2009b) has thus argued that the blueprint for the transformation of Shanghai into an international financial center can be understood as an attempt to liberalize the country's financial system in order to improve the allocation of capital and thus to enhance the economy's productivity. In this sense, Fang Xinghai, head of the Shanghai municipal government office responsible for the implementation of the plan, pointed out that the transformation of Shanghai into an international financial center could prove highly useful to the reform of China's domestic financial system. According to Fang (quoted after Kroeber 2009b), such a reform was urgently needed because China's financial system "is not so good at allocating capital efficiently" and would thus come to hamper China's development once the Chinese economy could no longer rely on exports as growth engine. In the words of Kroeber (2009b), the plan to establish an international financial center on the Chinese mainland can thus be seen "as analogous to China's entry into the World Trade Organisation eight years ago, which was used by reformers to engineer a host of domestic market reforms that would otherwise have been politically impossible."

3.2.2 China's System of Financial Repression

In order for Shanghai to succeed at transforming itself into an international financial center, China's financial system would have to undergo substantial reforms that would severely undermine the party-state's control over the country's political economy. To be able to assess the implications of financial system liberalization, the following sections look into the features of China's system of financial repression.

As Svenja Schlichting (2008: 29) has argued, the main characteristics of China's financial system can be explained with reference to "the institutional legacy of the command economy, the structures of China's political system and the path dependencies created by decisions made in the early reform years." Before the introduction of economic reforms in 1978, China's financial system was dominated by a banking sector whose main responsibility was the fulfilling of accounting tasks. With investment decisions made by the planning bureaucracy and financed from the government budget, the financial system remained subordinate to the real economy and was not designed to facilitate financial intermediation. Since the government owned both enterprises and banks and determined interest rate levels, budget constraints were soft and "the concept of credit [had] little practical meaning" (Schlichting 2008: 30).

When China's policymakers embarked on a path of economic reform, they chose not to break sharply with the structures of the planned economy, but to take a gradual approach to reform that allowed the country's state-owned enterprises to continue their dominant role in the economy. Arising from the leaders' determination "to secure stability, ensure employment, and guarantee continued control over production" (Schlichting 2008: 31), this decision necessitated a high degree of control over the financial system aimed at guaranteeing the SOEs' provision with cheap funding. For this reason, interest rates remained administratively controlled. Moreover, the authorities were careful to prevent the development of capital markets as alternative structures for resource allocation beyond the control of the party-state. As a result of the shift in SOE financing "from costless budgetary grants to interest-bearing, repayable loans" (Naughton 2007: 453), an enormous amount of nonperforming loans (NPLs) was created in the banking system that burdens it to the present day.

In the 1980s, the monobank that had dominated the financial system of the planned economy was broken up and divided into four commercial banks operated by the state. Known as Agricultural Bank of China (ABD), Bank of China (BOC), China Construction Bank (CCB) and Industrial and Commercial Bank of China (ICBC), these banks continue to dominate China's financial system to the present day. At the same time, the People's Bank of China (PBOC) began to transform itself into a central bank displaying increasing similarities with its counterparts in the developed world (Naughton 2007: 455). In the 1990s, three policy banks were established in an effort to free the commercial banks from their mandate to provide soft loans in line with the country's industrial policy, yet the foundation of these institutions failed to significantly alter the relation between the commercial banks and the party-state (Schlichting 2008: 55).[4]

China's leaders only began to tackle the problems of the state-owned commercial banks known as the 'Big Four' in the wake of the Asian Financial Crisis that made them realize the dangers emanating from a weak financial system. Starting from 1998, a first attempt was made to strengthen the banks' balance sheets focusing on the transfer of NPLs to asset-management companies (Naughton 2007: 461–464). In the years between 2004 and 2010, a second round of reforms was conducted in three steps: In the first step, the Big Four were recapitalized through the injection of foreign exchange reserves. The second step included their restructuring into joint-stock corporations owned by a subsidiary of the PBOC, Central Huijin Investment, and the Ministry of Finance (MOF) and the selling of stakes to foreign strategic investors.[5] In the last step, the banks were listed on the stock exchanges in Hong Kong and Shanghai. However, the party-state has retained majority stakes in the four banks that make up the heart of China's financial system and has thus secured its control over the allocation of funds via its influence on the banks' senior management based on the party's nomenklatura system (Schlichting 2008: 56–57).

While the reform of China's state-owned commercial banks has weakened the party-state's control over the allocation of credit in the 'normal mode' of Chinese politics, the party-state's control in the 'crisis mode' of politics has not decreased (Schlichting 2008: 216–218).[6] This became obvious in the wake of the global financial crisis when the authorities ordered the Big Four to implement the country's stimulus program and embark on a lending binge in order to fight the threat of a severe economic downturn. Moreover, the Big Four continue to provide the bulk of resources to SOEs that the country's leaders consider strategically important and thus play a crucial role in the implementation of the country's strategic development planning. Since the banking system is designed to support the state-owned sector of the economy, private companies only have very limited access to credit. Non-state companies are thus heavily dependent on alternative financing channels that can be found in the country's growing shadow banking system.[7]

As Barry Naughton (2007: 451–452) has emphasized, China's financial system has deepened significantly since the beginning of the reform policies. At the same time, it has remained very narrow since it continues to be dominated by the banking

[4] The three policy banks are China Development Bank, Export-Import Bank of China and Agricultural Development Bank of China.

[5] With the establishment of China's sovereign wealth fund, Huijin became a subsidiary of the China Investment Corporation.

[6] The distinction between the 'normal mode' and the 'crisis mode' of political decision-making in China has been introduced by Sebastian Heilmann (2004: 42–43).

[7] For analyses of the importance of alternative financing channels to non-state-owned firms see Allen et al. (2005, 2012), Ayyagai et al. (2008).

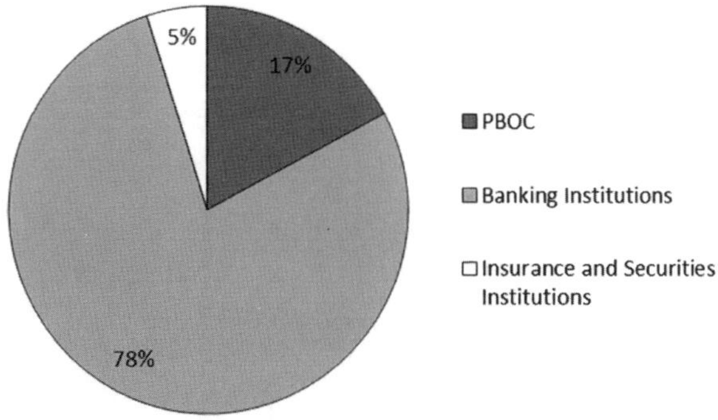

Fig. 3.3 Distribution of assets in China's financial sector (2012) (Source: PBOC 2013c)

sector.[8] At the end of 2012, China's banks held 78 % of the country's financial assets (see Fig. 3.3). At the same time, the Big Four accounted for 43 % of banking assets (see Fig. 3.4).[9] China's banks also continued to dominate the country's corporate financing channels, providing CNY 5,641 billion in bank loans to corporate customers. However, since the beginning of the reform of the country's corporate bond markets in 2005, corporate debt products have come to rival the importance of bank loans. In 2012, the issuance volume of corporate bonds already amounted to CNY 3,737 billion, while equity issuance played a negligible role (see Fig. 3.5).

China's financial system remains heavily repressed since the banks continue to operate in a highly protective interest rate framework. In the late 1990s, the PBOC started to liberalize the country's interest rate regime. However, this policy was put to a halt in 2004. As Nicholas Lardy (2008) has argued, the decision to stop the process of interest rate liberalization can be understood as a reaction to the costs of monetary sterilization resulting from China's growing current account surplus under a fixed exchange rate regime. To sterilize the inflationary impact of its interventions in the foreign exchange markets, the PBOC has increased the reserve requirement ratios of banks and mandated state-owned banks to purchase its central bank bills. According to Lardy, both instruments impose a tax on banks because interest rates on reserves and central bank bills are lower than interest rates on loans. Due to the guaranteed interest rate spread between deposits and loans, this practice did not jeopardize the health of the banking sector. However, if the PBOC had continued its liberalization of interest rates, it would have been necessary to

---

[8] According to Naughton (2007: 451), M2, a money measure that represents currency plus demand and savings deposits, increased from 32 % of GDP in 1978 to 162 % in 2005, a rate that is much higher than in most other economies. In the same period, household saving deposits increased from 6 % of GDP to 77 %.

[9] In addition to the state-owned commercial banks and policy banks, the Chinese banking system comprises joint-stock commercial banks that are owned by groups of government agencies, state-owned and non-state-owned enterprises as well as city commercial banks that are owned by city governments. Other banking institutions such as rural credit cooperatives and foreign banks only play a very limited role (Naughton 2007: 456–457).

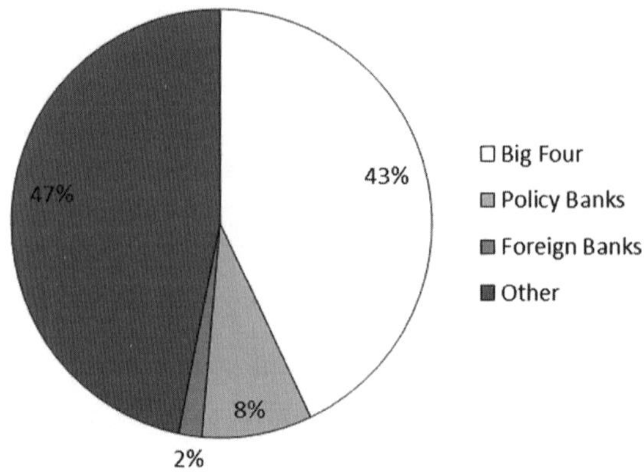

Fig. 3.4 Distribution of assets in China's banking sector (2012) (Sources: CBRC 2013, ABC 2013, BOC 2013, CCB 2013, ICBC 2013)

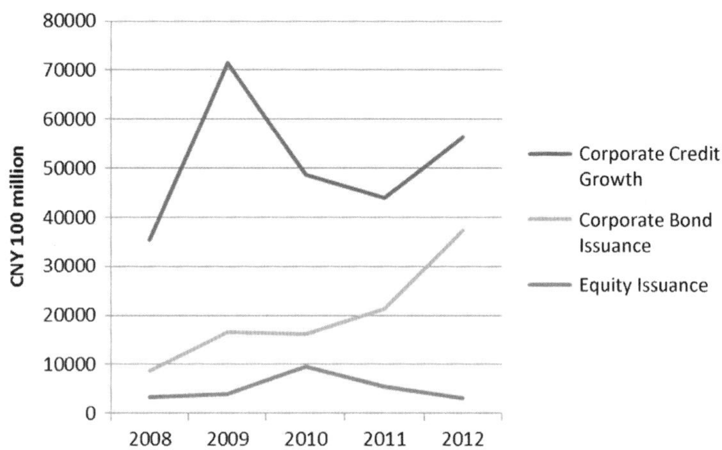

Fig. 3.5 Chinese corporate financing (Sources: PBOC 2013c, n.d.-a, b, c, d, e, f)

increase the interest paid on reserves and central bank bills to protect the banks' balance sheets. Lardy therefore argues that the government has in recent years been the main beneficiary of financial repression since the implicit tax on households resulting from a cap on deposit rates has allowed it to maintain an undervalued currency.[10]

After years of stagnation, the PBOC in 2012 resumed the process of interest rate liberalization, probably in a reaction to the economic woes that had befallen the country with the lackluster performance of its export sector in the wake of the

[10] Lardy (2008: 2) estimates that the implicit tax on household deposits amounted to CNY 255 billion, the equivalent of 4.1 % of GDP, in the first quarter of 2008.

global financial crisis. In June 2012, it raised the ceiling on deposit rates from 100 % to 110 % of its benchmark rate. At the same time, it lowered the floor for lending rates from 90 % to 80 % of its benchmark rate. One month later, the floor for lending rates was further decreased to 70 % of the benchmark rate (PBOC 2013a). In July 2013, the floor on lending rates was abolished. The PBOC reportedly had plans to remove the ceiling on deposit rates at the same time. However, the State Council prevented this much more substantial reform measure due to concerns over its possible ramifications for the country's state-owned banks and the state-owned sector of the economy (Anderlini and Hook 2013).

3.2.3 *China's Bond Markets*

What role do China's bond markets play in a financial system dominated by the banking sector and characterized by financial repression? A brief look at the history of China's bond markets will help us understand their present status. Before the introduction of economic reforms, China did not have any markets for securities. It was only when the government's growing demand for funds and its limited tax-collecting capacity resulted in the creation of government deficits that the idea to fund the national budget via the issuance of bonds was born. The Ministry of Finance issued its first government bonds in 1981, yet it continued to borrow from the PBOC for fiscal purposes until 1993. In the 1980s, SOEs were mandated to purchase government bonds since they were the only entities that had enough money at their disposal. Interest rates for bonds were set administratively with reference to the 1-year bank-deposit rate determined by the central bank. As part of the national credit plan, bond issues could be considered a form of taxation. A secondary market for government bonds did not exist and SOEs were required to hold the bonds until maturity (Walter and Howie 2011: 87–88; Bottelier 2004: 6).

When economic reforms in the 1980s resulted in a growth in household savings, an increasing amount of government bonds was sold directly to individual investors. The interest rate that households received on the bonds was slightly higher than the one that SOEs earned, which signaled the existence of "a real market situation" (Walter and Howie 2011: 88). However, this situation quickly came to an end when from 1987 inflation surged and banks were mandated to reign in lending. With cash-strapped households and SOEs desperate to sell their bonds, a completely unregulated secondary market emerged. Yet this market was rapidly closed by the authorities who moved the bond markets to the newly established exchanges in Shanghai and Shenzhen in order to be able to exercise a higher degree of control over prices and investors (Walter and Howie 2011: 88).

In the late 1980s, policymakers began to legalize China's bond markets and try to increase the attractiveness of government bonds for investors by reducing maturities and increasing coupon rates. In 1991, the first voluntary placement of government bonds took place. The development of China's bond markets further gained in significance when the government in 1993 stopped borrowing from the

PBOC (Bottelier 2004: 6). However, instead of continuing to increase the attractiveness of government bonds for investors, China's policymakers embarked on a different path. In the 1980s, household investors had purchased nearly two thirds of government bonds. Yet in the 1990s, the MOF started ordering the banks to buy the bulk of the bonds at interest rates slightly above the 1-year rate on their rapidly growing retail deposits – an arrangement that allowed the MOF to access household deposits at artificially low interest rates. When China's household investors in the mid-1990s lost their interest in shares and showed a renewed interest in bonds, they found that they had virtually no access to the market for government bonds that had been monopolized by the banks (Walter and Howie 2011: 103–106).

The limited access of individual investors to government bonds was cemented in 1997, when the PBOC mandated all commercial banks to shift their bond trading from the exchanges to the interbank market. In the wake of this decision, the interbank market became China's main market for debt, dominated by state-owned banks and open to other state-owned financial institutions. In the words of Walter and Howie (2011: 106), this shift from a market dominated by household investors to a market dominated by state-owned financial institutions meant that "bonds returned to their earliest stage, when the state was its own investor."

After years of stagnation, the development of China's bond markets only gained new momentum when the PBOC in 2005 began to reform the corporate bond market by introducing new products. China's corporate bond market has long been the least developed segment of the country's debt markets. Since 1984, domestic enterprises have been allowed to issue enterprise bonds (qiyezhai) with the approval of the PBOC. In 1993, regulation was shifted from the PBOC to the State Planning Commission (SPC) that tightened an already existing quota system and only granted issue rights to a small number of centrally-owned SOEs. In such a regulatory environment, it was impossible for China's corporate bond market to flourish (Bottelier 2004: 16–17).

First signs of a willingness to reform the corporate bond market could be found in a document issued by the State Council in 2004 that highlighted the importance of the capital markets and called for their further development (State Council 2004). Against this backdrop, the PBOC in 2005 moved to breathe new life into China's corporate bond markets. Convinced that "[i]f the practices of quota allocation, administrative approval and government intervention were to continue, the prospects for the bond market would be dismal" (Zhou 2006: 9), the PBOC under Zhou Xiaochuan arranged for the introduction of short-term financing bills (duanqi rongziquan) or commercial paper into the corporate debt market. In contrast to the NDRC's enterprise bonds, the issuance of this product under the supervision of the PBOC is not dependent on regulatory approval. Issuers are only required to have a credit rating and to register with the PBOC. However, just as in the case of other bond products, commercial paper can only be sold to institutional investors in the interbank bond market, but is not available to the general public (PBOC 2005).

Three years later, the National Association of Financial Market Institutional Investors (NAFMII), an industry organization established under the auspices of the PBOC, introduced 3-to-5-year medium-term notes (zhongqi piaoju) into China's

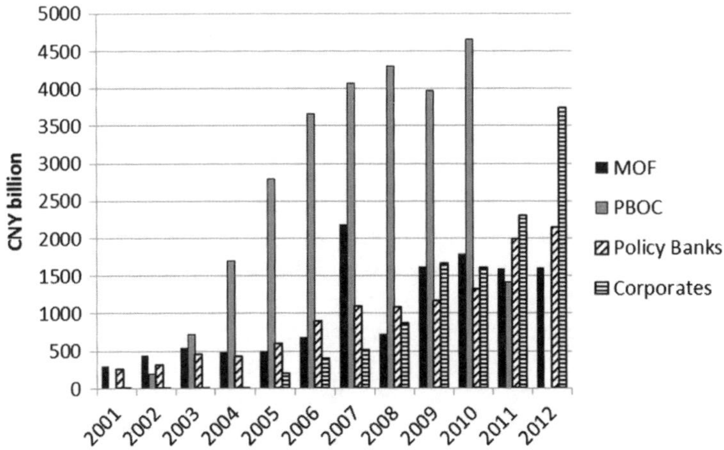

Fig. 3.6 Bond issuance volume by major issuers (Sources: China Bond n.d., PBOC 2013c)

corporate bond markets. Just as short-term financing bills, medium-term notes can only be traded on the interbank bond market. Issuers are not required to apply for regulatory approval, but only need to register with NAFMII (n.d.). In the following years, the PBOC and NAFMII continued to diversify the range of products available in China's markets for corporate debt.

In 2007, the China Securities Regulatory Commission (CSRC) emerged as another driving force in the reform of the country's corporate bond markets. The CSRC allowed listed companies to issue corporate bonds (gongsizhai) to be traded on the country's stock exchanges. Just as the NDRC's enterprise bonds, corporate bonds require regulatory approval. However, in contrast to the NDRC, the CSRC did not establish a quota system (Anderlini 2007b). In recent years, the introduction of new products has allowed for a significant growth in China's market for corporate debt (see Fig. 3.6).

Despite the development of the corporate bond market, China's debt markets have long been heavily dominated by the bond issuance of government agencies and state-owned financial institutions (see Fig. 3.6). Starting from 2005, an increasing amount of financial bonds has been issued by the China Development Bank (CDB), a policy bank mainly responsible for the financing of large infrastructure projects (see Fig. 3.6). Since the CDB is not allowed to take deposits, it exclusively relies on the bond markets for funding. Moreover, due to the growth in China's current account surplus and the ensuing necessity of large-scale sterilization measures to control the domestic money supply under a fixed exchange rate regime, the issuance of government bonds has in recent years been surpassed by the issuance of short-term central bank bills (see Fig. 3.6). The PBOC began to issue these bills in 2003, when it no longer had sufficient amounts of government bonds for its open market operations at its disposal. However, against the backdrop of a slowdown in the growth of reserves, it suspended the issuance of central bank bills in December 2011 and only resumed it in May 2013 (*People's Daily* 2013).

With total bond issuance skyrocketing from less than CNY 600 billion in 2001 to almost CNY 7,500 billion in 2012, China's bond markets have grown rapidly in recent years (see Fig. 3.6). However, as Walter and Howie (2011: 83–110) have argued, China's bond markets do not play a role in the pricing of risk and therefore fail to perform the function of real markets. The ultimate reason for this failure lies in the control of the party-state over the country's banking system. Since the state-owned commercial banks are obliged to buy the bonds issued by the MOF, their price is not set by the market, but fixed by the PBOC at an artificially low level. For this reason, there is almost no trading activity in the secondary market, since the banks would take losses if they sold their bonds because of the artificially low prices in the primary market. Without a market-based price for government bonds, there is no benchmark against which the prices of non-sovereign issuers could be determined. In the primary market for corporate bonds, prices are therefore set with reference to the 1-year deposit rate determined by the PBOC. Since this practice results in artificially low prices for corporate bonds, there is almost no trading activity in the secondary market for corporate debt. The banks therefore tend to hold the bonds until maturity and do not treat them any differently from the loans on their balance sheets, which is why Walter and Howie (2011: 91) have described China's bond markets as "thinly disguised loan market[s]."

3.2.4 China's Equity Markets

What role do China's equity markets play in a financial system in which the dominance of the state-owned banks has undermined the most crucial function of the bond markets? Also in this case a brief look at the equity markets' history will help us understand their present status.[11] The development of China's equity markets began in the 1980s, when companies searching for new avenues to raise funds came up with the idea of issuing shares to the public. The unregulated issuance of shares was initially tolerated by China's central government. Yet when at the end of the 1980s "China's retail investors set off a period of "share fever" centering on Shenzhen" (Walter and Howie 2011: 149) that gradually spread to other parts of the country, local governments were forced by Beijing to intervene in order to prevent social unrest. Instead of abolishing the new way of raising money, the central government decided to regulate the country's emerging equity markets by establishing formal stock exchanges in Shanghai and Shenzhen, thereby giving in to the wishes of the two municipalities that had already started building up equity market institutions in the late 1980s (Walter and Howie 2011: 148–149).

[11] For a detailed account of the development of China's equity markets see Walter and Howie (2003) and Heilmann and Gottwald (2002).

Beijing's decision to establish formal stock exchanges was motivated by the belief of leading policymakers that equity markets could support the government's efforts to reform the state-owned sector of the economy. It was hoped that the sale of minority stakes in SOEs would facilitate their restructuring and, even more importantly, provide them with a new source of funding. In line with this idea, the revenues of IPOs were usually provided to the listing firm or its parent instead of the national treasury. In the initial stages, the "development of the [equity] markets in China was thus clearly part and parcel of the process of state-enterprise reform, rather than being an alternative funding channel for independent and private firms" (Naughton 2007: 469).

In preparation of their IPOs, SOEs typically converted their profitable assets into a subsidiary. When the subsidiary was listed on the stock exchange, the government and the parent company kept a majority of the equity in the firm, and their shares were not allowed to be traded in the market (Naughton 2007: 469). Starting from 2001, attempts have been made to abolish the distinction between tradable and non-tradable shares, but it was only in 2005 that a compromise was reached that allowed each listed company to design its own plan for the conversion of non-tradable shares. These plans needed the approval of the companies' shareholders who usually required compensation since they feared that the conversion of non-tradable shares would drive down shareholder value (Naughton 2007: 474–475). Even though from a technical viewpoint, most shares have been converted, regulatory measures have been taken to ensure that the bulk of these shares remain in the hands of the government. These measures require that sales of more than 1 % of a company's equity capital be transacted privately instead of taking place at the exchanges. Besides, a 20 % capital gains tax on the profits on the sale of shares that were once non-tradable was introduced in 2010. Not least because of these measures, a big part of officially converted shares has never been traded on the market (Areddy and Ng 2010). [12]

Moreover, state entities continue to acquire new shares in the process of initial public offerings that allow them to benefit from the distorted pricing mechanism in the primary market. In order to ensure big increases in share prices on the day of listing, the China Securities Regulatory Commission (CSRC) sets prices artificially low. With profits guaranteed for those who get an allocation of shares of *any* company in the process of China's heavily oversubscribed IPOs, there is no "need for investors to understand companies and the industries in which they operate to arrive at a judgment as to valuation" (Walter and Howie 2011: 184). Since the investors who get the approval to participate in the IPOs are mainly state-owned enterprises, the loss that one SOE has to take due to the valuation of its shares below market demand benefits other SOEs, so that the state-owned sector as a whole does not take a loss. As Walter and Howie (2011: 187) have argued, the redistribution of capital among state entities can thus be considered one of the core functions of China's equity markets.

[12] For an overview of this reform see McGuinness (2009).

Even though China's equity markets have grown rapidly in the two decades since their establishment and have raised enormous amounts of funds for some of the world's largest companies, they still do not perform the most crucial functions of equity markets. Since the bulk of the companies that are listed on China's stock exchanges continue to be majority-owned by the government, China's equity markets fail to function as markets for corporate control that subject companies to the discipline of the markets.[13] Due to the party-state's majority stakes, the shares that are traded on China's stock exchanges do not represent an ownership interest in companies, and share prices do not represent a company's value, but "reflect market liquidity and demand" (Walter and Howie 2011: 190). For this reason, market movements are not so much driven by economic fundamentals as by regulatory changes that may affect market liquidity, which is why China's equity markets are commonly characterized as policy-driven markets. High trading volumes suggest that China's equity markets are proper markets, yet these high volumes only result from excess liquidity that is mainly controlled by agencies of the party-state. Due to a financial system that is characterized by financial repression, China's equity and real-estate markets are the only investment channels that can deliver a real return, which explains why they are rife with speculation (Walter and Howie 2011: 190–191; Naughton 2007: 473).

3.2.5 China's Approach to Capital Controls

China has only been able to maintain its system of financial repression by upholding capital controls that largely isolate the country from the international financial system. However, even though China continues to regulate capital flows to the present day, China's leaders have allowed for some liberalization measures over the course of the last three decades. China's approach to capital account liberalization has been characterized by two main features: Firstly, volatile portfolio flows have been subject to tighter controls than more stable direct investment flows. Secondly, the regulatory regime was initially biased against capital outflows, but has more recently shifted towards a more balanced management of capital flows (Ma and McCauley 2007: 2).

In the early 1990s, China's policymakers started to encourage inflows of foreign direct investment (FDI) in an effort to promote the country's economic development.[14] In the last two decades, FDI has accounted for the lion's share of Chinese capital inflows. Except for restrictions in some sectors that are classified as

[13] In recent years, a growing number of private companies have listed on Shenzhen's small and medium enterprise board that opened in 2004 and its board for growth companies that was established in 2009. However, the market capitalization of these boards still only makes up a tiny fraction of the total market capitalisation of China's equity markets.

[14] For a detailed analysis of the role of FDI in China's capital inflows see Prasad and Wei (2005).

strategic, China has almost completely liberalized FDI in the manufacturing sector. However, FDI in the service sector remains subject to tighter regulation, especially with regard to financial services and telecommunications (Lardy and Douglass 2011: 9).

While China's authorities established incentives for the inflow of FDI at an early stage of the reform process, outward direct investment (ODI) has long been subject to strict regulation. Only in 1999, when the 'Go Global' (zou chu qu) policy was announced, did the authorities start to promote ODI in order to secure the country's access to natural resources, promote the internationalization of China's companies, mitigate upward pressure on the renminbi and slow down the growth of China's foreign exchange reserves (Lardy and Douglass 2011: 9–10).

In contrast to the policies regarding direct investment flows, China's approach to portfolio investment flows has so far been highly restrictive. In 2002, China introduced the Qualified Foreign Institutional Investor (QFII) scheme that allows foreign institutional investors to invest in a certain range of domestic financial assets. Before the introduction of the QFII scheme, foreign investors could only invest in the insignificant B-share segment of China's equity markets that is denominated in foreign currency (Lardy and Douglass 2011: 10–11; Ma and McCauley 2007: 19).[15] In 2013, the quota limiting the total amount of funds that can be invested under the program was raised to USD 150 billion (*Reuters* 2013).

In 2006, China introduced the Qualified Domestic Institutional Investor (QDII) scheme that allows Chinese companies and households to invest in overseas securities via authorized financial institutions. Before the introduction of the QDII scheme, non-bank Chinese residents were barred from investing in overseas securities, while banks were only allowed to invest their dollar holdings in fixed-income securities. QDII investments were initially also restricted to fixed-income products, yet the product range was expanded to include equities in 2007 (Lardy and Douglass 2011: 11; Ma and McCauley 2007: 19). At the end of 2012, SAFE had granted approval to invest a total amount of USD 86 billion to 107 institutions (Yu 2013).

Even though China's regulation of portfolio capital flows remains highly restrictive, questions have arisen over the efficacy of these controls. As Prasad et al. (2006: 183; 192) have pointed out, capital controls tend to become less effective with a country's increasing integration into global trade that allows domestic and international investors to develop ways to circumvent controls. Evidence suggests that it is particularly difficult to maintain capital controls in the face of strong exchange rate pressure. Moreover, Prasad et al. (2006: 192–193) have emphasized that expectations of an appreciation of the renminbi have in recent years resulted in significant inflows of speculative capital. On the other hand,

[15] In addition to outward foreign direct investment and portfolio investment in the framework of the QDII scheme, Chinese outbound capital flows include the investment of China's foreign exchange reserves as well as cross-border lending by China's policy banks. These capital flows will be discussed in Chap. 5.

research by Ma and McCauley suggests that "China's capital controls remain substantially binding" (Ma and McCauley 2007: 22) even though "capital flows between China and the rest of the world do respond to interest rate differentials and to expected exchange rate changes" (Ma and McCauley 2007: 23). In a more recent study, McCauley (2011) confirmed these findings.

In recent years, a relaxation of China's capital controls that would grant individual investors direct access to international capital markets has been repeatedly discussed among China's policymakers. In 2007, the State Administration of Foreign Exchange (SAFE) announced the introduction of the so-called "Hong Kong Through Train" (ganggu zhitong che) pilot scheme under which individual investors were to be allowed to trade securities listed in Hong Kong via the operations of the Bank of China in Tianjin. According to the regulator, it was hoped that the scheme would relieve upward pressure on the renminbi while providing households with a broader range of investment opportunities. Besides, it was aimed at reducing excess liquidity in the country's financial system that was increasing inflationary pressures. Since the pilot scheme did not set a ceiling on capital outflows, it would have resulted in a de facto opening of the capital account in one direction (Anderlini 2007a).[16]

However, SAFE's announcement met with fierce opposition from other bureaucratic agencies. The China Banking Regulatory Commission (CBRC) and the China Securities Regulatory Commission (CSRC), who claimed they had not been properly consulted, were particularly opposed to the scheme since they feared that it could result in a lack of liquidity in China's banking system and its equity markets. SAFE's plan was therefore suspended later that year. However, in 2008, the PBOC's governor Zhou Xiaochuan indicated that the plan was still on track and could even be expanded to include investment destinations other than Hong Kong (Anderlini 2008c; McGregor and Mitchell 2007).

More than 3 years after the 'Through Train' scheme was put on ice, the city of Wenzhou announced a similar plan on its website, saying that it would allow individual residents to invest up to 200 million USD per year in overseas securities.[17] Even though SAFE did not publicly comment on the plan, it was widely believed that it had the blessing of the regulator. However, 2 weeks into its operation, the trial program was suspended by SAFE since Wenzhou's authorities had not been granted approval for its implementation (Anderlini 2011a, b; Ma 2011).

While the attempts of liberal-minded authorities to grant individual investors direct access to international capital markets have so far not been successful, China's efforts to promote the renminbi's role in international trade have led to further tentative steps towards capital account liberalization since they have

[16] According to one interviewee, a limit on the amount that individuals should be allowed to invest was planned from the very beginning but not clearly communicated (Interview No. 20).

[17] Under current regulation, Chinese individuals are only allowed to buy up to USD 50,000 worth of foreign exchange each year.

required improved access to renminbi-denominated financial assets for non-residents.[18] In July 2010, the introduction of a pilot scheme was announced that allows licensed Hong Kong subsidiaries of Chinese fund management and securities companies to invest offshore renminbi in China's capital markets. Originally dubbed as 'mini-QFII' scheme, the new pilot program differs from the original QFII insofar as the latter is not targeted at the investment of offshore renminbi but allows foreign institutional investors to convert foreign currencies into renminbi to invest them in China's capital markets. In December 2011, the CSRC published rules that allow for an initial CNY 20 billion to be invested in China's capital markets under the so-called renminbi-qualified foreign institutional investor (RQFII) program, with the amount that can be invested in equities capped at 20 % of the total (Konyn 2012; Ye 2012; Cookson 2010b). At the end of 2012, the quota was increased to CNY 270 billion. In the following year, the program was expanded to include institutional investors in London, Singapore and Taiwan (Reuters 2013).

Also in support of the renminbi's growing prominence in international trade, the PBOC in August 2010 launched a pilot project under which foreign central banks, banks in Hong Kong and Macau that conduct renminbi clearing and overseas banks involved in renminbi cross-border trade settlement can be granted access to China's inter-bank bond market (PBOC 2011c). Moreover, regulation of capital outflows was slightly liberalized when Chinese non-financial companies were allowed to issue renminbi bonds in Hong Kong. However, companies need to receive permission from the NDRC to issue bonds in the territory and be granted approval by SAFE for the remittance of proceeds to the mainland (Peng 2011). In their attempts to foster the renminbi's internationalization, China's authorities also designated a testing zone in Qianhai Bay in Shenzhen that allows banks in Hong Kong to apply for approval to offer loans to companies based in the zone (Yiu 2013). One year later, Shanghai was designated as another testing ground for experiments with financial liberalization (Barboza 2013).

Despite the numerous tentative steps towards capital account liberalization, China's authorities have so far focused on the development of Hong Kong as an offshore market for renminbi-denominated assets. They have thus tried to combine the advantages of a global trade currency with the benefits of a largely closed capital account that has allowed the country to secure at least a minimum of monetary policy autonomy under a fixed exchange rate regime and, above all, to maintain a system of financial repression that has limited the expenditures of the government and bolstered the state-owned sector of the economy.

[18] The liberalization measures aimed at the renminbi's internationalization will be analyzed in detail in Chap. 4.

3.2.6 Financial Repression and Structural Financial Power

Is the political economy of China's financial system compatible with the acquisition of structural financial power deriving from the international role of a country's financial markets? On the basis of the preceding analysis, an answer to this question can now be provided. China's financial system is dominated by a banking sector in which the most important players are all majority-owned by the government – an arrangement that allows the government to channel capital in a way that supports the state-owned sector of the economy and facilitates the implementation of industrial policy. State-ownership of the biggest banks and an administered cap on deposit rates do not only guarantee low funding costs for SOEs and low borrowing costs for the government, but also ensure low sterilization costs that have enabled the party-state to prevent a significant appreciation of the country's currency in the face of massive current account surpluses and allowed it to acquire an enormous amount of foreign exchange reserves. The very system of financial repression that has enabled the party-state to maintain a fixed exchange rate regime by suppressing sterilization costs has also necessitated the maintenance of a fixed exchange rate regime since it leaves no room for the development of a consumption-led growth model and therefore forces the authorities to promote a growth strategy focusing on investment and exports.

In the context of such a system of financial repression, bond markets with a significant market scale can only exist if they do not provide households with investment alternatives to bank deposits since such an alternative would result in an outflow of funds from the state-controlled banking sector. For this reason, China's policymakers have ensured that the country's debt markets are heavily dominated by securities issued by the government and quasi-governmental agencies whose interest rates can be set artificially low since the state-owned banks are mandated to buy them. China's bond markets thus fail to play a role in the pricing of risk and are hardly attractive to international investors.

Just as China's bond markets, China's equity markets do not pose a risk to the country's system of financial repression since their main function is to provide the state-owned sector of the economy with an additional funding avenue. With the bulk of listed companies majority-owned by the government, China's equity markets are not driven by economic fundamentals, but by policy decisions of the government, which is why they are highly volatile. For this reason, China's equity markets lack the potential to attract foreign investors who do not wish to play speculative games.

The maintenance of China's system of financial repression has not only relied on the hampering of the development of the country's financial markets, but has also been dependent on China's effective maintenance of capital controls that have ensured that China's household savings remain in the country's banking system. While it is theoretically possible to liberalize capital inflows while at the same time maintaining a tight regulation of outflows, China's financial markets could only become a dominant destination for international investors if the country's regulation of capital flows guaranteed a smooth withdrawal of funds at any time. However, such a regulatory regime would eventually result in an outflow of domestic savings in search of higher returns and hence undermine the repressive nature of China's financial system.

Since the liberalization of the country's financial markets is not compatible with the maintenance of China's system of financial repression, China will not be able to acquire structural financial power deriving from the international attractiveness of financial markets as long as it is not willing to subject its financial system to radical reforms. China's system of financial repression also prevents China from acquiring structural financial power deriving from the establishment of a domestic currency as an international store of value since that would also require the internationalization of China's financial markets. However, China's financial system has allowed the party-state to contain sterilization costs and thereby provided it with the power to delay the costs of adjustment to balance of payments surpluses. Besides, the ability to contain sterilization costs has enabled China to accumulate the massive stockpile of foreign exchange reserves that is the source of its relational financial power.

With China's system of financial repression ultimately serving to maintain the CCP's tight grip over the country's economic and political system, voluntary change is unlikely since it would result in a radical change of China's political economy that would harm the vested interests of many of the most influential players. However, while it can be assumed that there is strong opposition among China's elite to the radical change that would result from a restructuring of the country's financial system, it cannot be denied that especially in the financial bureaucracy liberal-minded reformers can be found who are keen to introduce a higher degree of liberalization. If these reformers, in the context of the country's fragmented authoritarianism, are given permission to realize some of their ambitions, consequences unforeseen by China's senior leaders might well ensue that could result in a radical change of the country's financial system. While the PBOC's plan to undermine the country's capital controls by liberalizing individual outward portfolio investment did not gain acceptance, attempts aimed at liberalizing the interest rate regime and reforming the bond markets have been more successful. Perhaps most importantly, by allowing the PBOC to experiment with controlled currency internationalization, China's senior leaders might already have unleashed forces beyond the control of the country's authorities that could eventually compel Beijing to give in to liberalization pressures.

Moreover, China's political economy could become subject to pressures that would make the liberalization of its financial system inevitable. In the face of the recent slowdown in export growth, the sustainability of the country's growth model has already become highly doubtful. In order to maintain sufficiently high growth rates and thus to sustain the regime's legitimacy, China's leaders might eventually be compelled to walk the talk and embark on a consumption-led growth strategy that is not compatible with the current system of financial repression. However, while the possibility of a radical change in China's financial system cannot even be ruled out for the near future, we have to bear in mind that such a change would result in a radical restructuring of the country's political economy. A China with significant structural financial power at its disposal might therefore well be considered much less of a threat in the western world than today's China with its substantial relational financial power.

3.3 Financial Repression and Liberalization Pressures

The political economy of China's present financial system bears striking similarities with the political economy of Japan's financial system in the postwar era. Just as China's financial system, Japan's financial system was designed to ensure the state's ability to conduct industrial policy via the control over the allocation of credit. It was characterized by a dominance of the banking sector and the suppression of capital markets, just as its Chinese counterpart. In order to guarantee low funding costs for strategically important sectors of the economy, the Japanese state also relied on the administrative setting of interest rates so that households were forced to bear the costs of industrial development. However, while the Japanese state's control over the allocation of credit resulted from the dependence of the banks on the BOJ for the provision of funds, the Chinese party-state has ensured its control through the continuous state-ownership of the banks that allows it to influence their lending decisions.

Starting from the 1970s, Japan's financial system was increasingly subject to liberalization pressures that initially resulted from a growing government deficit. While the government mandated the banks to absorb its growing debt, the banks were not willing to subsidize the government at ever increasing costs and hence demanded reforms aimed at reducing their burden. In response to this quest, the MOF facilitated the development of a secondary bond market, made first tentative steps towards the liberalization of interest rates and introduced competition into the financial system when it started to woo investors with increasing interest rates on its bonds. In addition to these measures, the liberalization of capital controls and the ensuing issuance of growing amounts of corporate securities in overseas markets further undermined Japan's system of regulatory control. While foreign pressure to liberalize was only important insofar as it forced the authorities to react to structural changes that they were already well aware of, US pressure to revalue the yen indirectly contributed to further steps towards liberalization since the BOJ reacted to the yen's appreciation with a loose monetary policy that drove up the value of Japan's capital markets and prompted a surge in financial innovation.

Even though the first steps towards financial system liberalization had already been taken in the second half of the 1980s when Japan became the world's largest creditor, the country's financial system remained one of the most heavily regulated systems in the developed world. The Japanese creditor state was thus not in a position to rival American structural financial power. Japan might have acquired a significant degree of structural financial power if liberalization had continued, yet in the wake of the bursting of the asset price bubble, reform was no longer high on the agenda. When Japan's policymakers finally embarked on a strategy of substantial reform in 1996, the country's economy was already so deep in the doldrums that the acquisition of structural financial power was nothing but a remote possibility.

In contrast to the experience of the Japanese authorities, China's policymakers have so far been spared serious liberalization pressures. China has not only been able to keep its budget deficit under control, an ability that has at least partially resulted from the fact that the government has extensively relied on lending by the country's state-owned banks to achieve fiscal policy objectives. Moreover, due to its ownership of the banks, the party-state has been in a position to mandate them to absorb not only the government's debt, but also the bills issued by the PBOC that have allowed the country to maintain a current account surplus under a fixed exchange rate regime. Even if China's budget deficit substantially widened in the years to come, it can therefore be assumed that the party-state's control over the banks would prevent the build-up of serious liberalization pressures. Also in contrast to Japan, China has so far refrained from significantly liberalizing the capital account. China's companies therefore do not have the chance to shift the market for corporate finance to less regulated markets overseas and thus push the government into liberalization measures, even though the permission to issue bonds in Hong Kong may be considered a first step in this direction. Last but not least, its relative political independence has allowed China to resist pressures to revalue the renminbi and to allow foreign financial institutions to play a more prominent role in its financial system.

On a more basic level, the countries' different approaches to the control over the allocation of credit explains why Japan was faced with growing liberalization pressures while China has so far not been confronted with serious challenges. While the state's control in the case of Japan resulted from the dependence of the banks on the BOJ for the provision of funds, the Chinese party-state has guaranteed its control through the continuous state-ownership of the banks. In contrast to Japan's system of administrative guidance, China's system hence does not rely on a continuous shortage of capital that creates a dependency relationship between the banks and the state's financial authorities. Quite on the contrary, it has proven sustainable in the context of steadily growing financial resources. The deeper reason for these different approaches can be found in the ultimate objectives of the classic developmental state exemplified by Japan on the one hand and the instrumental developmental state exemplified by China on the other hand: While the former pursues the goals of securing rapid economic growth, technological autonomy and international competitiveness as ends in themselves, the latter only embraces these objectives with the ultimate goal of securing the ruling elites' grip on power. For this reason, control over the allocation of credit lost in importance in the case of Japan when the country had reached a certain degree of development, and the authorities were thus not radically opposed to a liberalization of the financial system. In China's case, however, control over the allocation of credit ultimately aims at ensuring the CCP's continuous control over the country's political economy, which is why many senior leaders remain heavily opposed to financial system liberalization.

Chapter 4
Financial Repression and Currency Internationalization

According to the framework developed in Chap. 2, the main sources of structural financial power are the international status of a state's financial markets and the global role of its currency. Chapter 3 has already explained why the acquisition of structural financial power deriving from the international role of financial markets is not compatible with the political economy of China's financial system. The question if a state's currency can attain a prominent international role is partly dependent on the ability of its financial markets to attract international investors, yet it is also influenced by other factors. This chapter will thus give an overview of the determinants of currency internationalization on the basis of which it will analyze the renminbi's potential to internationalize and thus complete the assessment of China's potential to acquire structural power in global finance.

Section 4.1 looks into the literature on currency internationalization that identifies confidence in a currency's stable value, open, deep and broad financial markets and extensive transactional networks in the global economy as the main factors determining a currency's potential for internationalization. Section 4.2 examines the reasons for Japan's failure to establish the yen as a global core currency. Section 4.3 reviews China's criticism of the dollar's role in the international monetary system and provides an overview of China's motives for currency internationalization. Drawing on the determinants of currency internationalization identified in the first section of the chapter, it then assesses the renminbi's potential to internationalize. Against this backdrop, it sheds light on the policy measures that China's authorities have taken to promote the renminbi's internationalization. It concludes with a reflection on China's experiment of "currency internationalization under controlled convertibility" (Subacchi 2010: 1). Section 4.4 compares China's approach to currency internationalization with the Japanese approach.

S. Heep, *China in Global Finance*, Global Power Shift,

DOI 10.1007/978-3-319-02466-0_4,

4.1 Determinants of Currency Internationalization

The following sections provide an overview of the different aspects of currency internationalization, explain the economic as well as the political determinants of currency internationalization and introduce the concept of negotiated currencies.[1]

4.1.1 Aspects of Currency Internationalization

As Cohen (1971: 13–14) has pointed out, we can distinguish between 3 different aspects of currency internationalization in the private and the official realm that correspond to the three basic functions of domestic money. If a currency functions as an international medium of exchange, the private sector can employ it for the settlement of international transactions, while the public sector can use it for interventions in the foreign exchange markets. If a currency functions as an international unit of account, it can be used by the private sector for the denomination of internationally traded goods and financial assets, while it can be used by the public sector as a standard of value in which to express exchange rate parities or as a monetary anchor against which the domestic money can be pegged. If a currency functions as an international store of value, the private sector can hold it as an asset, while the public sector can include it in its foreign exchange reserves (Helleiner 2008: 355–356; Cohen 1971: 13–14). Even though different factors may contribute to different aspects of currency internationalization, every single aspect of internationalization is supportive of the others. For this reason, the internationalization of currencies is usually explained in aggregate terms. However, this does not mean that it is not possible for a currency to assume international standing in one of the above mentioned areas without assuming international standing in the others (Helleiner 2008: 356–357).

4.1.2 Economic Determinants of Currency Internationalization

It is generally agreed that there are three key economic factors contributing to currency internationalization (Chinn and Frankel 2005; Cohen 2004; Tavlas 1991). Firstly, a currency's internationalization depends on the confidence of foreigners in its stable value that mainly derives from "a proven track record of relatively low inflation and inflation variability" (Cohen 2004: 10) as well as low exchange rate volatility. This aspect is particularly important to a currency's function as a store of

[1] Section 4.1 largely follows Helleiner (2008).

value and a unit of account. The second factor contributing to a currency's internationalization is the existence of well developed and open financial markets within the issuing country that attract private and public investors on a significant scale. Finally, and most importantly, the issuing country needs to maintain extensive transactional networks in the global economy "since nothing enhances a currency's acceptability more than the prospect of acceptability by others" (Cohen 2004: 11). A country's share in world output and world trade thus plays a crucial role in determining whether its currency will play an international role. Moreover, due to the network externalities associated with the international use of a single currency, "an international currency can assume a global role that is well out of proportion to the issuing country's size in the world economy" (Helleiner 2008: 359) and may thus make it difficult for newcomers to assume international standing.

4.1.3 Political Determinants of Currency Internationalization

Even though the key determinants of currency internationalization are all economic in nature, politics also plays a role in a currency's assumption of international status. As Helleiner (2008: 360–366) has pointed out, we can distinguish between the influence of politics on the economic determinants of currency internationalization and the direct influence of politics on a currency's international role. As far as confidence in a currency's stable value is concerned, Andrew Walter (2006: 57) has noted that "a commitment to a low-inflation monetary policy is unlikely to be credible in the absence of institutional factors that constrain its use." According to Walter (2006: 57), these institutional factors "could include the delegation of monetary policy to an independent central bank or the support of a dominant political constituency for conservative monetary policies." More generally, institutions of limited, constitutional government contribute to international confidence in a currency's stable value.

Political factors also influence the development of financial markets that make a currency's international use attractive. As has been explained in the preceding chapters, well developed and open financial markets are not compatible with a political system in which the state engages in comprehensive development planning. Besides, Walter (2006: 57) has pointed out that conditions of limited, constitutional government as well as pro-creditor legal frameworks are important prerequisites for the development of financial markets of international significance. Political factors can also influence the issuing country's transactional networks in the global economy, for example if the government promotes the creation of payments and clearing systems to facilitate the international use of the domestic currency (Helleiner 2008: 362).

As Helleiner (2008: 362) has emphasized, "the international political reach of the issuing state may also boost the country's economic transactional networks."

Sterling's global role accordingly did not only result from Britain's dominant role in international trade and finance, but was further encouraged "by the economic activities of the increasingly far-flung official posts of the British empire" (Helleiner 2008: 362). Similarly, the dollar's function as international core currency was not only promoted by private US trade and investment abroad, "but also by the dramatic growth of US overseas aid, technical assistance and military spending" (Helleiner 2008: 362). Finally, political factors also influence the emergence of international currencies via the issuing country's current account position. In a world of fiat money, countries that deliberately embark on export-led growth strategies will not be able to establish their money as the main international reserve currency (Kroeber 2009a).

4.1.4 Internationalization of 'Negotiated Currencies'

It has already been pointed out that the influence of politics on currency internationalization is not limited to the indirect influence via economic determinants. Helleiner (2008) has reminded us that it is useful to recall Strange's (1971) typology of international currencies in this context. Strange (1971) distinguishes between top currencies, master currencies, negotiated currencies and neutral currencies, arguing that politics plays a prominent role with respect to the international status of master currencies and negotiated currencies, whereas the dominant position of top currencies and the prominent role of neutral currencies mainly result from their economic attractiveness. According to Strange (1971: 4), master currencies are established "when an imperial or hegemonial state imposes the use of its currency on other political entities, whether they are allied states, dependent protectorates, or colonies." Negotiated currencies, on the other hand, are not forced upon others, but are also used for political rather than economic reasons. They are "characterized by the need of the issuing state to bargain or negotiate diplomatically with the users about the terms and conditions of its use" (Strange 1971: 4–5) that commonly involve the offer of military protection or financial incentives. However, the international standing of negotiated currencies does not necessarily result from explicit negotiations, but might rely on "an implicit understanding" (Strange 1971: 5) among the countries involved. While Strange (1971) suggested that negotiated currencies are usually currencies in decline, Helleiner (2008: 366) has emphasized that the characteristics of negotiated currencies may also apply to currencies on the rise.

Any analysis of negotiated currencies will have to take into account the politics of both the state that tries to maintain or establish its currency in the international arena and the states that may accept it as a monetary leader. Follower states may influence the international standing of a currency by including it in their foreign exchange reserves, by using it as a monetary anchor or by settling transactions in their international trade in that currency. Besides, "[t]he attitude of follower states towards the private use of the dominant foreign currency *within* their domestic borders may also be significant" (Helleiner 2008: 364).[2] Whether a potential follower state chooses to support a potential monetary leader depends on factors at the domestic level, the state level and the systemic level. At the domestic level, private actors with close economic ties to the issuing state may lobby for the support of a currency in order to lower transaction costs. At the state level, similarities between the political and the economic system of the issuing state and the potential monetary follower may encourage policymakers' support for a currency. Perhaps most importantly, the potential followers' security position within the international system may influence policymakers' decisions at the systemic level (Helleiner 2008: 365; Strange 1971: 18).

As far as the potential monetary leader is concerned, policymakers' decisions to negotiate their currency's standing may likewise be influenced by factors at the domestic, the state and the systemic level that may also play a role in determining their willingness to promote the international use of their currency indirectly by boosting its economic attractiveness. At the domestic level, economic actors may lobby for the internationalization of the domestic currency in order to lower transaction costs. On the other hand, they may oppose currency internationalization due to fears of a loss of competitiveness of the country's export sector (Helleiner 2008: 365). Besides, policymakers' may choose to boost their currency's international standing in an attempt to appeal to the domestic constituency by playing to their nationalistic feelings. In addition, the particular interests of bureaucratic agencies that would be affected by the internationalization of the domestic currency may also have a bearing on policymakers' decisions. Concerning the state level, Cohen (2004: 20–24) has argued that decisions may be influenced by the possible consequences of currency internationalization with regard to domestic monetary policy, seigniorage gains, political symbolism and the distribution of financial power between states. Last but not least, at the systemic level, policymakers may be influenced by their country's position within the global political economy (Helleiner 2008: 365).

4.2 Japan's Failure to Internationalize the Yen

The following sections analyze Japan's approach towards the internationalization of the yen in the 1980s and 1990s. They provide an overview of Japan's foreign exchange controls in the early postwar years and then look into the effects of the Yen-Dollar Agreement on the yen's internationalization, shed light on the yen's internationalization in the wake of the Plaza Agreement and analyze Japan's changing attitudes towards currency internationalization following the Asian Financial Crisis.

---

[2] For a detailed analysis of the latter aspect see Helleiner (2003).

4.2.1 Foreign Exchange Controls in the Early Postwar Years

In the first decades after the war, Japan maintained a system of tight foreign exchange controls to uphold its system of financial repression and to make sure that the limited amount of foreign currency was available for the purchase of necessary imports (Rosenbluth 1989: 53). Both current and capital account transactions were exclusively conducted in foreign currency, and the yen's use was confined to that of a purely domestic currency. It was only in the early 1960s when Japan's balance of payments position began to improve that the first cautious liberalization moves were made. A yen exchange system was introduced that allowed for the use of the yen in external settlements. At the same time, the yen achieved current account convertibility for non-residents with the introduction of free-yen deposit accounts. In 1964, the yen achieved full current account convertibility when Japan accepted its IMF obligations. However, strict exchange controls and a distinction between domestic yen and free yen remained in place, and the authorities shied away from promoting the role of the yen as an international currency (Takagi 2011: 75; Kunieda 1995: 1).

By the 1970s, continuing high growth rates had turned Japan into an economic heavyweight in terms of its share in world output and international trade. Yet against the backdrop of the 1973 oil crisis and Japan's ensuing balance of payments difficulties, the MOF displayed significant resistance towards the internationalization of the yen, fearing that it could destabilize the exchange rate and hence put Japan's economic growth in jeopardy. It was only in 1980 when Japan had recovered from the oil crises and was running a substantial current account surplus that the Foreign Exchange and Foreign Trade Control Law was revised and the status of foreign exchange transactions was changed from 'restricted in principle' to 'free in principle'. However, the revised law allowed the government to impose controls necessary for the management of the balance of payments and the exchange rate and a wide range of transactions thus continued to be subject to regulatory approval (Takagi 2011: 76–77; Kunieda 1995: 1–2).

4.2.2 The Effects of the Yen-Dollar Agreement

It was only in the mid-1980s that the internationalization process gained momentum. Among the reasons for the acceleration was political pressure by the United States for the internationalization of the yen that "signalled a remarkable *volte face* in United States sentiment towards Japanese economic development" (Leyshon 1994: 128–129). In the first decades after the war the US had supported Japan's economic growth not least by allowing the yen-dollar exchange rate to remain unchanged between 1949 and the end of the Bretton Woods regime in 1971. Yet against the backdrop of Japan's growing current account surpluses, the US became convinced that Japan was benefiting from an undervalued yen that provided it with an 'unfair' advantage in international product markets. It was argued that the isolation of Japan's financial system from the international financial architecture allowed Japan to maintain low interest rates that did not only provide its companies with capital cost advantages, but also encouraged large outflows of capital resulting in a further depreciation of the yen (Leyshon 1994: 129).

In the negotiations leading to the 1984 Yen-Dollar Agreement, the US therefore pushed for a deregulation of Japan's financial system, arguing that this would assimilate Japanese macroeconomic conditions to those in other industrialized countries (Leyshon 1994: 129). Moreover, US representatives claimed that the deregulation of Japan's financial markets would increase the attractiveness of yen assets and thus lead to an appreciation of the Japanese currency (Kunieda 1995: 2). To further these goals, the US also pushed for a liberalization of the Euroyen market, assuming that a growth in offshore yen investment options would not only increase foreign demand for yen-denominated financial assets and hence drive up the yen's value but would also "increase the arbitrage opportunities between the international and domestic markets, and thus vitiate artificial restrictions on any financial instruments in Japan for which there were close substitutes overseas" (Rosenbluth 1989: 79).

Against the backdrop of the liberalization moves that followed the signing of the Yen-Dollar Agreement, Japan's financial markets attracted a growing number of foreign investors due to the country's booming economy, its low inflation rate and its appreciating currency. Moreover, the share of yen-denominated bonds issued in the Euromarkets more than doubled in the years between 1985 and 1990. However, most of the Euroyen bonds were issued by Japanese companies and acquired by Japanese investors, and the share of foreign holdings in the bond and equity markets remained negligible. The yen's internationalization had thus only gained very limited momentum (Hilpert 1998).

As has been pointed out in Chap. 3, the reason why US pressure to liberalize Japan's financial system was influential was that it "altered the balance between the domestic coalitions formed in the Japanese arguments about reform" (Moran 1991: 111). To a lesser degree, conflicting domestic attitudes had also emerged with respect to the internationalization of the yen. Most importantly, there was increasing disagreement between Japan's monetary authorities regarding the issue of currency internationalization. Traditionally, both the MOF and the BOJ had been opposed to the yen's internationalization since they feared that it would result in constraints on domestic monetary policy and upward pressure on the yen that would undermine the authorities' control over the allocation of credit and put the country's export-led growth in jeopardy. However, against the backdrop of an increasing liberalization of the country's financial system and ever growing current account surpluses, the MOF had come to appreciate the opportunity to take advantage of the yen's internationalization to introduce a higher degree of market discipline into the domestic financial system. The BOJ, on the other hand, continued its resistance to the yen's internationalization (Rosenbluth 1989: 51–52; 79–80).

The first steps towards the liberalization of Japan's financial system were already complicating the BOJ's implementation of monetary policy that mainly relied on the provision of credit to banks at the discount window and intervention in the interbank market. For this reason, the central bank was pushing for the development of a market in short-term government securities that would allow it to engage in open-market operations. However, the MOF refused to give in to the BOJ's wish since a market for government bills would have made the management of Japan's growing public debt both more difficult and more costly. Besides, it did not want to burden the banks that feared that a market for treasury bills would further erode their deposit base (Rosenbluth 1989: 63–64).

It has been argued that the failure to develop a market for government bills or, more generally, a functioning money market, was one of the main obstacles to the establishment of the yen as an international reserve currency since it severely limited the options available to foreigners wanting to invest in yen-denominated assets (Helleiner 2000: 241). However, while the structure of Japan's sovereign debt certainly hampered the yen's internationalization, the mere introduction of a market for government bills would not have compensated for the fact that Tokyo remained "the most tightly regulated of the world's great financial capitals" (Moran 1991: 105) and that the capacity of Japan's financial markets to attract international investors hence remained very limited.

4.2.3 Currency Internationalization in the Wake of the Plaza Agreement

While the effects of the Yen-Dollar Agreement on the yen's internationalization remained limited, the yen's global role was indirectly bolstered by US pressure for Japanese support in the fight against the growing American trade deficit. By 1985, the US had eventually come to realize the effects of the strong dollar on the US current account position and started to push for its devaluation. In September 1985, the finance ministers of the Group of Five agreed to intervene in the foreign exchange markets in order to achieve a controlled depreciation of the dollar, thereby giving in to US pressure. As a result of the Plaza Agreement, the value of the yen soared to unexpected levels, rising from JPY 240 to JPY 170 to the dollar within a period of only 7 months. This rapid appreciation "led to a large outflow of Japanese financial capital from 1985 onwards as money flowed out into what had suddenly become much cheaper investments" (Leyshon 1994: 130–131). Two years later, when the Louvre Accord was agreed upon by the Group of Seven in an attempt to stabilize the foreign exchange markets, Japan was pressured into holding interest rates below those in other core countries in order to stimulate its economy and thus to further reduce the US trade deficit. In the wake of this agreement, the volume of Japanese capital flowing abroad increased still further (Leyshon 1994: 130–131).

The realignment of the yen-dollar exchange rate in the short term benefited US manufacturers at the expense of their Japanese counterparts. Japanese exports, which had become ever more important to the country's economy, declined by almost 16 % from 1985 to 1986, resulting in a significant slowdown of economic growth (Itoh 1990: 177). Against this backdrop, a surge in Japanese overseas investment took place as Japanese companies began to establish new production sites in East and South East Asia in an effort to lower production costs. Japan's overseas investment in turn increased Japanese bank loans to the region "as the banks followed their old customers abroad" (Katada 2008: 402). Japanese aid flows into East Asia also grew significantly. As a result, yen-denominated liabilities reached new heights in countries such as Indonesia, the Philippines, Malaysia, Thailand and South Korea. In the late 1980s, they began to surpass dollar-denominated liabilities, which prompted the central banks in the region to increase the share of yen holdings in their foreign exchange reserves.[3] Besides, Japan's growing capital outflows into East Asia boosted the yen's role in Japan's trade, not least because they increased the volume of imported goods produced by Japanese companies located in East Asia for the country's domestic market (Helleiner 2000: 241–242).

As Helleiner (1992: 435, 2000: 241) has emphasized, the Plaza Agreement also contributed to a changing attitude of Japan's monetary authorities towards the yen's internationalization since the loose monetary policy pursued to smooth the fall of the dollar and the ensuing experience of the bubble economy made them realize the dangers of the country's dependence on the US currency. Against this backdrop, Japanese government officials started to question the dollar-based international financial system and to declare their support for a more important international role of the yen and the IMF's special drawing rights in the late 1980s. At the same time, the BOJ began to promote the development of a liquid short-term money market to increase the yen's attractiveness for non-residents. Even though the BOJ's efforts remained limited, "they marked an important first step in a process that was crucial if Japan was to promote the yen as an international currency" (Helleiner 2000: 241).

4.2.4 Changing Attitudes Following the Asian Financial Crisis

Against the backdrop of the 1997 Asian Financial Crisis, the yen's internationalization gained further momentum. While the US insisted that the crisis was caused by Asian 'crony capitalism', Japanese leaders were convinced that it had resulted from volatile capital flows and an over-reliance on the dollar. Due to their export-led growth strategies, most of the countries afflicted by the crisis had pegged their monies to the US currency. However, since the late 1980s, their trade with Japan

[3] As Saori Katada (2008: 402) has pointed out, the increase in official holdings of the yen was to some extent the direct result of the yen's appreciation.

had become increasingly important. As a result of the dollar's appreciation by roughly 50 % against the yen between 1995 and 1997, these countries were hence confronted with growing balance of payments problems (Katada 2002: 89–90; Helleiner 2000: 243–244). In the eyes of Japanese policymakers, the crisis had thus drawn attention to "the need to ensure that growing intraregional trade was matched by increasingly close exchange rate management within the region" (Helleiner 2000: 243–244).

As Saori Katada (2002: 90–93) has pointed out, Japan's efforts to internationalize the yen in the wake of the Asian Financial Crisis were motivated by economic as well political reasons. The economic turmoil in the countries afflicted by the crisis severely struck Japan's already depressed economy since it slowed down Japanese exports to the region. Besides, both Japanese manufacturers and Japanese banks were highly exposed to the countries suffering from the crisis due to the effects of the yen's appreciation in the wake of the Plaza Agreement. There were thus strong material incentives for Japan to contribute to the region's economic stabilization. Yet in addition to these motives, Japan also had an "ideational stake" (Katada 2002: 92) in the region's recovery. Japanese policymakers claimed that they had promoted the region's economic success "by providing foreign aid, direct investment, and a development model to follow" (Katada 2002: 92) that they did not want to see discredited by the US diagnosis of the source of the crisis. For this reason, they had to offer a solution that was not in line with the Washington Consensus that prescribed drastic liberalization measures. Last but not least, Japan's desire to internationalize the yen was further reinforced by its determination to strengthen Tokyo as an international financial center in the wake of the 1996 'Big Bang' liberalization moves (Katada 2002: 98).

Starting from 1998, Japan's policymakers took a range of measures aimed at boosting the yen's regional standing. Japan's Miyazawa Plan, designed to support the countries that had been struck by the crisis, tried to encourage the yen's use in the region by providing yen-denominated funding. Moreover, Japan offered to guarantee sovereign yen-dominated bonds and loans, thus moving "Japanese aid policy explicitly into promotion of yen internationalization as a national priority" (Grimes 2003: 60). Besides, Japan tried to strengthen the yen's role in the region by promoting yen-denominated swap agreements in the context of the Chiang Mai Initiative. In an attempt to increase the attractiveness of yen-assets to foreign investors, the maturity of government securities was diversified and non-residents were exempted from withholding taxes. Last but not least, the country's settlement systems were improved in order to facilitate cross-border transactions (Katada 2002: 102; Helleiner 2000: 243).

However, despite Japan's efforts to internationalize its currency, the yen's international role has failed to gain in importance in recent years. While its international use increased from the late 1980s into the early 1990s, its importance started to decline in the mid-1990s (Katada 2002: 98–101).[4] The main reasons for

[4] The only exception from this development was the increase in the use of the yen in the settlement of Japanese imports from Southeast Asia which continued into the late 1990s (Katada 2002: 101).

the failure of Japan's currency offensive were Japan's economic stagnation since the bursting of the bubble at the start of the 1990s and the problems resulting from the financial meltdown. Yet as Katada (2008: 409–410) has pointed out, Japan's efforts to boost the yen's international standing also suffered from the response of Japan's private sector. Foreign exchange transactions have turned into lucrative business both for the country's banks and for its trading and manufacturing companies. Moreover, Japan's export sector has been unwilling to support the yen's internationalization due to fears that it might undermine the country's international competitiveness. Besides, the yen's role as a trade currency has also been hampered by the fact that Japan's imports are dominated by natural resources that are traditionally priced in dollars.

Last but not least, Japan's efforts to boost the yen's standing in East Asia have met with resistance in the region. Anti-Japanese attitudes resulting from Japan's role in the Second World War have made it difficult for Japan to establish itself as a regional monetary leader. Even more importantly, East Asian countries have been hesitant to accept a more important role of the yen due to their reliance on the US as their major export market and their main security partner (Katada 2002: 86–87).

4.3 China's Approach to Currency Internationalization

The following sections examine China's currency offensive in the wake of the global financial crisis. They review China's criticism of the dollar's role in the international monetary system and provide an overview of China's motives to promote the renminbi's internationalization. Drawing on the determinants of currency internationalization identified in the first section of the chapter, they then assess the renminbi's potential to establish itself on the global stage and examine the steps that the Chinese authorities have taken to promote the renminbi's internationalization. The section concludes with a reflection on China's experiment of controlled currency internationalization.

4.3.1 China's Criticism of US 'Monetary Hegemony'

Against the backdrop of the global financial crisis, China's elite engaged in a harsh criticism of the dollar's dominant role in the international monetary system. In March 2009, PBOC governor Zhou Xiaochuan (2009) publicly called for an end of the current international monetary system. On the eve of a summit of the Group of Twenty, an essay was posted on the PBOC's website in which Zhou (2009) claimed that the "outbreak of the crisis and its spillover to the entire world reflect the inherent vulnerabilities and systemic risks in the existing international monetary system." Without explicitly referring to the US dollar, Zhou pointed out that the weakness of a system that relied on the domestic money of a single country lay in the fact that the issuing country's domestic monetary policy goals were not reconcilable with its international responsibilities: If the issuing country tried to fight domestic inflation, it failed to meet international liquidity demands. Yet if it tried to stimulate domestic demand, it ran the risk of creating excess international liquidity.

For this reason, Zhou (2009a) called for the creation of "an international reserve currency that is disconnected from individual nations and is able to remain stable in the long run," thereby reviving a proposal by John Maynard Keynes who had suggested the introduction of a supranational currency in the run-up to the 1944 Bretton Woods conference. For the sake of reforming the current monetary system, Zhou suggested expanding the role of the International Monetary Fund's Special Drawing Rights (SDR), a unit of account that was introduced by the Fund in 1969 but failed to play a prominent role after the breakdown of the Bretton Woods regime. While Zhou (2009) acknowledged that the creation of an international currency was "a bold initiative that requires extraordinary political vision and courage," he made concrete suggestions on how to broaden the scope of the use of SDRs, calling for the introduction of a settlement system between SDRs and other currencies, the creation of financial assets denominated in SDRs and an improvement of their valuation. Even though he did not explicitly mention the renminbi, he advocated for the inclusion of the currencies of all major economies in the currency basket determining the value of the SDR, implying that China's currency should be given some weight. Last but not least, Zhou (2009) suggested to create an "open-ended SDR-denominated fund" that would allow for the exchange of dollar reserves into SDRs that could be managed by the IMF.[5]

Three months after Zhou's (2009) proposal attracted the attention of the global financial community, China's central bank repeated its criticism of the international monetary system and its excessive reliance on the dollar. This time around, China's attack was accompanied by a warning to the US concerning its adoption of loose monetary and fiscal policies in response to the financial crisis and a call for enhanced supervision of the issuers of the leading reserve currencies (Garnham 2009). When Chinese State Counselor Dai Bingguo (quoted after Parker et al. 2009) met the leaders of the Group of Eight in July 2009 to discuss the state of the global economy, he also joined into the criticism, pronouncing that we "should have a better system for reserve currency issuance and regulation, so that we can maintain relative stability of major reserve currencies exchange rates and promote a diversified and rational international reserve currency system." In early 2011, even China's president Hu Jintao expressed his concern. On the eve of a state visit to Washington, Hu (quoted after McGregor 2011) pointed out that the "monetary policy of the United States has a major impact on global liquidity and capital flows and therefore, the liquidity of the US dollar should be kept at a reasonable and stable level."

[5] The proposal to create an SDR-denominated fund is a revival of the substitution account idea that was negotiated in the IMF in the late 1970s (Bergsten 2009).

The official Chinese criticism of the international monetary system and the 'irresponsible' economic policies of the United States was shared by many Chinese economists. A scholar at the influential Institute of World Economics and Politics (IWEP) at the Chinese Academy of Social Sciences (CASS) noted that the US was "sowing the seeds of inflation and dollar depreciation" (Zhang 2009a: 1) with its loose monetary policy. Even more pointedly, IWEP's influential director Yu Yongding described America's expansionary monetary policy as "almost crazy" (2008: 2). Moreover, Chinese criticism of the leading role of the US in the international monetary system was not only widespread among the elite, but also shared by the wider public (Murphy and Yuan 2009: 6). In a survey by the popular website Sina, out of 369,205 respondents, almost 90 % were in favor of using a supra-sovereign reserve currency to end the 'hegemony' of the dollar, and more than 95 % subscribed to the view that the Federal Reserve's monetary policy during the financial crisis was detrimental to the interests of other countries (Sina 2012).

China's criticism was to a great extent motivated by concern over its foreign exchange reserves. When the US embarked on a monetary policy of quantitative easing, Chinese policymakers, economists and the broader public alike feared that this policy would trigger dollar depreciation and inflation and thus erode the value of China's reserves. Besides, the US 'bashing' of China's policymakers also aimed at assuaging the public's dissatisfaction by blaming Washington for the outbreak of the crisis that had led to a slump in Chinese exports and rising unemployment. Last but not least, China's reform proposal also signaled Beijing's willingness to become a more active player on the global scene (Heep and Hilpert 2009: 6).

4.3.2 Motives for the Internationalization of the Renminbi

China's concern over Washington's monetary policy of quantitative easing and its implications for the value of China's foreign exchange reserve did not only prompt China's elite to engage in a harsh criticism of the international monetary system, but also played a major role in the decision to encourage a global role of the renminbi. Worried about potential losses in the country's reserves, China's policymakers decided to push for a prominent role of the renminbi in international trade that would slow down the growth of reserves and allow the country to lend in its own currency in the future.

At least equally important to the decision to promote the renminbi's international use was the fact that the global financial crisis made Beijing realize the dangers of the country's reliance on the dollar. When the financial upheaval triggered a repatriation of dollars into the US financial system, the ensuing dollar shortage in the global economy contributed to a sharp decline in China's exports that threw millions of migrant workers into unemployment.[6] For this reason,

[6] For an analysis of the global dollar shortage during the global financial crisis see McGuire and von Peter (2009).

China's authorities decided to bolster the renminbi's standing in global trade in order to stabilize the operating environment of the country's export sector. Besides, China's promotion of the renminbi in international trade has also been influenced by a desire to eliminate exchange rate risks and lower transaction costs. Against the backdrop of a slump in US consumer demand and the increasing importance of the European Union and the developing world as trading partners, the renminbi's de facto peg to the dollar no longer offered sufficient protection against exchange rate fluctuations, and the renminbi's internationalization thus appeared to provide a welcome means to protect China's export sector.

In addition to the rather uncontroversial motives for the promotion of the renminbi's internationalization mentioned above, it has also been argued that liberal-minded policymakers have been pushing for the renminbi's internationalization in order to facilitate the reform of China's financial system. It is believed that especially the reformers at the PBOC expect a more important international role of the renminbi to unleash liberalization pressures onto the financial system similar to the pressures that China's entry into the WTO put on the real economy a decade ago (Dyer et al. 2010; Pilling 2010). This hope is shared by a number of liberal-minded Chinese economists and journalists. In an article in the influential magazine *Caijing*, it was argued that the internationalization of China's currency would contribute to the development of China's financial sector and simplify the transition to a flexible exchange rate regime (Chen et al. 2009). In a similar vein, Ha Jiming, chief economist of China's leading investment bank CICC, pointed out that the renminbi's internationalization would facilitate the development of an international financial center on the Chinese mainland (Zhang and Li 2009). Likewise, IWEP's director Yu Yongding emphasized the risks that an internationalized currency would pose to the country's financial institutions, yet also pointed out that the renminbi's internationalization could contribute to an increase in their competitiveness (Liu 2009).

However, the decision to promote the renminbi's internationalization has not only been influenced by economic factors, but also by political considerations. Most important in this regard has been the widespread desire to turn China into a 'rich and powerful country' (fuqiang guo) capable of rivaling and eventually overtaking the US. Against this nationalistic background, the replacement of the greenback with the 'redback' (hongbi) is regarded a powerful symbol of China's emergence as a major player in the global political economy. Comments with a nationalistic touch were thus very common in the Chinese debate on the renminbi's internationalization. As one commentator put it, "China currently still lacks a 'ticket' to the transformation into an economic powerhouse: the transformation of the renminbi into the monetary standard currency in the international monetary system" (Yuan 2009). Zhang Tiegang (2009b), professor at China's Central University of Finance and Economics, contended that the renminbi's internationalization was ultimately dependent on the development of China's comprehensive national power. If China's efforts to internationalize its currency succeeded, this would not only contribute to the pluralization of the international monetary system, but would also strengthen China's influence on the development of the rules of the international system. While China should currently actively seek to become a member of the international community by playing by the rules of the game, it should change these rules at a later stage before it could finally reach a position that would allow it to establish its own rules. In a similar vein, Li Daokui (quoted after *Zhongguo Qiyejia Wang* 2010), Director of Tsinghua University's Center for China in the World Economy, expressed his trust in the government's ability to turn the renminbi into a competitive international currency within the next 10–15 years and pointed out that "the internationalization of the renminbi is a historical trend that cannot be evaded or avoided."

Last but not least, Chinese analysts have speculated that the PBOC's push for the renminbi's internationalization was also influenced by bureaucratic politics (Interview No. 45). One interviewee emphasized that in the years before the crisis, the PBOC conducted the country's monetary policy almost without interference from higher ranks of the government. However, when the crisis caused a slump in China's GDP growth, China's senior leaders reportedly held the PBOC responsible, claiming that it had failed to react to the crisis by adjusting its monetary policy. As a result, the responsibility for China's monetary policy is said to have been transferred from the PBOC to the Central Leading Small Group for Finance and Economics, a high level informal party body. In reaction to this development, the PBOC has reportedly tried to bolster its standing by gaining new areas of influence: Well knowing that the liberalization of the exchange rate regime would meet insurmountable resistance especially among the more conservative government officials at the NDRC, the PBOC started to lobby for the internationalization of the renminbi.

4.3.3 Assessing the Renminbi's Potential to Internationalize

The following section draws on the determinants of currency internationalization identified in the first section of the chapter to assess the renminbi's potential to internationalize and explain how this potential is influenced by the political economy of China's financial system.[7]

4.3.3.1 China's Transactional Networks in the Global Economy

A country's extensive transactional networks in the global economy are the most important determinants of currency internationalization since they play a decisive role in promoting a currency's use as an international settlement currency and a monetary anchor. Judging from this factor, the renminbi's potential to become one of the world's leading currencies is significant. In the years from 2000 to 2012,

[7] Dobson and Masson (2009) provide a similar assessment.

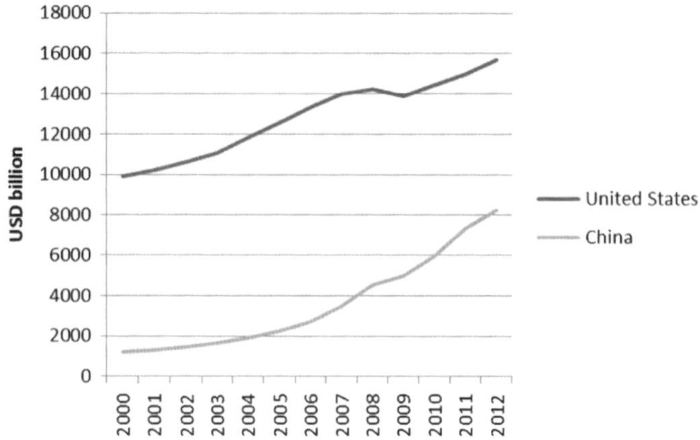

Fig. 4.1 Chinese GDP in comparison (in current USD) (Source: World Bank: World Development Indicators)

China's GDP increased from USD 1,198 billion to USD 8,227 billion, thus turning the country into the world's second-biggest economy after the United States (see Fig. 4.1). Since China's GDP per capita is still very low in comparison to that of developed countries, China's economy has not yet reached its full potential and will probably continue to grow rapidly in the years to come, even though it might grow at a slower pace (see Fig. 4.2). Assuming an annual growth rate of 8 % for China and 2.5 % for the US, China will overtake the US in 2020 as the world's leading economy (*Economist* 2011: 6).[8] Against this backdrop, the renminbi's chances to become one of the world's leading currencies look very promising.[9]

China's trade in goods and services has also grown at a rapid pace. In the years from 2000 to 2011, it increased from USD 531 billion to USD 4,294, thus rapidly approaching the position of the US (see Fig. 4.3). Even though China will probably not be able to uphold its current export growth, its import growth is likely to accelerate. Besides, China has long been one of the world's leading destinations for foreign direct investment, and the country's transactional networks have in recent years also been boosted by its growing importance as outward foreign direct investor. Due to China's prominent position in Asian production networks, the renminbi is well suited to begin the process of internationalization by establishing itself as a regional settlement currency. In this regard, it is important to point out that China's regional trade could further be boosted by growing Chinese investment

[8] This calculation is further based on the assumption of an inflation rate of 4 % in China and 2 % in the US and a 3 % annual appreciation of the CNY against the USD.

[9] It goes without saying that the renminbi's chances to internationalize are also heavily influenced by the development of the US dollar as the global core currency. For an analysis of the dollar's current position in the international financial system, see the collection of essays in Helleiner and Kirshner (2009). On the political implications of a possible decline of the dollar see Kirshner (2008).

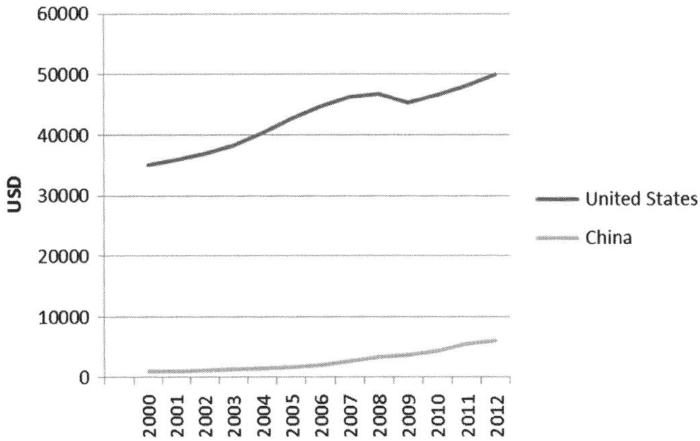

Fig. 4.2 Chinese per capita GDP in comparison (in current USD) (Source: World Bank: World Development Indicators)

activities in the region's manufacturing sector that would lead to an increase in intra-company trade. Last but not least, China's increasingly prominent role as international aid donor could also bolster the renminbi's international standing if China decides to denominate its grants and loans in renminbi instead of dollar.

4.3.3.2 Confidence in the Renminbi's Value

Particularly with regard to a currency's role as a store of value and a unit of account, confidence in its stable value plays a crucial role in determining its potential for internationalization. Judging from the renminbi's track record of inflation, its chances to develop into a leading international currency look promising. China has experienced a relatively low level of inflation for an emerging economy during the last decade (see Fig. 4.4). Moreover, limiting inflation has been a major goal of Chinese macroeconomic policymaking since the late 1980s, and the country's authorities can be considered sufficiently committed to preserving the renminbi's value in order to maintain political stability.[10]

However, the renminbi's potential to play a prominent role on the global stage looks more limited if we take into account the lack of institutional arrangements ensuring that the renminbi's inflation rate will not significantly rise in the years to come. Among the more important constraints is the fact that China's financial system does not feature an independent central bank. Even though the PBOC is officially in charge of formulating and implementing the country's monetary policy, it remains subject to the control of the State Council under the guidance

[10] For a detailed analysis of the political economy of inflation in China see Shih (2007).

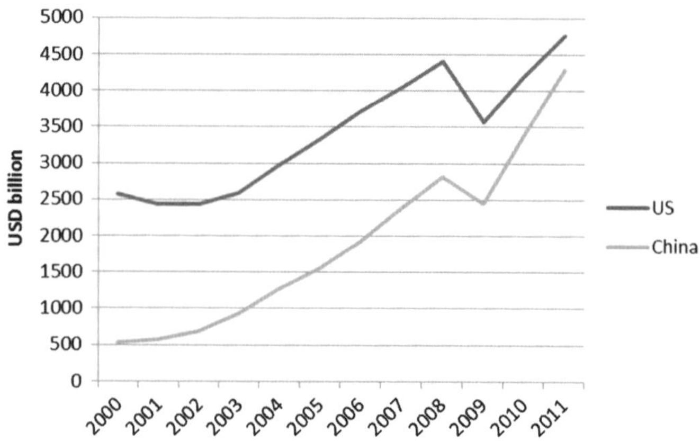

Fig. 4.3 Chinese total trade in comparison (Source: World Bank: World Development Indicators)

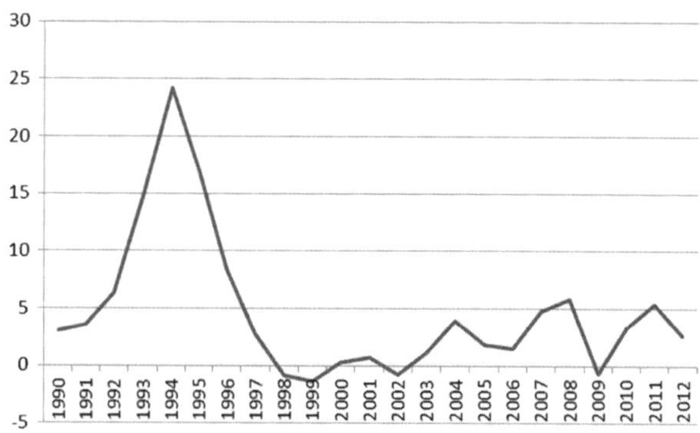

Fig. 4.4 Chinese CPI inflation (annual percent) (Source: World Bank: World Development Indicators)

of CCP organs. On a more general level, China lacks the institutions of limited, constitutional government that strengthen the confidence in a currency's stable value. While the latter are considered conducive to political stability, China's political model of authoritarian one-party rule is believed to be much more fragile. Even though the CCP has so far been able to keep a tight grip on power, there is persistent concern over growing social tensions that might come to threaten China's political stability.[11] Moreover, even if the CCP succeeds at maintaining regime stability, the mere possibility of a breakdown of the country's political system might prove detrimental to the confidence of international investors in the renminbi's value.

[11] For an outlook of China's political future that highlights the stability of China's regime see Nathan (2003). For a more pessimistic outlook see Pei (2008).

4.3.3.3 Development of China's Financial Markets

The main obstacle to the renminbi's internationalization is the lack of financial markets capable of attracting international investors on a significant scale. Instead of institutions of limited, constitutional government and pro-creditor legal frameworks, China features a political model of authoritarian one-party rule that is not conducive to the development of financial markets. Moreover, as has been explained in Chap. 3, the political economy of China's financial system does not allow for the development of financial markets operating beyond the control of the party-state since that would undermine the country's system of financial repression. The underdeveloped nature of China's financial markets is mainly a hindrance to the establishment of the renminbi as a reserve currency, but also hampers the renminbi's development into a major trade currency since foreigners need to be able to hold and trade safe and liquid renminbi-denominated financial assets in order to be able to invoice and settle in renminbi.

4.3.3.4 Liberalization of the Exchange Rate Regime

The spectacular growth of China's export sector has taken place under a quasi-fixed exchange rate regime. Until July 2005, the renminbi was pegged to the US dollar. At that time, the PBOC announced a switch to a managed floating regime based on a basket of currencies that allowed for daily bilateral exchange rate movements within a certain range (Frankel 2009: 3). In subsequent years, the Chinese currency appreciated against the dollar, yet this trend came to an abrupt halt when the global financial crisis hit China's export sector, thus revealing the importance that China's authorities continued to attribute to the exchange rate. However, in the following year the renminbi resumed its appreciation. In a report released in 2013, the IMF argued that the renminbi was only moderately undervalued by 5–10 % (IMF 2013: 9).

If China's authorities decided to liberalize the country's financial system and abolish its capital controls in order to attract international investors to the country's financial markets, they would have to liberalize the exchange rate regime in order to maintain the country's monetary policy autonomy. Not long ago, such a reform would probably have resulted in an accelerated appreciation of the renminbi that would have undermined the export sector's competitiveness. However, since the renminbi is no longer considered to be significantly undervalued, it can be assumed that a liberalization of the exchange rate regime would have no significant ramifications for the performance of China's export sector under present circumstances.

4.3.3.5 The Renminbi as a Negotiated Currency

Currencies on the rise can be assisted by the issuing country if it offers incentives for the support of its currency that are unrelated to the currency's inherent economic attractiveness. In this regard, China is well positioned to bolster the renminbi's international standing. In recent years, China has emerged as a major provider of funds to the developing world. From 2009 to 2010, China lent more money to developing countries than the World Bank (Dyer et al. 2011). China could well use its increasingly important role as a creditor to the developing world to 'convince' its debtors to allow the renminbi to play a more prominent role in their trade and investment activities or as a monetary anchor, especially if the country started to lend in renminbi instead of dollars. Besides, perceived similarities concerning the politico-economic system between China and its creditors as well as a shared resentment to US hegemony may further encourage the latter's support for the renminbi. Last but not least, China could also offer military protection in exchange for a support of the renminbi's global role.

4.3.4 Policy Measures Promoting the Renminbi's Internationalization

Having examined the conditions under which the renminbi could develop into a leading international currency, this section analyzes the policy measures that Beijing has taken in the wake of the global financial crisis in order to bolster the renminbi's global standing. These measures were mainly aimed at promoting the renminbi as an international settlement currency. As a result of the growing importance of China as a trading partner in the region, the use of the renminbi in China's neighboring countries had already increased significantly in the years before the outbreak of the crisis. However, China's authorities had initially refrained from formulating a policy on the renminbi's overseas use (Bottelier 2009).

At the height of the financial crisis, the State Council explicitly addressed the internationalization of the renminbi for the first time. In December 2008, it announced the introduction of a pilot scheme for the use of the renminbi as a settlement currency in international trade transactions. Starting from July 2009, selected companies from Shanghai, Guangzhou, Shenzhen, Zhuhai and Dongguan in Guangdong province have been allowed to settle their trade with companies in Hong Kong, Macao and ASEAN member states in renminbi (PBOC 2010b: 12). In 2010, the scheme was expanded to include 20 Chinese provinces and municipalities and their trading partners in every country in the world and was broadened to include all transactions under the current account (PBOC 2011b: 11). In 2011, it was expanded to cover the whole country (PBOC 2012b: 14). One year later, all

Table 4.1 Selected swap agreements involving the renminbi

Swap partner country	Amount swapped	Date of agreement
Hong Kong	CNY 200 billion	January 2009
Malaysia	CNY 80 billion	February 2009
Belarus	CNY 20 billion	March 2009
Indonesia	CNY 100 billion	March 2009
Iceland	CNY 3.5 billion	June 2010
Singapore	CNY 150 billion	July 2010
New Zealand	CNY 25 billion	April 2011
Uzbekistan	CNY 0.7 billion	April 2011
Mongolia	CNY 5 billion	May 2011
Kazakhstan	CNY 7 billion	June 2011
Korea	CNY 360 billion	October 2011
Hong Kong	CNY 400 billion	November 2011
Thailand	CNY 70 billion	December 2011
Pakistan	CNY 10 billion	December 2011
United Arab Emirates	CNY 35 billion	January 2012
Malaysia	CNY 180 billion	February 2012
Turkey	CNY 10 billion	February 2012
Mongolia	CNY 10 billion	March 2012
Australia	CNY 200 billion	March 2012
Ukraine	CNY 15 billion	June 2012

Sources: PBOC (2010a, 2011a, 2012a, 2013a)

restrictions on Chinese companies wanting to settle their international trade in renminbi were removed (PBOC 2013b: 14).

China has tried to bolster the renminbi's international standing by concluding currency swap agreements with emerging market economies. The PBOC signed its first bilateral swap contracts under the framework of the Chiang Mai Initiative. By the end of 2007, China had concluded swap agreements with Japan, Korea, Thailand, Malaysia, the Philippines and Indonesia. However, the renminbi was only used in the arrangements with Japan, Korea and the Philippines, while all the other arrangements involved the dollar instead of the renminbi (Yu and Gao 2011: 196). Yet when a number of China's trading partners were facing liquidity problems in the wake of the global financial crisis, Beijing decided to strengthen its financial cooperation with these countries by providing them with renminbi that would allow them to continue their trade with China if they ran out of dollars (see Table 4.1).

How successful have China's measures been so far? According to the PBOC (2012b: 15, 2013b: 14–15), international trade settled in renminbi amounted to CNY 2,081 billion in 2011 and rose to CNY 2,938 in 2012, thus accounting for almost one tenth of China's total international trade. In the early days of the pilot scheme, import settlement in renminbi strongly prevailed over export settlement, reflecting the fact that the renminbi in Hong Kong (CNH) traded stronger against the US dollar than the renminbi on the mainland (CNY). Garber (2011) has thus argued that the renminbi's internationalization in the early days was driven by the desire of international investors to profit from the renminbi's appreciation and the eagerness of Chinese importers and non-Chinese exporters to benefit from the exchange rate differential between the CNY and the CNH. However, more recently, the use of the renminbi in the settlement of imports and exports has become more balanced (PBOC 2013b: 15).

Even though China has concentrated its efforts on the establishment of the renminbi as an international settlement currency, the closed structure of the country's financial markets has been an obstacle to the renminbi's internationalization since its use in international trade requires that foreigners have access to renminbi-denominated financial products. As has been pointed out in Chap. 3, Beijing has taken some cautious steps towards allowing foreign investors limited access to financial markets on the mainland in order to promote the renminbi's internationalization. However, Beijing's main focus has been on the development of a renminbi offshore market in Hong Kong.

The first step towards the creation of such a market was already taken in 2004, when 32 licensed banks started offering renminbi deposits as well as currency exchange and remittances services in the former British crown colony. Three years later, Chinese policy and commercial banks were granted permission to issue renminbi-denominated bonds in Hong Kong (Yu and Gao 2011: 197–199). In an effort to support the policies aimed at establishing the renminbi in international trade, the pace of reform accelerated substantially. In September 2009, China's Ministry of Finance for the first time issued government bonds in Hong Kong. The first batch was only worth CNY 6 billion, yet issuance volumes increased to CNY 8 billion in 2010, CNY 20 billion in 2011 and CNY 23 billion in 2012 (*Xinhua* 2012; Rabinovitch 2011; Cookson 2009). In July 2010, permission was given to any company in the world to open a renminbi bank account in Hong Kong and to freely exchange the currency. Besides, financial institutions in the territory were allowed to create investment products denominated in renminbi and restrictions on the type of corporations that can be granted loans denominated in renminbi were removed (Cookson 2010c). Since August 2012, Hong Kong banks have also been allowed to offer renminbi services to non-resident personal customers (HKMA 2013: 41). At the end of 2012, the combined amount of outstanding certificates of deposit and customer deposits in renminbi in Hong Kong accounted for CYN 620 billion (HKMA 2013: 42).

The most important developments have taken place in the territory's corporate bond market. Since February 2010, non-Chinese corporations as well as offshore branches of Chinese corporations have been allowed to issue renminbi bonds in Hong Kong's so-called 'dim sum' market. However, issuers still need to gain approval from the State Administration of Foreign Exchange (SAFE) to move the proceeds to the mainland. In August 2010, the US fast-food chain McDonald's was the first foreign company to raise funds in the former British crown colony, followed 3 months later by the Asian Development Bank as the first international financial institution to issue renminbi bonds in the territory (Cookson 2010a).

In August 2011, during a Hong Kong visit of China's Vice Premier Li Keqiang that aimed at underlining the territory's importance to the mainland's objective of internationalizing the renminbi, PBOC governor Zhou Xiaochuan announced that Chinese non-financial companies would be allowed to issue renminbi bonds in

Hong Kong and that the quota for issuance of renminbi bonds by Chinese companies in Hong Kong would be raised to CNY 50 billion, to be split in half between financial and non-financial companies (Peng 2011). After receiving permission from the National Development and Reform Commission (NDRC), the state-owned iron and steel company Baosteel in November 2011 became the first non-financial Chinese company to issue renminbi bonds in Hong Kong. Also in the case of Chinese companies issuing bonds in the territory, approval needs to be granted by SAFE for the remittance of the proceeds to the mainland (Zheng 2011).[12] In 2012, the total amount of renminbi debt securities excluding certificates of deposits issued in Hong Kong was worth CNY 127 billion (HKMA 2013: 51–52).[13]

4.3.5 *Experimenting with Controlled Currency Internationalization*

With their attempt to internationalize the renminbi within a system of capital controls, China's policymakers have entered completely unknown territory. As McCauley (2011: 3) has pointed out, capital controls neither prevented the British pound from playing an important international role between 1945 and 1979, nor did they undermine the US dollar's role as a core currency between the mid-1960s and the early 1970s. However, these currencies had been established on the global stage when there were no capital controls to circumscribe their global use, and their international role only had to be *maintained* within the newly emerging regime of capital controls.

Judging by our assessment of the renminbi's potential to internationalize, the chosen strategy to try and establish the renminbi in international trade while at the same time maintaining a tight regime of capital controls appears promising. China's large and growing transactional networks in the global economy and its tremendous financial resources that allow it to 'negotiate' the renminbi's international standing imply that the renminbi is well positioned to assume a prominent role as an international medium of exchange. On the other hand, China's lack of an institutionalized commitment to a low-inflation monetary policy and the relatively high potential for political instability associated with its political system are detrimental to the confidence of foreigners in the renminbi's stable value. Moreover, the development of financial markets that are capable of attracting international investors on a significant scale is not compatible with China's system of financial

[12] Hong Kong's offshore renminbi bond business has been challenged by London, Taiwan and Singapore who have already seen bonds issued in the Chinese currency.

[13] China has also established programs that allow for the use of the renminbi in direct investment activities. In 2012, OFDI settled in renminbi amounted to CNY 30 billion, while FDI settled in renminbi reached CNY 254 billion (PBOC 2013b: 15).

repression that is ultimately designed to guarantee the party-state's control over the country's political economy. Without a significant change of the political economy of the Chinese party-state, the renminbi will therefore only be able to play a limited role as an international store of value or an international unit of account. Against this backdrop, the Chinese proposal to transform the IMF's Special Drawing Rights into the world's leading reserve currency appears to be a reasonable supplement to the policies aimed at promoting the renminbi's global standing.

4.4 Wholesale Rejection Versus Controlled Internationalization

By the late 1980s, Japan's transactional networks in the global economy and its first cautious steps towards the liberalization of its financial markets would have allowed the country to bolster the yen's role as an international currency. However, Japan's authorities chose to discourage the yen's internationalization out of concern that a global role of the yen would undermine the country's monetary autonomy, jeopardize its export-led growth model and threaten the authorities' control over the allocation of credit and hence their ability to engage in industrial policymaking. When financial policymakers became less hostile to the idea of a more important international role of the yen on the ground that an internationalized currency could foster the reform of the country's financial system, disagreement between the Ministry of Finance and the Bank of Japan concerning the structure of the country's public debt prevented Japan from taking a more assertive stance in its currency policy. The Asian Financial Crisis made Japan's authorities realize the dangers of their reliance on the dollar. Yet when they finally started pushing for a more prominent international role of the yen, the country's economic decline meant that it was already too late for the yen to become one of the leading global currencies.

Judging from the political economy of the Chinese developmental state, China's policymakers should be expected to try and prevent a global role of the renminbi on the very grounds that discouraged Japan from promoting the yen as an international currency. However, against the backdrop of a long-standing tradition of policy experimentation and encouraged by strong nationalistic feelings, China has chosen a different approach. Instead of engaging in a wholesale rejection of currency internationalization, Beijing has embarked on a strategy of promoting the renminbi's role in international trade while at the same time maintaining the country's capital controls. This strategy of promoting "currency internationalization under controlled convertibility" (Subacchi 2010: 1) has allowed the authorities to pursue an incremental approach to the renminbi's internationalization that leaves room for the experimentation with a variety of pilot schemes that can be put on ice if they threaten the stability of China's domestic financial system. China's approach to currency internationalization has thus followed the Chinese policy-making formula that Heilmann (2009: 451) has described as "extensive policy experimentation with long-term policy prioritization" or "foresighted tinkering."[14]

By allowing liberal-minded reformers at the PBOC to experiment with controlled currency internationalization and using Hong Kong as a testing ground while at the same time maintaining a tight grip on the renminbi's exchange rate and the country's capital controls in accordance with the preferences of the more conservative officials at the NDRC, China's senior leaders have also succeeded at reconciling differences between important players in the country's bureaucracy. China's experiment of controlled currency internationalization is a risky endeavor that could unleash forces beyond the control of the country's policymakers and undermine the stability of its financial system. However, if China's currency experiment succeeds, China will benefit from a stabilization of the operating environment of its export sector and the establishment of the renminbi as a powerful symbol of China's rising economic and political clout while at the same time mitigating the risks of currency overvaluation and monetary policy constraints that result from a currency's international role under full convertibility. Yet in terms of structural financial power, the renminbi's establishment as an international medium of exchange will not significantly bolster China's clout since structural financial power almost exclusively derives from a currency's role as an international store of value.

[14] For a comprehensive account of this policy formula see Heilmann (2008) as well as Heilmann and Perry (2011).

Chapter 5
Financial Repression and Relational Financial Power

This chapter analyzes the developmental state's potential to develop relational power in global finance. According to the definition provided in Chap. 2, relational financial power is a state's ability to influence the behavior of other states directly through its financial relations with them either by applying financial pressure or by providing financial incentives. The main mechanisms for the exercise of relational financial power that are at a creditor state's disposal are the provision of credit as far as incentives are concerned and the withdrawal of credit or the refusal to provide credit as well as the dumping of a debtor state's currency in order to manipulate its exchange rate as far as pressure is concerned. A state's creditor status can thus be considered its main source of relational financial power (Helleiner 1989, 1992; Strange 1990). The main determinants of a creditor state's relational financial power are the size and the duration of its capital outflows, the government's control over these outflows and the creditor state's vulnerability to its major debtors (Helleiner 1989: 345). In addition to these determinants, it needs to be taken into account that a creditor state's relational financial power is also influenced by the debtor's vulnerability to the creditor that depends on the alternative sources of credit at the debtor's disposal and the nature of the debtor's exchange rate regime (Drezner 2009: 18–20).

This chapter is organized according to these considerations. Section 5.1 looks into the relational power deriving from Japan's emergence as a net creditor in the 1980s. Section 5.2 analyzes the reasons for China's accumulation of foreign exchange reserves and its resulting emergence as a creditor state, looks into China's debate on its growing stockpile of reserves and sheds light on the bureaucratic rivalries between China's sovereign wealth managers as well as their investment strategies. Against the backdrop of these examinations, it assesses China's relational financial power potential by putting the size of China's reserves in a comparative perspective, by estimating the probable duration of China's capital outflows and by analyzing the government's control over these outflows as well as the mutual vulnerability of China and the US as its major debtor. Last but not least, it looks into China's attempts to exercise its relational financial power.

S. Heep, *China in Global Finance*, Global Power Shift,
DOI 10.1007/978-3-319-02466-0_5,

Section 5.3 compares China's relational financial power with the relational financial power of the Japanese developmental state.

5.1 Japan as a Creditor

The following sections analyze the reasons for Japan's emergence as a net creditor, look into the Japanese state's control over the country's capital outflows and examine Japan's vulnerability to the US as its major debtor.

5.1.1 Japan's Emergence as a Creditor

When Japan emerged as a major creditor in the global financial system, many international relations scholars were convinced that the country was bound to replace the US as the world's leading financial power (e.g. Gilpin 1987: 328–336). From the early postwar years to the beginning of the 1980s, Japan had almost continuously been a net borrower. However, Japan's international investment position suddenly changed in 1982 when the country started to run significant current account surpluses. Only 4 years later, Japan had turned into the world's largest net creditor and was accumulating external financial assets on a great scale. During the late 1980s, Japan's annual long-term capital export was worth close to USD 100 billion. By the end of 1990, its external assets had reached a value of USD 328 billion (Helleiner 1989: 343, 1992: 422–423, 2000: 230–231; Gilpin 1987: 328–330). This development seemed to usher in a new era in global finance since "it coincided with America's descent into debtor status for the first time in the post-1945 period" (Helleiner 2000: 231). In the words of Gilpin (1987: 328), "Japan [had] supplanted the United States as the dominant creditor nation and financial power."

The ultimate reason for Japan's emergence as a creditor can be found in the political economy of the Japanese developmental state that relied on a system of financial repression to facilitate rapid economic growth. Within this system, a high savings rate allowed the authorities to provide industrial sectors considered strategically important with an ample amount of funds for investment, as has been explained in the preceding chapters. When economic growth started to slow down in the 1970s and the demand for corporate investment decreased, the authorities refrained from substantially reforming the country's financial system for the sake of maintaining control over Japan's economic development. Even though the financial system was increasingly subject to liberalization pressures, elements of financial repression remained firmly in place.

Due to the decline in corporate investment, Japan's massive amount of savings had to be channeled into new outlets and a new engine of growth had to be found. In reaction to the economic downturn in the 1970s, the government thus embarked on a strategy of Keynesian demand management to achieve economic recovery. Until the late 1970s, a considerable portion of Japan's excess savings was hence absorbed by a growing government deficit (Helleiner 1989: 344). Yet starting from the early 1980s, it became evident that the country's newfound embrace of Keynesianism was no longer sustainable. As Makoto Itoh (1990: 173) has pointed out, Japan had come to rely on the issuance of treasury bonds for more than 30 % of its revenue, which made it ever more challenging for the government to service its debt without radically increasing tax rates.[1]

Against this backdrop, Japan was forced to find yet another way to revive its struggling economy. Even though the country's system of financial repression had by then already begun to erode due to the rapidly growing government deficit, it remained one of the most tightly controlled financial systems in the capitalist world (Moran 1991: 105). Moreover, the Japanese authorities continued to encourage the high savings rate that had been one of the pillars of its system of financial repression. Since Japan's policymakers were not willing to subject the country's political economy to substantial reform, they hence did not have a choice but to embark on an export-led growth strategy that, in contrast to a growth strategy focusing on consumption, was compatible with the political economy of its financial system.[2] For this reason, Gilpin (1987: 329–330) has argued that

> [t]he causes of underconsumption and a falling rate of profit on domestic investment [. . .] had much more to do with internal Japanese politics than with the inevitable laws of the motion of capitalism. If the interests of the ruling Liberal Democratic Party had been different, Japan could easily have used the capital to improve the quality of Japanese life. Unwilling to make the needed domestic reforms, Japanese capitalism [. . .] required a 'colony' to rid itself of these financial surpluses.

Following the recovery of the US economy under the Reagan Administration beginning in 1983, Japan's exports began to expand on a massive scale, a development that was supported by a considerable appreciation of the dollar against the yen. In the US, "a massive tax cut without a complementary reduction of expenditures of the federal government had resulted in a huge and continuing budget deficit" (Gilpin 1987: 330). Due to the low level of domestic savings, this deficit had to be financed through external borrowing. With the increase in US interest rates resulting from the growing budget deficit, the US had no difficulty attracting foreign and especially Japanese capital in search for profitable investment opportunities. The US had thus embarked on "an economic recovery financed by foreign creditors" (Gilpin 1987: 331) that strengthened the dollar and undermined the competitiveness of American exporters, which in turn reinforced the country's reliance on foreign creditors in general and Japanese investors in particular (Itoh 1990: 174–175; Gilpin 1987: 330–331).

[1] According to Itoh (1990: 173), treasury bonds accounted for only 12 % of revenue in the US and for a mere 9 % in the UK.

[2] The Japanese shift to an export-led growth model was already initiated in the mid-1970s, yet only reached full bloom in the 1980s.

5.1.2 State Control over Japan's Capital Flows

For the assessment of the Japanese developmental state's relational financial power, one of the most crucial questions concerns the degree of control that the state exercised over the export of Japanese capital. In this context, it is important to point out that since the country's emergence as a creditor was paralleled by a gradual liberalization of the capital account, the foreign currency earned by Japanese exporters was not channeled into the country's foreign exchange reserves and thus into the hands of the public sector, but remained with the country's private investors.

According to Helleiner (1989: 346–349), the close ties between Japan's financial institutions and its bureaucracy led many observers to believe that the state was highly influential in the country's financial investment activities in general and its capital exports to the US in particular. While the actual involvement of the Japanese state into the country's overseas investments remains difficult to assess, it is obvious that it had the potential to influence the country's financial flows since Japanese rather than foreign financial institutions were managing the country's surplus, which allowed the Japanese state to influence investment decisions not only via discretionary power, but also via regulation and tax policies (Helleiner 1989: 349). Japan was thus in a better position to turn its creditor status into relational financial power than the member countries of the OPEC, whose foreign investment in the 1980s "was primarily placed in bank deposits and thus was recycled through the market by Western commercial banks" (Gilpin 1987: 329).

5.1.3 Japan's Vulnerability to Its Major Debtor

For an assessment of the Japanese developmental state's relational financial power, the country's vulnerability to its major debtor also needs to be examined. In this regard, it is important to draw attention to the fact that Japan was lending in dollars and was thus vulnerable to possible depreciations in the value of its debtor's currency. Besides, Japan was dependent on the US as its major export market that allowed it to pursue an export-led growth strategy. It has therefore been argued that the Japanese government encouraged Japanese financial investment in the US in order to ensure the sustainability of its growth strategy by financing US consumption of Japanese products. As Taggart Murphy (1996: 161) put it:

> By buying such high quantities of Treasuries, the Japanese were ultimately financing their own exports [. . .]. The terms were very favorable to the Americans because ultimately they did not have to earn the dollars to pay back the financing; they could just print more of them. Dangerous it might be, but it permitted the Japan export machine to continue roaring along.

Last but not least, it has been pointed out that the power arising from Japan's creditor status was limited by the country's military dependence on the US that led many observers to consider Japan's financial assistance to the US as the price that it had to pay for America's military support (Murphy 1996: 161; Helleiner 1989: 345).

However, Helleiner (1992: 434) has argued that despite Japan's dependence on the US in economic as well as security affairs, the country became less willing to accommodate US financial interests when the costs of its financial support began to rise. According to Helleiner, the withdrawal of Japanese funds from the US in mid-1987 could at least partially be explained by the frustration of Japanese policymakers with the lack of US commitment to cut the country's budget deficit. While this deficit had initially prompted the dollar to soar until the central bank intervention following the Plaza meeting, the ensuing fall of the dollar and the mirroring rise of the yen were now turning into a major concern for Japanese policymakers. For this reason, Japanese officials were less willing to encourage a continuation of the flow of Japanese funds into the US since these funds enabled America to sustain its deficit and thereby contributed to the problem of the skyrocketing yen.

Moreover, Helleiner (1992: 436) has pointed out that the tightening of monetary policy that started in 1989, when Mieno Yashushi was installed as new Governor of the Bank of Japan, ultimately undermined Japan's financial support of the US. Since 1985, Japan had pursued a loose monetary policy in an effort to smooth the fall of the dollar in the wake of the Plaza Accord. However, this policy had become too costly for Japan since it had resulted in the creation of the asset bubbles that would ultimately deliver a serious blow to the country's economy. The new policy was designed to burst the bubble, but it also triggered a withdrawal of Japanese funds from the US since it caused interest rates to rise and equity prices to collapse, so that the country's financial institutions had to bring back funds in order to meet reserve requirements. Due to concerns that the withdrawal of funds would antagonize the US, Mieno's policy was highly controversial. However, Mieno's stance prevailed, and "the subordination of Japanese monetary policy to the external goal of supporting the dollar was finally ended" (Helleiner 2000: 234).

5.2 Investing China's Foreign Exchange Reserves

Just as in the case of Japan in the 1980s, China's increasing importance in global finance is mainly a result of its emergence as a major international creditor (Chin and Helleiner 2008: 88). It was only in 2004 that China became a net creditor (Ma and Zhou 2009: 5). However, China's net foreign assets have grown rapidly in recent years (see Fig. 5.1). At the end of 2012, they amounted to USD 1,736 billion. The most striking feature of China's international investment position is the dominance of foreign exchange reserves. At the end of 2012, they amounted to USD 3,312 billion or about three quarter of its total international assets (see Table 5.1). Due to the importance of China's reserve assets, they will be the focus of the analysis of China's creditor status. The following sections give an

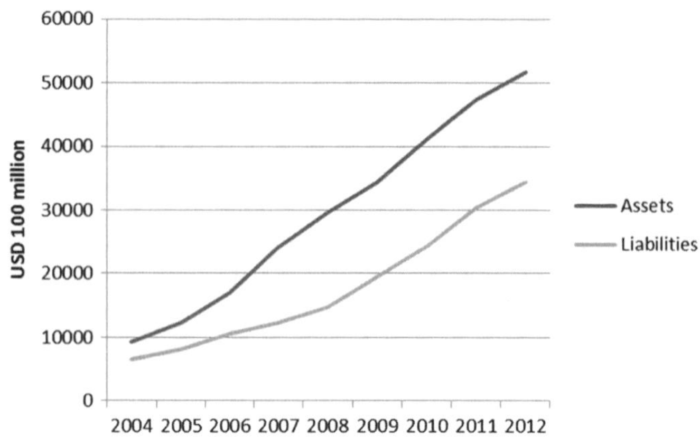

Fig. 5.1 China's international investment position (Source: SAFE 2013b)

overview of the functions of foreign exchange reserves, examine the reasons for China's reserve accumulation and assess the relational financial power deriving from China's creditor status.[3]

5.2.1 *Functions of Foreign Exchange Reserves*

In order to be able to assess the relational financial power deriving from China's accumulation of reserves, we need to understand the functions that reserves perform and be able to determine the amount of surplus reserves at China's disposal. Foreign exchange reserves can be defined as "official public sector foreign assets [...] readily available to and controlled by the authorities for meeting a defined range of objectives" (IMF 2004: 1), including the management of the exchange rate, the provision of foreign currency liquidity in times of crises and the support of the government with regard to its foreign exchange needs. Since reserves need to be held in safe and liquid assets, the portfolio of central banks usually consists of short-term government bonds or money market instruments denominated in US dollars or euros (Park 2007: 4).

By definition, a change in foreign exchange reserves is equal to the sum of the current account balance and the capital account balance. A country can hence accumulate foreign exchange reserves by running a current account surplus, a capital account surplus or a combination of both. However, this does not mean that the level of reserves cannot be influenced by a country's monetary authorities. Quite on the contrary, a change in reserves results from the monetary authority's

[3] Section 5.2 partially draws on Heep (2009a, b, 2008).

Table 5.1 China's international investment position (2012) (USD 100 million)

Net position	**17,364**
A. Assets	**51,749**
1. Direct investments abroad	5,028
2. Portfolio investment	2,406
3. Other investment	10,437
4. Reserve assets (foreign exchange)	33,879 (33,116)[a]
B. Liabilities	**34,385**
1. Foreign direct investments	21,596
2. Portfolio investments	3,364
3. Other investment	9,426

Source: SAFE (2013b)

[a]In addition to foreign exchange, reserve assets include monetary gold, special drawing rights and the country's reserve position in the IMF

interventions in the foreign exchange market which influence the country's capital account balance. The extent to which the monetary authority intervenes in the market is determined by a country's exchange rate regime, whereby greater exchange rate flexibility implies a lower degree of intervention and hence a slower accumulation of reserves (Park 2007: 4–5). While the accumulation of reserves is usually motivated by a demand for self-insurance against the possible consequences of future financial crises, it can also result from interventions in the foreign exchange market aimed at preventing the domestic currency from appreciating in order to ensure the competitiveness of the country's export sector.[4]

The accumulation of reserves is associated with a variety of costs. Since a growth of reserves usually results from a current account surplus, one price that has to be paid is a reduction of imports relative to exports. Besides, a growth of reserves is usually associated with sterilization costs in the form of interest that the central bank has to pay on the domestic debt that it issues to neutralize the inflationary impact of the reserve accumulation. These sterilization costs often exceed the interest that the monetary authority earns on the investment of its reserves, thus resulting in a net loss on the central bank's balance sheet. Costs can also result from an appreciation of the domestic currency that implies a loss of the value of reserves in local terms that might put the central bank's balance sheet in jeopardy. Last but not least, opportunity costs arise with the accumulation of reserves since the resources that are needed to purchase them could be put to alternative uses (Green and Torgerson 2007: 7–10).[5]

Several benchmarks can be used to determine the adequacy of a country's reserves. The traditional indicator measures reserves in months of imports, whereby three to four months of imports are usually cited as benchmark. This benchmark is particularly useful for countries whose access to capital markets is limited.

[4] For a detailed discussion of the motives for the accumulation of reserves see Aizenman and Lee (2006).

[5] For a detailed discussion of the costs of reserve accumulation see Mohanty and Turner (2006).

Money-based measures can be applied to countries that face a high risk of capital flight. It has been suggested that reserves equivalent to 5–20 % of M2 should be considered appropriate (Green and Torgerson 2007: 3–4). The so-called Greenspan-Guidotti rule, according to which reserves should be equal to a country's external debt with a maturity of up to 1 year, is the most commonly used benchmark for measuring vulnerability to capital account crises and is considered "the single most important indicator of reserve adequacy in countries with significant but uncertain access to capital markets" (IMF 2000: 15–16).

5.2.2 China's Foreign Exchange Reserves

China has long suffered from a scarcity of foreign exchange reserves. However, in the early 2000s, China's reserves embarked on a tremendous growth trajectory. From 2000 to 2012, China's stockpile of reserves grew by more than USD 3,000 billion (see Fig. 5.2). This rapid accumulation of reserves has mainly been driven by China's current account surplus and thus reflected the country's export-oriented growth strategy. However, especially in the years from 2009 to 2011, China's capital account surplus also contributed significantly to the build-up in reserves, a development that mainly resulted from huge inflows of foreign direct investment (see Fig. 5.3).

As Dooley et al. (2003: 2) have argued, China's accumulation of reserves reflects the conscious choice of a development strategy based on "export-led growth supported by undervalued exchange rates, capital controls and official capital outflows in the form of accumulation of reserve asset claims." According to this so-called Bretton Woods II hypothesis, China's policy choice of providing financial support to the US to ensure the ability of the American market to absorb large quantities of Chinese exports has allowed the US to maintain a massive current account deficit (Dooley et al. 2003: 6).

The choice of this very development strategy by Chinese policymakers can be explained with reference to the model of the developmental state. Relying on a system of financial repression to channel the country's funds into industrial development and to ensure the party-state's control over the country's political economy, China's leaders had to embark on a growth model complementing a focus on investment with the promotion of exports that resulted in massive current account surpluses and the accumulation of a huge stockpile of reserves. As has been explained in Chap. 3, its tight control over the country's financial system has allowed the party-state to sterilize the monetary impact of the accumulation of reserves to a large extent by mandating state-owned banks to purchase them and by hiking reserve ratios to levels that were only sustainable within a system of administratively guaranteed spreads. China's system of financial repression has thus enabled the party-state to continue its export-led growth strategy by preventing an appreciation of its currency through the accumulation of an unprecedented stockpile of reserves.

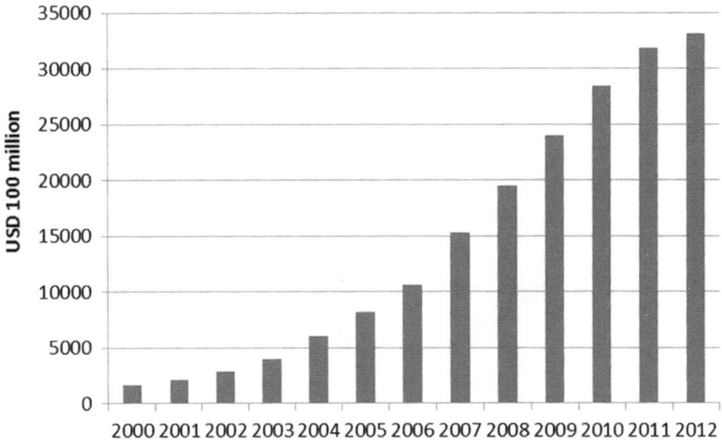

Fig. 5.2 China's foreign exchange reserves (Sources: SAFE 2012b, 2013c). These figures do not include the foreign exchange reserves that are managed by China's sovereign wealth fund, the China Investment Corporation)

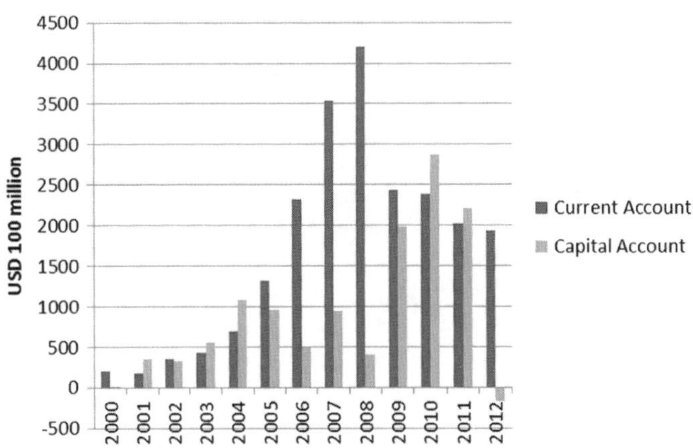

Fig. 5.3 China's twin surplus (Sources: SAFE 2012a, 2013a)

Since the accumulation of China's reserves has not resulted from precautionary motives, China has come to hold a vast amount of excess reserves according to the most commonly used benchmarks for the measurement of reserve adequacy. At the end of 2012, China's stockpile of reserves was equivalent to more than 21 months of imports and more than six times the amount of China's external short-term debt. Even if we assume that a country's foreign exchange reserves should cover three months of imports as well as the entire external short-term debt, China's excess reserves amount to USD 2,355 billion.[6] China's choice of an export-led growth strategy has thus resulted in the accumulation of a huge amount of foreign assets on the basis of which the country could develop considerable relational financial power.

5.2.3 *Debating China's Creditor Status*

The following sections look into the overriding topics of the Chinese debate on the country's foreign exchange reserves: concern over the reserves' value and possible investment strategies.

5.2.3.1 Concern over the Value of Reserves

China began to discuss its huge amount of excess reserves in 2006, when the government established a Small Group for the Protection and Increase of the Value of Foreign Exchange Reserves with representatives of 14 different government agencies (Wang 2007a). Until then, China's reserves had mainly been invested in low-yielding US Treasury and agency bonds and, to a smaller extent, in bonds denominated in euro and yen.[7] As the name of the Small Group suggests, its establishment reflected the growing concern among Chinese policymakers over the increasing costs of reserve accumulation that mainly resulted from the renminbi's appreciation against the dollar that had begun with the reform of the exchange rate regime in 2005, but also from growing sterilization costs.[8] For this reason, the Small Group recommended to establish a sovereign wealth fund that should invest a portion of China's excess reserves in riskier asset classes and diversify away from the US dollar in order to increase the return on China's reserves, thereby helping to cover the costs of sterilization and preventing a further decline in the value of reserves measured in renminbi. This recommendation was

[6] According to SAFE (2012c), China's external short-term debt amounted to USD 501 billion at the end of 2011, the latest date for which statistics were available. According to MOFCOM (2013), China's imports amounted to USD 1,818 billion in 2012. The above approach of calculating excess reserves follows Jen and St-Arnaud (2007).

[7] Agency bonds are issued by agencies that are sponsored by the US government. These bonds are backed, but not guaranteed by the government. The most prominent agencies are the Federal National Mortgage Association (Fannie Mae) and the Federal Home Loan Mortgage Corporation (Freddie Mac).

[8] As long as interest rates in China were lower than in the US, the PBOC was making a profit by issuing renminbi bills while investing its reserves in US Treasuries. However, since 2008 the PBOC had to pay more on the renminbi bills than it earned on its Treasuries due to a reversal in monetary cycles (McGregor 2008a).

accepted by the government and led to the creation of the sovereign wealth fund China Investment Corporation in September 2007 (Guo 2007b).

The government's concern over a loss in the value of China's reserves was shared by the circle of Chinese scholars and journalists who took part in the debate on China's reserves. Scholars at the influential Institute of World Economics and Politics (IWEP) expressed their worries about the possibility of a "tremendous loss in the international purchasing power of China's foreign exchange reserves" (Zhang and He 2009: 103). Based on the amount of reserves that China had accumulated by the end of March 2008, they pointed out that a depreciation of the nominal exchange rate by 10 % would result in a decline of the domestic value of reserves equivalent to 5 % of China's GDP in 2007. They also drew attention to the rising costs of sterilization that put the PBOC's balance sheet in jeopardy. Moreover, they highlighted that the build-up of reserves was associated with huge opportunity costs defined as the gap between the high yield of FDI in China and the low yield of the investment of China's reserves.[9] The authors therefore suggested that the government should either introduce a more flexible exchange rate regime that would slow down the accumulation of reserves or embark on a new investment strategy in order to increase the returns on China's reserves (Zhang and He 2009: 102–103).

However, several commentators also drew attention to the fact that the appreciating renminbi and the rising costs of sterilization meant that even a riskier investment strategy could not guarantee a profit on the investment of China's reserves. Ba (2007: 30) thus pointed out that China's sovereign wealth fund would have to achieve an annual return of at least 10 % to be able to make up for the loss resulting from the appreciation of the renminbi and to cover the costs of sterilization. Others offered a fundamental criticism of China's export-led growth strategy. Fang (2007: 18) thus highlighted that the accumulation of foreign exchange reserves meant that China's population did not sufficiently benefit from the country's economic growth since a huge portion of the nation's earnings was being invested abroad instead of being used to improve the living standard of the people.

China's concern over the value of reserves grew with the onset of the global financial crisis. When the US mortgage lenders Fannie Mae and Freddie Mac were teetering on the brink of bankruptcy, China's leaders realized that they could no longer take the safety of China's reserves for granted. Even though Fannie Mae and Freddie Mac were eventually bailed out by the US government, China still had to endure heavy losses on its holdings of US agency bonds. Besides, plummeting share prices of US financial institutions meant that China's sovereign wealth fund also suffered big losses on its investments.[10] In the light of these events, China's top

[9] According to Zhang and He (2009: 102), the average annual return on FDI in China was 22 % in 2005, while the interest on US Treasury bonds fluctuated between 3 % and 6 % from 2001 to 2007.

[10] The CIC's loss-making investments included the acquisition of a stake in the private equity firm Blackstone and the investment bank Morgan Stanley as well as the investment in a money market fund, the Reserve Primary Fund.

government officials expressed their worries about the safety of China's reserves. In January 2009, Vice Premier Wang Qishan (quoted after Dean et al. 2009) called on the US to "take all necessary measures to stabilize its economy and financial markets to ensure the security of China's assets and investments in the U.S." Two months later, Prime Minister Wen Jiabao (quoted after Dyer and Beattie 2009) told an international audience that he was "a little bit worried", requesting the US "to maintain its good credit, to honour its promises and to guarantee the safety of China's assets."

Against the backdrop of the crisis, the call of China's academic community to diversify away from the dollar and to stop investing in US Treasury bonds was also growing louder. Yu Yongding (2008), a former advisor to China's central bank and then head of the Institute of World Economics and Politics, drew attention to the fact that the growing US budget deficit and the increasing supply of Treasury bonds resulting from the Federal Reserve's monetary policy of quantitative easing was likely to trigger a fall in the price of US government securities. Moreover, he pointed out that the Fed's loose monetary policy might well result in serious inflation that would reduce the purchasing power of China's reserves. One of the remedies suggested by Yu was that the US should start issuing 'Panda Bonds' denominated in renminbi that would allow China to continue its financial support of the US government without having to be concerned about a loss in the purchasing power of its reserves.

5.2.3.2 Envisioned Investment Strategies

Not only the preservation of the value of China's excess reserves was high on the agenda of China's elite. Policymakers, scholars and journalists also devoted considerable thought to the question of how China's excess reserves could be used to support China's development. The three government agencies that were particularly in favor of a strategic investment of China's excess reserves were the powerful planning agency, the National Development and Reform Commission (NDRC), the Ministry of Commerce (MOFCOM) as well as the managing agency of China's state-owned enterprises, the State-owned Assets Supervision and Administration Commission (SASAC).

In line with China's policy to try and turn the most successful state-owned enterprises into global champions, SASAC's chairman Li Rongrong advocated that China's sovereign wealth fund should use the reserves under its management to support their overseas investment activities (McGregor 2007).[11] This idea initially did not seem to have too many supporters in government circles, but was later on even endorsed by the Prime Minster (Anderlini 2009). However, much more

[11] According to one interviewee (Interview No. 38), the CIC does not rule out joint overseas investments with Chinese companies, but is not planning to grant loans to Chinese companies for their overseas investment activities.

popular among China's elite was the proposal that China's reserves should be invested in a way that would secure China's supply with raw materials. While officials at the NDRC argued that China should use its excess reserves for the establishment of a strategic oil reserve, others pleaded for strategic investments in resources, for the acquisition of stakes in resource companies and the investment in commodity futures (Interview No. 13; No. 21; Chang and Li 2007; He and Zhang 2007: 21).

Participants in the debate also advocated that China's sovereign wealth fund should try to gain expertise in the area of wealth management by investing in equities and purchasing stakes in foreign financial institutions, arguing that skilled wealth managers were urgently needed in China's ageing society (He and Zhang 2007: 21). In this context, it was also suggested that China should use its excess reserves to set up a sovereign pension fund (Zhu and Lin 2008). Others demanded that a portion of China's reserves be used to acquire stakes in companies that would give China access to important technology (Guo 2007a: 60; Jiao 2007: 104). In a similar vein, the use of reserves for the purchase of technology products and services that were needed for China's development was considered (*Financial Times* 2009; Zhong 2007: 32). Besides, it was suggested that the managers of China's excess reserves try to contribute to the stabilization of the Chinese economy by investing in assets that would gain value when China's economy was experiencing a downturn (Jiao 2007: 104; Li 2007: 55).

Against the backdrop of the global financial crisis, a more ambitious plan was put forward by Xu Shanda, an economist who used to run China's State Administration of Taxation. Xu called for the creation of a 'Chinese Marshall Fund' that should lend China's excess reserves to developing countries in Africa, Asia and Latin America to improve living standards in these regions and thus to create new export markets (Dyer 2009). A similar idea was put forward by the deputy governor of China's central bank, Hu Xiaolian (quoted after Dyer 2009), who suggested at a meeting of the Group of Twenty in September 2009 the creation of a "supra-sovereign-wealth investment fund" whose investment of foreign exchange reserves in developing countries should aim at creating "new engines in global recovery and growth."

5.2.4 Investment Agencies

The following sections look into the organization, financing and investment strategies of China's most important sovereign wealth managers, the China Investment Corporation and the State Administration of Foreign Exchange.

5.2.4.1 The China Investment Corporation

As a result of the debate on the investment of China's reserves, China's sovereign wealth fund was established in order to increase the return on China's excess reserves through an investment in riskier asset classes and a diversification away from the dollar. While China's elites agreed on the necessity of a change in the investment of China's excess reserves, the question of which government agency should be in control of the funds that were designated for a change in the management of reserves was highly disputed. The main contenders in the debate were the central bank and the Ministry of Finance. While the PBOC considered itself entitled to manage the new fund since it had traditionally been responsible for the investment of China's reserves, the MOF tried to legitimize its claim for control of the new fund by drawing attention to the role that finance ministries in other countries played in the management of reserves, thereby particularly highlighting the case of Japan. The discussion was further complicated by the fact that the MOF at the same time also questioned the PBOC's control of China's state-owned financial companies when it proposed the establishment of a Financial Assets Commission (jinrong guoziwei). According to the Ministry's plans, this commission would have absorbed the Central Huijin Investment Company that had been set up as a subsidiary of the PBOC in 2003 to recapitalize state-owned banks and brokers and to foster the reform of the financial sector. In the end, China's senior leaders rejected the Financial Assets Commission plan, but decided to create a sovereign wealth fund largely independent from the PBOC (Eaton and Zhang 2010: 493–494).

China's sovereign wealth fund was then established as a state-owned company with ministry status that reports directly to the State Council, which appoints the members of the CIC's board of directors, its board of supervisors and its executive committee. The CIC's first chairman, Lou Jiwei, formerly served as Vice Minister of Finance, while its president, Gao Xiqing, was Deputy Chairman of China's National Council for Social Security Fund. With the Ministry of Finance, the PBOC, the National Development and Reform Commission and the Ministry of Commerce, almost all the government agencies that had an interest in the management of China's excess reserves were represented in the CIC's initial leadership. However, the MOF was in the most influential position because it provided the CIC's funding. It thus did not only achieve a victory over the PBOC, but also won out over the National Development and Reform Commission that had lobbied for the establishment of a sovereign wealth fund under its authority but had lost the bureaucratic battle due to the fact that it did not have the right to issue bonds and therefore did not have anything to offer in exchange for the PBOC's reserves (Interview No. 21).

To provide the nascent sovereign wealth fund with a capital base, the MOF in 2007 issued special government bonds worth CNY 1.55 trillion. It then exchanged these bonds for USD 200 billion in foreign exchange reserves from the PBOC that it channeled to the CIC. This complicated funding procedure was a reaction to the growth in the money supply – resulting from the accumulation of reserves – that began to accelerate in 2007. Against this backdrop, the issuance of special government bonds was aimed at draining excess liquidity from the banking system. Due to the fact that the MOF had not been appointed as the CIC's official shareholder, it refused to assume responsibility for the payment of interest on these bonds. To cover its expenses, the Ministry thus insisted that the CIC cover the debt service on the special government bonds, meaning that the sovereign wealth fund would be under the immense pressure to achieve a daily profit of about CNY 300 million just to break even (Walter and Howie 2011: 129–132; Eaton and Zhang 2010: 495; Heep 2008: 57–58).

With the establishment of the CIC, the MOF indirectly gained control of the Central Huijin Investment Company. As a subsidiary of the PBOC, Huijin was established in 2003 to facilitate the reform of China's state-owned commercial banks. From 2004 to 2005, the PBOC injected a total of USD 60 billion into three of the country's most important commercial banks through Huijin, thus acquiring major stakes in Bank of China, China Construction Bank and Industrial and Commercial Bank of China (Feng 2006: 37). When the CIC came into being, it spent a third of its capital base to take over Huijin from the PBOC. As a subsidiary of the CIC, Huijin also became principal shareholder of the policy bank China Development Bank and Agricultural Bank of China (ADB) by investing about USD 20 billion of the CIC's capital base into each of these institutions (*People's Daily* 2008; China Development Bank 2008). Against the backdrop of these developments, Walter and Howie (2011: 132) have argued that the establishment of the CIC and its takeover of Huijin have resulted in "the restoration of the financial system to the pre-2003 status quo and a further weakening of the PBOC and the market-reform camp."

Due to Huijin's investments, China's sovereign wealth fund initially only had slightly more than USD 90 billion to invest in international markets. In financial terms, the CIC has clearly benefited from taking over the highly profitable Huijin which allows it to use the dividends it receives from China's state-owned financial institutions to cover the debt service on the MOF's bonds. Yet on the other hand, the takeover of a strategic holding company has rendered the fund's claim to be a purely commercial investor doubtful (Eaton and Zhang 2010: 496). Moreover, as Shih (2009: 340) has argued, this financial arrangement might prove another serious obstacle to the reform of the banking sector since it will create incentives for the CIC to "behave as a major lobbying group for Chinese state banks" that tries "to persuade the government to limit competition in the banking sector, slow down foreign entry, set interest rates to give banks a healthy spread, and bail out the banks if non-performing loan ratio rises."

In an effort to underline the separation between the CIC and Huijin and to "clarify the division of responsibilities" (CIC 2012: 5), the CIC's investment portfolio was transferred to a newly created subsidiary, CIC International, in September 2011. Since then, CIC International has been responsible for the management of the company's overseas assets. Following this organizational overhaul,

CIC International received an additional USD 30 billion to further diversify the country's foreign exchange reserves (CIC 2012: 5).

The CIC's first series of overseas investments focused heavily on US financial institutions. The fund first stepped into the limelight with a USD 3 billion investment in the US private equity firm Blackstone, followed by a USD 5.6 billion investment in the US investment bank Morgan Stanley. Due to the turmoil on global financial markets, the CIC had to suffer heavy losses on its initial investments and was confronted with severe criticism not only by China's leaders, but also by China's populace who accused it of wasting the people's hard-earned money. In 2008, the sovereign wealth fund therefore embarked on a more cautious strategy and decided to keep the majority of its global portfolio in cash funds including bank deposits, money market funds and short-term notes (CIC 2009: 33–35). However, in the same year, it also invested 4 billion dollars in a fund run by the US private equity firm JC Flowers that was targeted at struggling financial institutions in the West without announcing this investment to the public (Interview No. 13; No. 15; Sender 2008b). Thanks to its stakes in the domestic banking sector, the CIC achieved a return of almost 7 % on its total capital in 2008 even though the return on its global portfolio was negative (CIC 2009: 34). In the following years, the CIC's investment activities focused on publicly traded equities and direct investments in the infrastructure, energy, mining and real estate sectors (CIC 2013: 31). At the end of 2012, 64 % of the CIC's overseas portfolio was managed externally (CIC 2013: 36). From its inception in 2007 to the end of 2012, the company's overseas portfolio achieved a cumulative annualized return of 5 % (CIC 2013: 35).

5.2.4.2 The State Administration of Foreign Exchange

The State Administration of Foreign Exchange (SAFE) is the subsidiary of the PBOC that has traditionally been responsible for the management of China's foreign exchange reserves. SAFE mainly invests China's reserves in secure and liquid asset classes that only achieve a modest return. While it does not disclose the composition of its portfolio, conclusions regarding its dollar holdings can be drawn from the Treasury International Capital (TIC) data that are released by the US Department of the Treasury. Because of China's capital controls, it can be assumed that the majority of US securities purchased by Chinese entities are part of SAFE's portfolio. However, due to the fact that purchases of SAFE's offshore subsidiaries and third-party fund managers are not included in the Treasury's data on China, TIC data tend to underestimate the true amount of China's official dollar holdings (Setser and Pandey 2009: 2).

According to the TIC data, the bulk of China's holdings of US securities consists of long-term government securities. Until 2011, China increased its holdings of treasuries, yet 2012 saw a reduction in the amount of treasuries in China's portfolio. China increased its holdings of agencies until 2008, but then started to decrease their amount (see Fig. 5.4). In terms of their share of the total amount of China's foreign exchange reserves, US securities have been significantly reduced in recent

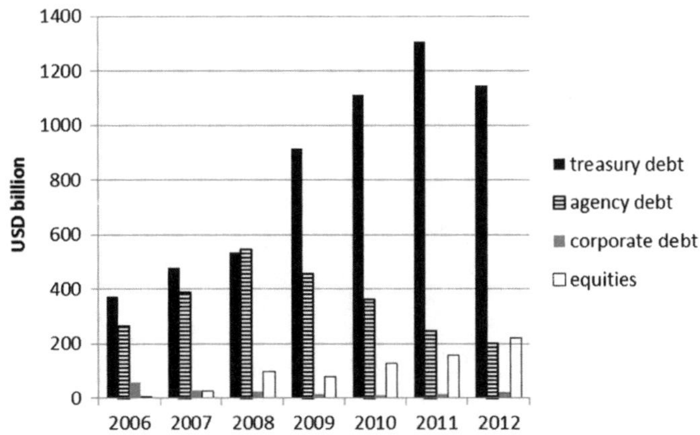

Fig. 5.4 Chinese holdings of US securities (Source: TIC n.d.)

years – from 66 % in 2006 to 48 % in 2012 (see Fig. 5.5). It can be assumed that this diversification away from the dollar went along with an increase in the holdings of securities denominated in euro.

Due to a lack of reliable sources of information, no details are known regarding the composition of the part of China's reserves that is invested in non-dollar assets. It can be assumed that they are mainly invested in securities denominated in euros and, to a smaller extent, in Japanese yen and British pounds. With the growth of China's reserves, SAFE has been slowly diversifying out of the dollar and into the euro. It reportedly accelerated its diversification into the euro in 2009 due to concerns about the dollar's value. One year later, there were rumors that SAFE was trying to reduce its euro holdings in the face of the euro zone's debt crisis (Oakley and Anderlini 2010). However, according to research by the British bank Standard Chartered, SAFE has purchased a significant amount of AAA-rated bonds issued by the European Financial Stability Facility, an investment vehicle established by the members of the euro zone to support struggling economies in the currency union. To a lesser scale, it has reportedly acquired AAA-rated bonds issued by the European Financial Stability Mechanism backed by the EU Commission (Noble 2011). In addition to its diversification into the euro, SAFE also increased its holdings of Japanese government debt and, to a smaller extent, Korean government bonds (Anderlini et al. 2010; Garnham 2010; Nakamoto and Cookson 2010). Besides, SAFE almost doubled its stock of gold between 2003 and 2009 to more than 1,000 t, thereby becoming the world's fifth largest holder of the precious metal (Anderlini and Blas 2009).

With the rapid growth of China's reserves, SAFE has not only been diversifying its assets away from the dollar into other currencies, but has also shifted some of the reserves under its management into riskier asset classes than government securities. Against the backdrop of the CIC's establishment, SAFE was reportedly granted approval by the State Council to invest up to 5 % of the reserves under its

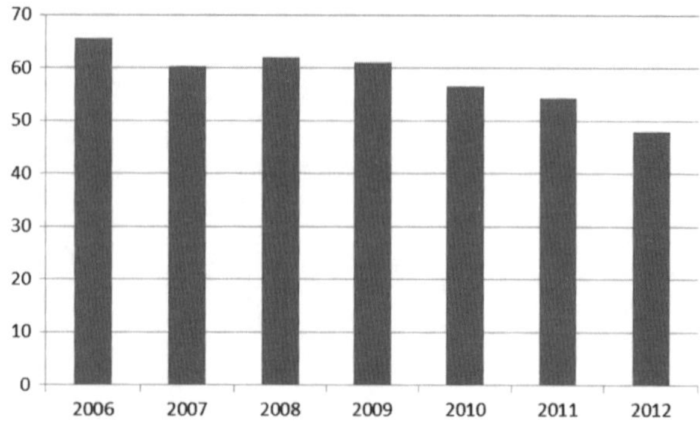

Fig. 5.5 Chinese holdings of US securities in percent of Chinese reserves (Sources: SAFE 2012b, 2013c; TIC n.d.). Data provided by SAFE refer to the end of each year, while TIC data refer to the end of June of each year)

management into non-fixed income financial assets (Interview No. 3; No. 15). China's holdings of US equities increased markedly between 2006 and 2008, were then cut back in 2009, presumably in a reaction to the heavy losses on these investments resulting from the global financial crisis, and then started to increase again (see Fig. 5.4). In 2008, SAFE acquired small stakes in Australian, French and British companies, with a focus on financial companies and the resource sector (Anderlini 2008b). In the same year, it also invested USD 2.5 billion in a fund run by the US private equity firm TPG on which it also had to suffer significant losses (Interview No. 15; Sender 2008a). In 2011, it was revealed that SAFE had acquired a stake of just above 3 % in the German company Munich Re, the world's largest provider of reinsurance (Wilson and Anderlini 2011).

SAFE's equity investments came as a surprise since investments in riskier and less liquid asset classes were supposed to be carried out by the CIC. However, increasing sterilization costs and the falling value of reserves measured in renminbi have burdened the PBOC's balance sheet and led to concern that it might have to ask the Ministry of Finance for a capital injection that would probably weaken the PBOC's position in the bureaucracy (Zhang 2008). For this reason, it is believed that SAFE has been trying to achieve a higher return on the reserves under its management by embarking on a riskier investment strategy. Besides, SAFE has presumably been attempting to demonstrate its ability to achieve higher returns than the CIC in order to prevent further transfers of reserves to the sovereign wealth fund (Heep 2009b).

5.2.5 *China's Relational Financial Power*

The following sections examine China's relational financial power by putting the size of China's excess reserves in a comparative perspective and by estimating the probable duration of China's capital outflows. In addition, they analyze the party-state's control over these outflows as well as the mutual vulnerability of China and the US as its major debtor. Last but not least, they try to deepen our understanding of China's relational financial power by looking into attempts of the Chinese creditor state to exercise this power.

5.2.5.1 Size and Duration of China's Capital Outflows

At the end of 2012, China's excess reserves amounted to USD 2,355 billion. China could have used this huge stockpile of reserves to finance 14 % of America's enormous outstanding public debt. Alternatively, with as few as 28 % of its stockpile of excess reserves, China could have financed the European Stability Mechanism set up to fight the eurozone's debt crisis. China could also have used a mere 7 % of its excess reserves to provide the developing world with an amount of aid equivalent to the total official development aid provided in 2011. Against the backdrop of this comparison, it becomes obvious that China's relational financial power is considerable if it is judged by the mere size of its excess reserves (see Fig. 5.6).

As far as the duration of Chinese capital outflows in the form of reserves is concerned, the situation is less clear. China's rapid accumulation of reserves has resulted from a surplus in the current account reflecting the success of China's export sector and, to a lesser extent, from a surplus in the capital account reflecting China's attraction of FDI. China's reserves will only continue to grow if the country maintains these surpluses, yet it is difficult to make any predictions in this regard. As far as inflows of FDI are concerned, rising labor costs might result in a relocation of production sites from China to other countries that are more competitive in this regard. Yet increasing wages seem to have been offset by improvements in productivity so far. Moreover, while rising labor costs might result in production shifts in the case of labor-intensive sectors, high-technology companies are increasingly attracted by China's infrastructure and the skills of China's workers (Brown 2011). China might therefore well be in a position to continue receiving significant FDI inflows. On the other hand, China's growing overseas investment will probably reduce its capital account surplus in the years to come.

However, the single most important factor determining the future pace of China's reserve accumulation and its creditor status is the development of the country's current account surplus. Relying on a system of financial repression to secure the CCP's tight control over the country's political economy, China's policymakers did not have a choice but to embark on a growth model heavily relying on investment and exports that resulted in massive current account surpluses and the accumulation of a huge stockpile of reserves. Since a fundamental reform of this system would harm the vested interests of many of the most influential players, the prospect of voluntary change appears unlikely. However, China's political economy could become subject to pressures that would make the liberalization of its financial system inevitable. In the face of the recent slowdown in export growth and the resulting decline in the current account surplus, the sustainability of the country's growth model has already become highly doubtful.

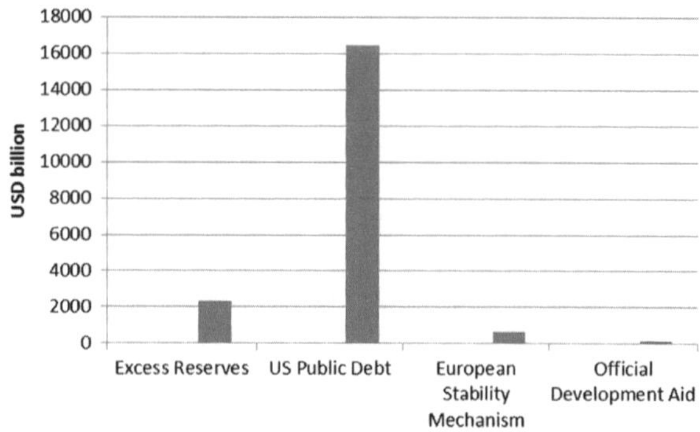

Fig. 5.6 China's excess reserves in comparative perspective (end of 2012) (Sources: US Treasury 2012; OECD: Query Wizard for International Development Statistics). Data on the amount of official development assistance refer to 2011, the latest year for which statistics are available)

With a liberalized financial system, China might still be able to run significant current account surpluses and thus maintain its creditor status, yet with an open capital account and a flexible exchange rate, this surplus would no longer be funneled into the country's reserves, but would be held by the private sector. This shift of foreign assets from the public to the private sector would have significant ramifications for the degree of control that the state maintains over the direction of China's capital outflows, thereby affecting a crucial determinant of the relational financial power deriving from China's creditor position. It can therefore be assumed that a Chinese creditor state with a liberalized political economy and a concentration of foreign assets in the hand of the private sector would appear much less of a threat in the eyes of potential debtors.

5.2.5.2 Control of the Party-State over China's Foreign Assets

The fact that China's foreign assets are dominated by official reserves allows the government to exercise a degree of control over the country's capital outflows that is substantially higher than it was in the case of Japan where private financial institutions directed the flow of funds, or in the case of Saudi Arabia that recycled its surplus via Western banks (Chin and Helleiner 2008: 98–99). However, the fact that the Chinese state is in control of the country's capital outflows should not be confused with the idea of a center of power making investment decisions based on a strategic master plan. As the previous sections have shown, the fragmented structure of authority and the bureaucratic rivalries characteristic of China's political economy also play a role in the management of the country's sovereign wealth. The reason why China's fragmented authoritarianism matters for the question of its relational financial power is that the government agencies involved in the management of China's reserves are usually more concerned with the improvement of their standing within the bureaucratic system than with the increase of power of the Chinese state as a whole. It is therefore unlikely that China's investment agencies will pursue investment strategies that might increase China's relational financial power at the expense of decreasing returns on their investment that might put their balance sheets in jeopardy and undermine their standing within the bureaucratic system.[12] However, even though bureaucratic rivalries do play a central role in China's routine policy making, we also have to be aware of the fact that China's decision making process in times of crises tends to be highly centralized. While a costly exercise of power in normal times appears unlikely, a strategic exercise of relational financial power in situations that threaten the survival of China's regime can therefore not be ruled out.[13]

5.2.5.3 China's Vulnerability to Its Major Debtor

Any assessment of China's relational financial power has to take China's vulnerability to its major debtor into account.[14] The main reason for China's vulnerability to the US is the fact that China is lending in the debtor's currency, which makes it vulnerable to depreciations in the value of the dollar. Due to the massive size of their dollar holdings, China's sovereign wealth managers run the risk of triggering a depreciation of the dollar whenever they try to diversify away from the US currency on a substantial scale. China would therefore have to pay dearly for any attempt to exert financial pressure on the US by withdrawing its investment or by deliberately dumping its dollars in order to manipulate its exchange rate. In Kirshner's (1995: 117–119) terminology, China has thus been "entrapped" by the US. Through the country's acquisition of a massive stock of dollar-denominated assets, China's monetary interests have been transformed in a way that has aligned them to the interests of its major debtor. China's relational financial power has thus been constrained by the continuing structural financial power of the US, and "China has become a central part of the dollar bloc" (Chin and Helleiner 2008: 92).

A withdrawal of Chinese funds from US financial markets could also have unwelcome consequences for China's export-led growth strategy. According to the Bretton Woods II hypothesis, China has been investing in US securities in order to finance American consumption of Chinese exports. A withdrawal of Chinese funds from the US could therefore dampen China's economic growth prospects.

[12] Helleiner (2009) has argued that the behavior of sovereign wealth funds is generally driven by domestic rather than foreign policy considerations.

[13] For the distinction between a "normal mode" and a "crisis mode" of political decision making in China see Heilmann (2004: 42–43).

[14] It could be argued that, for the sake of analytical clarity, a distinction between the creditor's power and the price that it would have to pay for the exercise of its power is necessary. In this sense, a creditor's vulnerability to its debtor would not determine its degree of relational financial power, but would only influence the costs that are associated with the exercise of its power. Yet the problem with this distinction is that the association of high costs with a possible power exercise decreases its probability, thereby reducing the creditor's power by making its threats less effective. Put differently, while a creditor's vulnerability to its debtor does not affect its ability to inflict costs on the debtor that might result in a change of behavior, it weakens its ability to push the debtor into a specific change of behavior that is desired by the creditor.

However, "this strategic rationale for financial support becomes less compelling" (Chin and Helleiner 2008: 95) with the ongoing diversification of China's trade and the increasing role of the EU and the developing world in its trade relationships.

5.2.5.4 The Vulnerability of China's Major Debtor to China

For an assessment of a creditor state's relational financial power, the vulnerability of its debtor also needs to be taken into account. As Drezner (2009: 18) has pointed out, the ability of a creditor to exercise financial leverage on its debtor crucially depends on the question if the debtor has alternative sources of credit at its disposal. As has been explained in Chap. 2, the US enjoys an 'exorbitant privilege' in this regard that results from the dollar's role as international core currency and the pulling power of American financial markets. Alan Greenspan, the former chairman of the Federal Reserve, thus assumed that a reduction in the purchases of Treasury securities by foreign central banks would not result in a funding problem since official investors would be replaced by private investors (Setser 2008: 15). However, others have drawn attention to the fact that instead of offsetting a change in the purchases of foreign central banks, private investors could also follow into the footsteps of reserve managers, thereby inflicting substantial costs on the US government (Setser 2008: 16). In any event, it should not be assumed that there are no limits to the ability of the US to secure foreign financial support. The rapid growth of the US budget deficit in the wake of the global financial crisis has not dried up alternative sources of credit so far since the crisis has also caused consumption levels to decline, thereby reducing the US current account deficit and bolstering domestic sources of credit. However, America's reliance on Chinese financial support might increase in the long run if US government spending rises to a point where it can no longer be matched by an increase in domestic savings (Drezner 2009: 20–21; 44–45).

In addition to the question of alternative sources of credit at the disposal of the debtor, the debtor's currency regime also influences the creditor's ability to influence the behavior of the debtor. As Drezner (2009: 20) has pointed out, debtors maintaining a fixed exchange rate regime are particularly vulnerable to the exercise of a creditor's relational financial power since the latter can force them off their currencies' pegs. However, if the debtor maintains a floating exchange rate regime, the creditor can only inflict serious costs upon the debtor by triggering a massive depreciation of the latter's currency that also inflicts significant costs on the creditor. China's financial leverage over the US is thus significantly weakened by the dollar's floating exchange rate regime.

5.2.5.5 China's Attempts to Exercise Its Relational Financial Power

How has China so far tried to use its relational financial power, and how successful have its attempts to influence its major debtor been? Drezner (2009: 31–42) has analyzed the attempts of China's authorities to push the US into protecting the value of China's dollar-denominated financial assets in the summer of 2008. At that time, the US mortgage lenders Fannie Mae and Freddie Mac, to which China's sovereign wealth managers were heavily exposed, were teetering on the edge of bankruptcy. According to Drezner, Chinese pressure contributed to the decision of the US Treasury to put the mortgage lenders into a government conservatorship. However, the Treasury neither provided explicit guarantees for the mortgage lenders' bonds, nor did it yield to China's insistence to provide special protection for China's investment in US financial institutions, private equity funds and money market funds whose market values had also significantly decreased. Moreover, the US simply ignored China's attempts to compel the US to pursue more restrictive monetary and fiscal policies to prevent a further loss in the value of China's reserves.

The unwillingness of the US to give in to the pressure of one of its major debtors can be explained by the fact that it was aware that China would inflict serious costs upon itself by a significant diversification out of the dollar.[15] Secondly, the US knew that China's ability to diversify was limited by a shortage of alternative investment opportunities. Besides, the US probably took it for granted that it still had alternative sources of credit at its disposal. However, while China's ability to influence US policy decisions has been limited so far, its financial leverage over its major debtor might grow stronger if China decides to speed up the pace of its reserve diversification and a further growth in the US budget deficit increases the government's external borrowing needs. China's major debtor might then become much more willing to give in to its creditor's wishes (Drezner 2009: 45).

Not surprisingly, China has been more successful in its attempts to yield policy concessions from countries with fewer alternative sources of credit. A case in point was China's purchase of dollar-denominated Costa Rican government bonds in 2008 that prompted Costa Rica to sever ties with Taiwan and establish diplomatic relations with Beijing (Anderlini 2008a). China also succeeded in securing its supply with commodities by providing loans to foreign entities. In 2009, China granted Russian oil companies USD 25 billion in loans in return for their agreement to supply oil from new fields in Siberia for the next 20 years. The deal was struck during the financial crisis when Russia's energy giants were facing massive refinancing needs (Belton 2009). In the same year, China signed an agreement with Brazil's oil company Petrobras according to which it would provide loans of up to USD 10 billion for the development of Brazil's oil and gas reserves in its coastal waters in return for the supply of oil (Wheatley 2009b). China struck similar loan-for-oil deals with Kazakhstan and Venezuela.[16]

[15] It can be argued that a creditor's attempt to push its debtor into guaranteeing its assets is a special case insofar as the threats of investment withdrawal are not credible in this context since a withdrawal would lead to the very loss in value that the threat is supposed to prevent in the first place.

[16] Even though these loans were not provided by China's sovereign wealth managers but by China Development Bank, the still involved the use of China's foreign exchange reserves.

China's growing foreign exchange reserves have also allowed the country to bolster its ties with other developing countries by increasing its foreign aid in Asia, Latin America and Africa. Since it is willing to provide preferential loans without requiring painful economic restructuring measures from its debtors, Beijing is often considered a more attractive creditor than the IMF or the World Bank who are in many cases the only alternative sources of credit at the disposal of developing countries. By shifting its financial support from the US to the developing world, China could therefore strengthen its financial leverage to a considerable degree.

To the great astonishment of many observers, China has so far refrained from trying to extract concessions from the eurozone by providing substantial funds to support the members of the currency union in their fight against the sovereign debt crisis. It can be assumed that China's hesitancy in this regard results from the fact that the idea of risking the hard-earned money of a developing country in an effort to rescue profligate western nations is highly unpopular among the Chinese public. In this sense, Li Daokui (quoted after Anderlini and Milne 2011), an economics professor at China's renowned Tsinghua University and a member of the PBOC's monetary policy committee, has pointed out that "[i]t is in China's long-term and intrinsic interest to help Europe because they are our biggest trading partner but the chief concern of the Chinese government is how to explain this decision to our people." According to Li, (quoted after Anderlini and Milne 2011) "[t]he last thing China wants is throw away the country's wealth and be seen as just a source of dumb money."

5.3 Financial Repression and the Power of Creditors

The potential of both the Chinese and the Japanese developmental state to acquire structural financial power has been severely limited by the countries' systems of financial repression. However, these very systems have been highly conducive to the acquisition of relational financial power. Relying on systems of financial repression to channel the countries' funds into industrial development and to ensure the states' control over the economy, the policymakers of both countries had to promote a growth model relying on investment and exports that resulted in massive current account surpluses and thus turned the countries into net creditors. China's variety of a system of financial repression that combines a credit-based system and government-administered prices with state-ownership of the dominant financial institutions has proven particularly advantageous to the development of relational financial power since it has allowed the party-state to accumulate surpluses in the form of foreign exchange reserves without losing control over the monetary impact of reserve accumulation and has thus provided it with an usually high degree of control over the country's capital outflows.

The fact that China's foreign assets have so far been dominated by foreign exchange reserves has allowed the government to exercise a degree of control over the country's capital outflows that is substantially higher than it was in the case of Japan where private financial institutions directed the flow of funds. Yet even in China's case, senior leaders are not unconstrained in their decisions concerning the investment of the country's external assets, but have to consider the bureaucratic interests of the government agencies that manage the country's sovereign wealth. Besides, it is uncertain if China can maintain this high degree of control over the country's capital outflows in the long run. China will continue to export capital as long as it runs a current account surplus. Yet its capital exports will only be dominated by foreign exchange reserves as long as the country refrains from liberalizing its financial system and allowing its current account surplus to be matched by outward investment by the private sector.

As far as their vulnerability to their major debtor is concerned, both China and Japan have suffered from American structural financial power. By lending in their debtor's currency, both countries have made themselves vulnerable to a depreciation of the US currency. Caught in the dollar trap, they have not been able to diversify their assets without risking significant losses on their holdings. Besides, America's unrivalled ability to raise funds has allowed it to largely resist the pressures of its creditors. However, in the face of rising costs associated with their investments, both China and Japan have become increasingly reluctant to continue their financial support of the US.

Due to the government's control of China's capital outflows, China can already be considered a more powerful creditor than Japan was in the 1980s, and it might well increase its relational financial power if it decides to shift its financial support to weaker debtors by diversifying its existing dollar holdings. However, even though China may have a higher degree of relational financial power at its disposal, it is not necessarily more willing to exercise its power. Ever since the beginning of the debate on China's excess reserves in 2006, China's elite has been trying to find ways to use these reserves that would contribute to the development of China's economy. Considering the fact that China is still a developing country, this focus of the debate is not surprising. While investment strategies that aim at development objectives may involve the use of its relational financial power, as was the case in China's loan-for-oil deals, they can also reduce this power, as would be the case if China spent its reserves to build a strategic oil reserve.

Moreover, China's concern over losses in the value of its reserves should not be underestimated. Since the PBOC has to sterilize the inflationary impact of its reserve accumulation by issuing domestic currency bills, an increase in the accumulation of reserves always goes along with an increase in public sector liabilities. It is therefore unlikely that China will embark on costly investment strategies to project its relational financial power since this would put the balance sheets of China's sovereign wealth managers in jeopardy and threaten their position within the bureaucratic hierarchy. Besides, substantial losses on China's reserves would result in anger on behalf of China's population who consider China's reserves as the fruits of their labor, thereby undermining the government's legitimacy. However, while a costly exercise of relational financial power is unlikely under normal circumstances, China might be willing to pay the price for an investment strike aimed at foreign policy objectives when facing a severe crisis. In a strategic dispute with the United States over Taiwan, China could consider the dumping of its dollar holdings a justifiable means of warfare. It therefore makes a crucial difference that China, in contrast to Japan, is not an ally of its major debtor.

Chapter 6
Developmental States in the Bretton Woods Institutions

As has been explained in Chap. 2, institutional financial power is a state's ability to influence the behavior of other states through the policy decisions of international financial institutions in general and the International Monetary Fund and the World Bank in particular. The main sources of a state's institutional financial power are its voting share, its contribution of funds as well as its representation among the staff and management of these institutions (Woods 2003b). The main mechanism for the exercise of institutional financial power is a state's influence on the provision of credit via these institutions and the conditions upon which this provision of credit relies. If a state exercises its institutional financial power in a manipulative way, the objectives of its power exercise usually lie in the realm of economic interests. However, in principle any policy objective may be achieved through the exercise of institutional financial power.

This chapter is organized according to these considerations. Section 6.1 portrays the structures of power within the IMF and the World Bank by analyzing the distribution of voting shares, the contribution of funds and the composition of staff and management. Section 6.2 examines Japan's attempts to increase its institutional financial power and its challenge to the Washington Consensus in the 1980s and 1990s. Section 6.3 assesses China's institutional financial power by analyzing its increasing voting share in the Bretton Woods institutions, examining its growing financial contributions and considering its improving representation among staff and management. Last but not least, it sheds light on the policies that China has been promoting in the IMF and the World Bank. Section 6.4 compares China's policies towards the IMF and the World Bank with the policies of the Japanese developmental state.

S. Heep, *China in Global Finance*, Global Power Shift,
DOI 10.1007/978-3-319-02466-0_6,

6.1 Structures of Power in the IMF and the World Bank

The following sections analyze the distribution of voting shares, the contribution of funds as well as the composition of staff and management in the Bretton Woods institutions since these factors determine the distribution of institutional financial power between the institutions' members.

6.1.1 Voting Shares

A country's voting share is its most important source of institutional financial power. Both the IMF and the World Bank operate on a principle of weighted voting "designed to reflect the position of each member country in the global economy" (IMF n.d.-a). Each member country is assigned a quota that determines its financial commitment to the institutions, its voting share and, in the case of the IMF, its access to the institution's resources. In addition to the votes that reflect member countries' quotas, votes also comprise basic votes aimed at guaranteeing a minimal influence of members who do not play a significant role in the global economy. Member countries are entitled to borrow up to 200 % of their quota annually and 600 % cumulatively. In times of severe crises, additional resources can be made available (IMF 2012b).

The redistribution of quotas among member countries usually requires a general quota increase that may be decided in the course of the general quota reviews that take place at least every 5 years. The issues addressed in these reviews are the appropriateness of the IMF's funds judged against the balance of payments financing needs of its member countries as well as changes of the relative importance of its member countries in the world economy. On rare occasions, there have been ad hoc redistributions of quotas outside the context of general quota increases. Changes in quotas require the approval by an 85 % majority of the total voting power as well as the consent of the member countries affected (IMF 2012b).

Even though the notion of a formula suggests that the allocation of votes is a purely technical matter, quota allocation "has always been deeply political" (Woods 2003a: 958). As Rapkin and Strand (1997: 272) have pointed out, quotas are "determined by negotiation rather than a mechanical process." Over the course of time, several changes in the distribution of quotas have aimed at realigning quota shares with changes in the international political economy. When the Bretton Woods institutions were founded at the end of the Second World War, the US held a quota share of more than 30 % in the IMF and the World Bank, yet in the following decades its share gradually sank to 17 % (Helleiner and Momani 2007: 12). Nevertheless, the US remains the IMF's only shareholder with a quota share that gives it the power to veto major decisions. In recent decades, the US was followed by Japan, Germany, France and the United Kingdom as the Fund's biggest shareholders. However, the distribution of voting shares has changed significantly against the backdrop of the global financial crisis. The most recent reforms in the distribution of the institution's voting shares and the ensuing shift of quota shares to emerging market and developing countries will be discussed in the third section of this chapter.

Shareholding in the World Bank's main arm, the International Bank for Reconstruction and Development (IBRD) has until recently been largely determined by IMF quotas.[1] However, this parallelism has not been strictly maintained in the IBRD's capital increases over the last two decades. Shareholding in the IBRD has occasionally been adjusted to reflect the contribution of funds by individual member countries to the International Development Association (IDA), the World Bank's soft-loan facility for the world's poorest countries (World Bank 2010: 3). In 2010, the World Bank's members approved a reform of the Bank's voting rights system that makes it independent of the IMF's quota formula. Just as in the case of the IMF, this reform will lead to a shift of voting power to emerging market and developing countries. This reform will also be discussed in the third section of this chapter. Voting power in the IDA is independent of voting power in the IBRD and solely reflects the financial contributions of its member countries. However, the distribution of voting shares in the IBRD determines the structure of the IDA's Board of Directors, an arrangement that also applies to the International Finance Corporation (World Bank n.d.-a).

The rules governing both the IMF and the World Bank stipulate that decisions affecting the institutions' policies require a majority of 85 %, thus ensuring that the US as the institutions' biggest shareholder can veto major decisions and prevent a reduction of its voting power as well as an increase in the voting power of other members (Rapkin and Strand 1997: 273). As Kahler (1990: 100) has pointed out, due to the continuous decline in the US quota, this special majority has become increasingly important to the preservation of US influence over the Bretton Woods institutions. While policy decisions need a special majority, more routine decisions only require simple majorities.

The highest decision-making bodies in the Bretton Woods institutions are the Boards of Governors, consisting of one governor and one alternate governor for each member country. The Boards of Governors of the IMF and the World Bank usually meet once a year to discuss the institutions' work and make strategic decisions concerning their operations. Even though all powers of the IMF and the World Bank are vested in their Boards of Governors, most powers have been delegated to the Executive Boards that are responsible for the day-to-day work of the institutions. Among the rights that the Boards of Governors of both institutions retain are the right to approve the admittance of new members and amendments to the Articles of Agreement. In the case of the IMF, the Board of Governors also

---

[1] The World Bank Group comprises the International Bank for Reconstruction and Development (IBRD), the International Development Association (IDA), the International Finance Corporation (IFC), the Multilateral Investment Guarantee Agency (MIGA) and the International Centre for Settlement of Investment Disputes (ICSID). In this book, "World Bank" refers to the IBRD.

retains the right to approve quota increases and special drawing right allocations. In the case of the World Bank, the Board of Governors also retains the right to make changes in the capital stock, to determine the distribution of the Bank's income and to increase the number of Executive Directors. While all member countries are represented on the Boards of Governors, only the biggest shareholders have the right to appoint their own directors to the Executive Boards. The rest of the 24 Executive Directors are elected by groups of member countries (IMF n.d.-b; World Bank n.d.-b). Even though the Executive Boards of both the IMF and the World Bank operate by consensus, voting power is still relevant since it "is taken into account in determining the extent of consensus on any issue" (Woods 2003b: 111).

6.1.2 Provision of Funds

In contrast to the United Nations, the core funding of the IMF and the World Bank does not rely on annual contributions by their members. For this reason, they are more immune to the exercise of political pressure by members threatening to withhold contributions. However, some of the funds of each institution do rely on the willingness of its members to provide financial support, thus providing countries with small voting shares but plentiful financial resources with an opportunity to increase their say in the institutions (Woods 2003a: 961, 2003b: 98).

Most of the IMF's resources are provided through the payment of quotas by its member countries. These quotas are reviewed at least every 5 years, giving financially potent members the opportunity to exercise political pressure if a quota increase is deemed necessary. Besides, the IMF's borrowing capacity is bolstered by the New Arrangements to Borrow (NAB) – a multilateral borrowing arrangement that can be activated if the IMF's resources are considered insufficient to meet member countries' needs. The NAB was originally established in the wake of the Mexican financial crisis amid concern that more funds would be needed to successfully tackle future financial crises. Against the backdrop of the 2008 global financial crisis, the NAB was revamped and its total borrowing capacity was significantly increased. China, India, Brazil and Russia were among the countries that made the most significant contributions to the reformed NAB (IMF 2012c).[2]

The IBRD enjoys an even higher degree of financial independence from its members than the IMF since it primarily finances its lending to developing countries by raising funds in the world's financial markets. Its triple-A-rated bonds are

[2] The General Arrangements to Borrow (GAB), established in 1969 and comprising 11 industrial countries, can only be activated if the participants of the NAB have refused its activation. In addition to the expansion of the NAB, the IMF has signed bilateral loan and note purchase agreements with some of its member countries. In the case of NAB participants with bilateral credit lines, the latter are included in the total resources made available to the IMF under the NAB (IMF 2012c).

backed by the capital commitments of its members that function as guarantees vis-à-vis its creditors (World Bank n.d.-c). In contrast, the IDA's interest-free loans and grants to the world's poorest countries rely on the financial contributions of its members. The IDA's donors meet every 3 years to review the IDA's policies and to replenish its funds. The most recent replenishment of the IDA's resources took place in 2010, resulting in a record replenishment amounting to SDR 32.8 billion or USD 49.3 billion (World Bank n.d.-d).[3] As Woods (2003b: 101) has pointed out, the US as the IDA's biggest contributor has repeatedly "used threats to reduce or withhold contributions to the IDA in order to demand changes in policy, not just in the IDA but in the World Bank as a whole." This happened in the late 1970s, when the US pushed the World Bank into refusing to lend to Vietnam in the course of the negotiations on the IDA 6 replenishment as well as in 1993, when the US demanded the creation of an Independent Inspection Panel in the context of the IDA 10 Replenishment.

6.1.3 Staff and Management

With regard to staff policies, the IMF and the World Bank differ from most international institutions insofar as there are no nationality quotas guaranteeing that member countries are not only formally represented in the governing bodies of the institutions, but also informally among their professional staff (Woods 2003b: 108–110).[4] In addition, the fact that English was established as the institutions' single working language has inhibited the representation of different nationalities among the professional staff. Historians of the World Bank have thus argued that "from early on there was a tilt in the staff toward homogeneity" (Kapur et al. 1997: 1167), with staff policies distorting employment decisions by favoring English native speakers and graduates of universities teaching in English, thus embedding Anglo-Saxon liberalism into their operations.

In line with this argument, a 1991 study of the World Bank's Policy, Research and External Affairs Department found that nearly 80 % of senior staff had received their graduate degrees from American or British institutions, thus raising "the question of whether the professional research staff may not be excessively homogeneous and be looking at the world in one particular way" (Stern and Ferreira 1997: 587). Similarly, a breakdown of the IMF's senior staff by nationality in 1968 revealed that 32 of 54 employees were nationals of four English-speaking countries: the US (23), the UK (6), Canada (2) and Australia (1) (Strange 1973: 269). Another study conducted in 1996 showed that while only 41 % of IMF professionals were nationals from English-speaking industrialized countries, 90 % of the

[3] In addition to donor contributions worth SDR 21.1 billion (USD 31.7 billion), this amount includes reflows from credit repayments and IBRD transfers (World Bank n.d.-d).

[4] Section 6.1.3 largely follows Woods (2003b: 108–110).

staff with PhDs that were hired in the preceding year had received their degree from universities in the US or Canada (Clark 1996: 9).

As far as the formal rules of staff and management selection are concerned, both the head of the IMF and the World Bank are appointed by the institutions' Executive Boards. In practice, the Managing Director of the IMF has always been a Western European while the President of the World Bank and the IMF's First Deputy Managing Director have always been US nationals. According to the Articles of Agreement, the heads of the institutions appoint their professional staff upon approval by the Executive Boards. However, as Woods (2003b: 109) has pointed out, "the approval of the US is *de facto* necessary" for all decisions concerning senior personnel. Below the level of head of department, staff are appointed by senior management, yet "even at this more junior level, the United States has gone to some length to ensure that its own nationals have every incentive to work for the institutions" (Woods 2003b: 109).

6.2 Japan's Challenge to the Washington Consensus

The following sections look into Japan's push for a larger voting share in the IMF and the World Bank, analyze the country's challenge to the Washington Consensus and examine its Asian Monetary Fund proposal.

6.2.1 Fighting for a Larger Voting Share

Until the late 1970s, Japan did not play a major role in the Bretton Woods institutions. It was only in the early 1980s, when the country emerged as a leading international creditor and its contributions to the IMF and the World Bank increased significantly, that Japan began to push for an increase in its voting shares. As Rapkin and Strand (1997: 276) have argued, "this bid was but a recent chapter in Japan's long quest for international status and prestige commensurate with its objective accomplishments and capabilities."

In the early 1980s, Japan focused its efforts on the increase of its voting share in the World Bank. According to Ogata (1989: 18), "adjustment in the IBRD shareholding had a symbolic significance beyond the numerical size of the votes" and Japan's efforts to achieve a more influential position in the World Bank "were likened to the struggle over the revision of the unequal treaties in the Meiji period" by the country's financial authorities. Japan's bid for a more influential role initially met with heavy resistance by the US that was unwilling to agree to an overall increase in the World Bank's capital. According to Rapkin and Strand (1997: 280), the reserved attitude of the US resulted not only from budgetary concerns of the US Congress, but was also influenced by "the ideological disdain of the first administration of Ronald Reagan for international organizations."

In addition, the US linked its approval to a more prominent Japanese position in the World Bank to issues that had been troubling the countries' bilateral relations (Rapkin and Strand 1997: 281; Ogata 1989: 15). As has been explained in the preceding chapters, the US was determined to push Japan into financial market liberalization and currency internationalization in an attempt to reduce the US trade deficit. Washington thus decided to take advantage of Japan's desire to increase its voting share in the World Bank by intensifying its pressure for financial system reform. US officials publicly doubted Japan's ability to play a more responsible role in the Bretton Woods institutions due to the international isolation of its financial sector. As Treasury Secretary Donald Regan put it, "Japan is not acting like a number two nation as far as its financial markets are concerned" (quoted after Ogata 1989: 15).

In the face of this resistance, Japan made its contribution to the International Development Association contingent upon a significant increase of its voting share in the World Bank. However, in the negotiations leading up to the Yen-Dollar Agreement that took place at the same time, Japan also gave in to US liberalization pressures, mainly by introducing easier rules concerning the issuance of yen bonds in the Euromarkets (Emmott 1989: 102). Against this backdrop, the US finally agreed to a selective capital increase in the World Bank, and Japan could establish itself as number 2 in one of the world's most important international financial institutions (Rapkin and Strand 1997: 281–282; Ogata 1989: 15–16).

During the negotiations over the following IDA replenishment in 1986, Japan successfully applied the same strategy of linking its contribution to an increase in its voting share in the World Bank. This time Japan's pressure led to an increase of the country's voting share to 6.7 %. The US, which saw its voting share fall below the 20 % threshold, had made this redistribution conditional upon an increase in the World Bank's special majority to 85 % in order to sustain its veto (Rapkin and Strand 1997: 282).

After its successful bid for a more prominent position in the World Bank, Japan in the late 1980s began to push for a bigger say in the IMF, where its voting share was even less commensurate with its weight in the world economy. Japan started to work towards this objective at the annual meeting of the IMF and the World Bank in 1988, where the governor of the Bank of Japan, Sumita Satoshi, did not only present the Miyazawa Plan as a new strategy in the fight against the global debt crisis, but "also made a forceful case for increasing Japan's role in the IMF" (Rapkin and Strand 1997: 283). Japan was particularly frustrated with its position in the Fund since it had given in to pressures from the US and other nations for greater financial support and made significant financial contributions that were not taken into consideration in the calculation of voting rights. Against this backdrop, Japan's Minister of Finance, Hashimoto Ryutaro, warned that the Diet might not be willing to approve bills appropriating funds for the IMF if the country was denied a more influential position in the IMF (Rapkin and Strand 1997: 283).

Also in this case, the US initially opposed Japan's request for a more influential position, arguing that there was no need for a general quota increase that would allow for a shift in the distribution of quotas. Yet when Japan announced that it would provide USD 4.5 billion to support the US in its efforts to solve the developing world's debt problem according to the Brady plan, Washington embraced a more supportive position. In 1990, IMF member countries agreed on a 50 % quota increase and a redistribution of quotas that left the US in the number 1 position, while Japan and Germany had to share the second rank. Japanese officials seemed at least temporarily satisfied with the new power ranking in the IMF. However, the distribution of voting shares still failed to reflect the economic weight of the IMF's major member countries (Rapkin and Strand 1997: 284–285). In the words of Rapkin and Strand (1997: 285), "Japan's diplomatic exertions have improved its rank within the Bretton Woods institutions since 1980, but its voting share remains obviously misaligned in relation to the shares of the other G-5 countries."

6.2.2 *Challenging the World Bank*

Even though Japan was successful in its bid to increase its voting share in the World Bank in the 1980s, the country's newly gained "voting strength did not automatically translate into policy influence at the World Bank" (Katsuhiro 2007: 116). As Katsuhiro has argued, the reasons for Japan's lack of influence were manifold: Japan did not have the political experience required to form winning coalitions of member countries in order to imprint its preferences onto the institution. Moreover, the country lacked expert knowledge in official development assistance and was not sufficiently represented among the Bank's staff and management. With the World Bank's headquarters based in Washington, its use of English as single working language and its American style of decision-making, Japan struggled to find its voice in an institution in which it was the second-biggest shareholder (Katsuhiro 2007: 116–117). It was only in the 1990s that Japan tried to overcome these obstacles and increase its influence on the World Bank's policies, "not least by focusing on administrative and personnel issues, and by gaining the courage to give 'voice' to distinctly Japanese experience and approaches" (Katsuhiro 2007: 117).

Disagreements between Japan and the US had already emerged in the late 1980s, when Japan began to challenge the World Bank's neoliberal development policies. As Rapkin and Strand (1997: 289) have pointed out, "[t]he most important Japanese-American differences were over the appropriate role of the state in the economic development process, the boundary between the public and private sectors, and how these issues should be manifest in the policies of international financial institutions." Over the course of the 1980s, the Bretton Woods institutions had adopted what later came to be known as the 'Washington Consensus', a term that was coined by John Williamson, an economist at the Peterson Institute of International Economics in Washington. Williamson (1990) had identified a number of development policies focusing on fiscal discipline, privatization, liberalization and integration into the world economy concerning which he assumed there was agreement in the Washington community. As far as the World Bank was concerned, these ideas played a particularly prominent role in the newly established Structural Adjustment Loans that required borrowers to diminish the role of the state and to integrate the country into the global economy (Wade 1996: 5). In the eyes of Japan, the main drawback of this neoliberal approach was that it was exclusively based on the development experiences of the Western industrialized countries in general and the United States in particular, while "[t]he quite different experiences of Japan, and east Asia more generally, seemed to be ignored altogether" (Rapkin and Strand 1997: 290).

The tension between the World Bank and Japan culminated when the World Bank criticized Japan's bilateral development assistance for undermining the development objectives of the Bretton Woods institutions (Wade 1996: 4).[5] Over the course of the 1980s, Japan had emerged as one of the major providers of aid and investment in East and Southeast Asia. In the words of Robert Wade (1996: 7), Japan had used its newly gained influence to encourage its debtors "to think more strategically and in more interventionist terms than can be accommodated by World Bank ideas" and to promote the pursuit of an active industrial policy facilitated by a "regulated, 'non-liberalized' financial system capable of delivering concessional credit to priority uses." Guided by this new approach to development, the Ministry of International Trade and Industry (MITI) in 1987 published *The New Asian Industries Development Plan* that contained a blueprint for the industrialization of Southeast Asian countries.[6] In reaction to the need for an offshore relocation of Japanese production resulting from the appreciation of the yen in the wake of the Plaza Agreement, the plan announced that Japanese companies willing to invest in Southeast Asia would benefit from Japanese aid to the region. Subsidized targeted loans – also known as 'directed credit' – were to play a crucial role in this strategy. For the provision of these loans, Japan established the ASEAN-Japan Development Fund under the auspices of the Overseas Economic Cooperation Fund (OECF). Even though World Bank officials did not hide their discontent with Japan's development policy, Japan was not willing to change its course (Wade 1996: 7–8).

In 1989, the disagreement between the World Bank and Japan reached new heights when a vice-president of the Bank sent a letter to the president of the OECF in which he criticized the policy of directed credit since it "could have an adverse impact on development of the financial sector" and "would create unnecessary distortions and set back the financial sector reforms" promoted by the IMF and the Bank (quoted after Wade 1996: 8). When Japan's Executive Director at the World Bank protested against this official scolding, many Executive Directors from developing countries expressed their support for Japan's development strategy, yet the World Bank's management refused to relent. Unwilling to surrender, Japan's Ministry of Finance decided to make out its case by explaining Japan's understanding of structural adjustment (Wade 1996: 8–9).

---

[5] The remainder of this section largely follows Wade (1996).

[6] The plan is only available in Japanese.

In 1991, the OECF (1998) presented the *Issues Related to the World Bank's Approach to Structural Adjustment: A Proposal from a Major Partner.*[7] The report argued that governments should pursue industrial policies "to develop industries that can support long-term economic development" since "[t]o expect that the next generation of industries will pop up automatically through the activities of the private sector is overly optimistic" (OECF 1998: 65). Moreover, it highlighted the importance of "measures aimed *directly* at promoting investment" (OECF 1998: 64) within this context, pointing out that due to imperfections in the financial markets of developing countries, "it is indispensable for government to intervene to overcome the limits of market interest rates" (OECF 1998: 66).

At the same time, the MOF urged the World Bank to conduct its own study of East Asia's development experience and to reconsider its development paradigm in the light of its findings. The Bank's management was at first unwilling to give in to Japan's pressure, yet eventually agreed since Japan was not only willing to pay for the study, but also offered to give up its opposition to a directive on financial sector reform promoting comprehensive financial deregulation. In 1992, a team of almost exclusively American-trained World Bank economists began to work on the study that came to be known as *The East Asian Miracle* (World Bank 1993) and was published in the following year (Wade 1996: 17–18).

While the authors of the study remained faithful to the World Bank's promotion of neoliberal policies, they also acknowledged that some interventional policies in East Asia had had positive effects. In the foreword to the study, the Bank's President, Lewis Preston, accordingly claimed "that rapid economic growth in each economy was primarily due to the application of a set of common, market-friendly economic policies, leading to both higher accumulation and better allocation of resources" (World Bank 1993: VI). Yet he also admitted "that in some economies, mainly those in Northeast Asia, some selective interventions contributed to growth, and [the study] advances our understanding of the conditions required for interventions to succeed" (World Bank 1993: VII). Preston thus summarized the report's findings by arguing that "[t]he market-oriented aspects of East Asia's policies can be recommended with few reservations, but the more institutionally demanding aspects, such as context-based interventions, have not been successfully used in other settings" (World Bank 1993: VII).

The report's underlying policy of minimally accommodating Japan's demands for a more pragmatic stance regarding development strategies while at the same time insisting on the overriding importance of market-friendly policies was also applied to the question of financial repression. The authors argued that while "directed-credit programs have been catastrophic failures" in other regions, the policy of controlled credit allocation has "caused less damage to capital allocation and may have been beneficial" in East Asian states that "supplemented fundamentally sound capital market policies with improved selection and monitoring" (World

[7] As Wade (1996: 10, footnote 13) has pointed out, this was the OECF's first Occasional Paper in the 30 years of its existence.

Bank 1993: 274). They acknowledged "that credit programs directed at exports yielded high social returns and, in the cases of Japan and Korea, other directed-credit programs also may have increased investment and generated important spillovers" (World Bank 1993: 356). Yet at the same time, they stressed that "when interest rate subsidies were large, or export performance criteria were not imposed, directed credit often went to inefficient ventures and those with low social returns" (World Bank 1993: 356). Moreover, they were very explicit about their reservation against the promotion of specific industries, arguing that it "generally did not work and therefore holds little promise for other developing economies" (World Bank 1993: 354).

Japanese officials were not too pleased with this outcome. They blamed the authors of the study for having failed to bring Japanese economists onto the research team and argued that they had completely misunderstood Japan's development path. Besides, they were exasperated by the study's advice to other developing countries to learn from the success of the Southeast Asian economies of Singapore, Thailand, Malaysia and Hong Kong that in contrast to the developmental states of Japan, South Korea and Taiwan had engaged in comprehensive liberalization measures (Terry 2000: 86–87).

As Wade (1996: 35) has argued, Japan's failure to imprint its ideas of economic development onto the World Bank's policies "shows the determining importance of essentially American values and interests in the functioning of the Bank." According to Wade (1996: 35), US influence is not mainly exercised through the government's pressure on the Bank's management, but crucially derives from the Bank's professional norms and its "dependence on world financial markets, and the self-reinforcing congruence between the values of the owners and managers of financial capital and those of the US state". With the dominance of economists who received their training in North American or British universities and the dependence of the Bank on the favor of international financiers, neoliberalism was too firmly embedded in the institution to be swept away by an outsider with unorthodox views on development strategies, even though that outsider was the Bank's second-largest shareholder.

However, even though the World Bank "emerge[d] with its traditional paradigm largely unscathed" (Wade 1996: 5) the *East Asian Miracle* still brought about a minor change in the Bank's thinking. Not only could the change in the Bank's attitude towards directed credit in the 1990s be at least partially ascribed to Japanese pressure. More importantly, the study legitimized further research on the subject of industrial policy that could have resulted in more substantial changes in the Bank's policies if Japan's 'lost decade' had not destroyed the appeal of the developmental state (Terry 2000: 87–90; Wade 1996: 33).

6.2.3 Japan's Asian Monetary Fund Proposal

While the *East Asian Miracle* epitomized Japan's most serious challenge to the World Bank, the country expressed its most outspoken critique of the IMF's policies a few years later in the context of the Asian Financial Crisis. As Saori Katada (2002: 92) has pointed out, Japanese policymakers had an "ideational stake" in the region's recovery whose economic success they largely attributed to the provision of Japanese foreign aid and foreign direct investment in combination with "a development model to follow." They hence did not want to see the Japanese model of the developmental state discredited by the American argument that the crisis was caused by Asian 'crony capitalism'. Convinced that the main reasons for the outbreak of the crisis were the region's exposure to volatile capital flows and its overreliance on the dollar, they heavily opposed the IMF's prescriptions of drastic liberalization measures, instead promoting a response to the crisis focusing on a higher degree of financial regulation with a particular emphasis on the establishment of capital controls (Katada 2002: 92; Helleiner 2000: 235). Moreover, Japan was seriously affected by the crisis since both its manufacturers and its banks were highly exposed to the region due to the effects of the yen's appreciation in the wake of the Plaza Agreement. Besides, the crisis also dampened Japanese exports to the region. Japan's policymakers thus considered a generous provision of liquidity to be in the country's own material interest. The US, on the other hand, maintained only weak economic ties with East Asia and was thus highly reluctant to provide financial support, arguing that it would only increase the risk of moral hazard (Lipscy 2003: 97–98; Katada 2002: 90; Helleiner 2000: 235).

Due to its dominance in the IMF, it came as no surprise that America's stance prevailed and the IMF made its bailouts conditional upon comprehensive liberalization measures. The failure of their efforts to influence the IMF's response to the crisis was particularly exasperating in the eyes' of Japanese policymakers since the US obtained its preferred policy outcomes even though the funds provided through the IMF were mainly made available by Asian countries and in particular by Japan.[8] Frustrated with its inability to garner the IMF's support for its policy preferences, Japan set out to propose a regional alternative to the IMF, hoping that the pooling of reserves in an Asian Monetary Fund would allow for a more suitable response to regional financial crises. However, with the US heavily opposed to this plan due to fears that a regional alternative to the IMF would undermine the Fund's role in Asia, Japan soon had to withdraw its proposal (Lipscy 2003; Katada 2002; Helleiner 2000: 235–236).[9]

---

[8] In the case of the Thai rescue package, 55 % of the total funds were provided by Asian nations, including 23 % provided by Japan, while the IMF also provided 23 % (Lipscy 2003: 101).

[9] Even though Japan did not realize its proposal to set up a regional alternative to the IMF, the general idea guiding its plan was present in Japan's New Miyazawa Initiative and continues to live on in the currency swap arrangement among Japan, South Korea, China and the members of ASEAN known as the Chiang Mai Initiative.

6.3 China on the Rise in the Bretton Woods Institutions?

The following sections examine China's voting share in the IMF and the World Bank, analyze the country's contribution of funds and its representation among staff and management and look into the policies that it is promoting in the Bretton Woods institutions.

6.3.1 China's Voting Power in the Bretton Woods Institutions

The increase in China's voting power in the IMF and the World Bank can only be discussed in the context of the more general shift of voting shares to emerging market economies in the wake of the global financial crisis. The following sections therefore shed light on the reform processes that the IMF and the World Bank have undergone in recent years.

6.3.1.1 Voting Power in the IMF

After two decades in which the IMF played a highly influential role in the international financial architecture, it was "facing yet another crisis of legitimacy and purpose" (Helleiner and Momani 2007: 2) in the early 2000s. The institution's main problem was the fact that demand for its funds was in severe decline. Among the reasons for this development was the absence of severe financial crises at the beginning of the decade as well as the improved access of emerging market economies to funds provided by private lenders through international financial markets (Helleiner and Momani 2007: 2–3). Moreover, the IMF was facing increasing competition from China and other financially potent emerging markets that in contrast to the Bretton Woods institutions provided credit without demanding painful economic restructuring measures.

However, the fact that many emerging markets turned their backs on the Fund could also be attributed to the institutions growing legitimacy deficit. Most importantly, many East Asian countries had accumulated large amounts of foreign exchange reserves to ensure their independence from the Fund in reaction to its highly controversial role during the Asian Financial Crisis. While the Fund continued to play an important role with regard to the borrowing of low-income countries, its financial support was becoming ever less popular with emerging market economies. This development was particularly threatening to the institution since it did not only raise questions about its utility, but also posed a danger to its funding since its costs are covered by the income generated by its loans (Helleiner and Momani 2007: 2–4).

In the face of severe criticism and growing financial difficulties, reform was high on the IMF's agenda even before the outbreak of the global financial crisis. A change in the Fund's governance structures with an emphasis on a redistribution of voting shares and a more equitable composition of its Executive Board was considered to have the greatest urgency. At the IMF's annual meeting in Singapore in 2006, the Board of Governors thus endorsed ad hoc quota increases for China, South Korea, Mexico and Turkey, the four "most clearly underrepresented countries", as a "first step in the process of realignment" (IMF 2006). From the completion of the IMF's eleventh general quota review in 1998 until the 2006 reform, China's voting share accounted for 2.9 %. As a result of the reform, it increased to 3.7 %, turning the country, into the institution's sixth biggest shareholder after the US, Japan, Germany, France and the UK (IMF n.d.-d).

At the meeting in Singapore, the IMF's members had already agreed upon the necessity of a second round of reforms. Yet with the outbreak of the global financial crisis in 2007, the need for reform appeared even more urgent. One reason for the greater importance attributed to the reform was the fact that the Fund's decreasing popularity among emerging market economies, particularly in the Asian region, was believed to have been among the causes of the crisis: In an effort to insure themselves against the danger of future financial crises, a number of Asian countries had built up massive amounts of foreign exchange reserves and thus contributed to the creation of the global imbalances at the core of the global financial turmoil. It was therefore argued that emerging market economies should be given a bigger say in the IMF to increase its legitimacy and to regain the trust of Asian countries that had been lost in the wake of the Asian Financial crisis so that these countries would no longer accumulate reserves for the sake of protection.

Even more importantly, the crisis had revealed the increasing importance of emerging markets as growth engines of the world economy. While the better part of the developed world was teetering on the edge of recession, China succeeded at maintaining growth rates close to 9 % in the 2 years following the outbreak of the crisis. Unsurprisingly, China was among the countries that vehemently and repeatedly called for a shift of IMF quotas to emerging market and developing countries.

Against this backdrop, the IMF's members in 2008 endorsed a more comprehensive set of reforms, including a new quota formula, a second round of ad hoc quota increases based on this formula and an increase in basic votes to ensure an adequate representation of low-income countries. The replacement of the old set of 5 different formulas by a new single formula was aimed at improving the transparency of the IMF's governance. According to the new formula, a country's GDP, openness, variability and reserves determine its quota share, with the GDP variable understood as a blend of GDP converted at market rates (60 %) and at purchasing power parity exchange rates (40 %).[10] In the old formulas, GDP was measured solely at market prices, yet developing countries had long demanded an inclusion of

[10] In the new formula, average of GDP accounts for a weight of 50 %, economic openness for a weight of 30 %, economic variability for a weight of 15 % and reserves for a weight of 5 % (IMF 2008).

purchasing power parity exchange rates. The second round of ad hoc quota increases based on this new formula resulted in a 5 % shift in quota shares to emerging market countries. This shift was made possible by the agreement of several developed countries, including the US, Japan, Germany and Italy, to forego part of the quota increases for which they were eligible (IMF 2008).

Even with this change in the IMF's governance structure, the momentum for reform did not come to a halt. The shift in economic power from the developed to the developing world that was driving the reform process was epitomized by the replacement of the Group of Seven with the Group of Twenty, established in 2008 to include the most influential emerging market economies in the decisions affecting the world economy. With emerging market countries "being invited to take their places at the top table of global governance" (Beattie 2010) it seemed increasingly inappropriate that their representation in the IMF failed to match their economic weight. Besides, the reform process was also accelerated by the fact that China with the exacerbation of the crisis became ever more outspoken in its critique of the Fund. At the IMF's meeting in October 2009, the POBOC's Deputy Governor Yi Gang (2009: 3) thus argued that

> [t]he persistently misaligned quota shares and underrepresentation of emerging market and developing countries hamper Fund governance and even-handed surveillance. It undermines Fund legitimacy and effectiveness. The traditional unreasonable quota allocation and adjustment method have intensified the misalignment.

For this reason, Yi (2009: 3) called on the Fund to "complete in a timely manner [...] a shift of at least 5 percentage points of the quota shares in favour of the emerging market and developing country members," a target that had previously been set by the G20.

Against this backdrop, the IMF's members in 2010 reached an agreement on "a historical reform of the IMF" (Strauss-Kahn quoted after IMF 2010a). This agreement included a doubling of IMF quotas to USD 755 billion and a shift of more than 6 % of quota shares to emerging market economies and developing countries at the expense of overrepresented European countries and oil-producing countries.[11] Once implemented, this redistribution of votes will be mirrored in the composition of the Fund's Executive Board that will include two fewer seats for European countries and two additional seats for emerging economies (IMF 2010a).

According to Paulo Batista (2010), who at the time represented a group of 8 countries including Brazil on the IMF's Executive Board, European countries were pushed into accepting this set of reforms by the US, which had long been frustrated with European reluctance to agree to a power shift from overrepresented European to emerging market and developing countries. Even though the EU at the time of this step in the reform process only accounted for about 20 % of global gross domestic product, it held almost a third of IMF votes. Besides, European countries held 9 of the 24 seats on the IMF's Executive Boards. While the IMF's rules stipulate that the Board of Executives has 20 members, the Fund's Governors

[11] To a lesser degree, the quota shares of the US and other emerging markets were also affected by the shift (IMF 2010a).

have agreed to keep 24 places on the Board since 1992, when the number of IMF members increased due to the collapse of the Soviet Union. Against this backdrop, the US vetoed the continuation of this arrangement in order to push the European countries into agreeing to a reform benefiting emerging market countries at the expense of European countries, a radical step that reportedly "came as a complete surprise" since "the Europeans, in particular, simply did not believe America would go for such an extreme measure" (Batista 2010).

Once the reforms will be implemented, the four BRIC countries as the leading emerging markets will be among the IMF's top 10 shareholders. China will move from the number 6 to the number 3 position and see its voting share increase to 6.1 % (see Table 6.1). However, despite this massive shift in its quota share, China will still be underrepresented considering that it had already overtaken Japan as the world's second-largest economy before the reform was agreed upon.

6.3.1.2 Voting Power in the World Bank

With its distribution of voting shares basically mirroring the IMF's quotas, the World Bank was suffering from a similar legitimacy deficit as the Fund. In the case of the Bank, the reform process began with the formulation of the Monterrey Consensus at the United Nations International Conference on Financing for Development in 2002 that called for a more equitable representation of developing countries in multilateral institutions (UN 2003). However, just as in the case of the IMF's reforms, the process only gained momentum with the outbreak of the global financial crisis and the establishment of the G20. The first phase of the World Bank's voice reform was agreed upon at its annual meeting in 2008, when its members decided to double the number of basic votes and maintain their share in total votes at 5.55 % in order to ensure that developing countries and countries with economies in transition (DTCs) have a minimum degree of influence in the organization. Besides, member countries agreed to add an elected Executive Director for Sub-Saharan Africa on the World Bank's Boards (World Bank 2010: 2, footnote 2).

The main element of the second phase of the World Bank's voice reform was the decision to realign the distribution of shares via a selective capital increase that would allocate new shares to under-represented members on the basis of a new quota formula (World Bank 2010: 4). While China as well as other developing countries had called for parity between developing and industrialized countries on the Bank's Board of Governors that would have required a 7.4 % shift in voting power from industrialized to developing countries, the Bank's members only agreed upon an increase of 4.6 % in the voting share of developing countries (Stumm 2011).

According to the new formula, 75 % of the Bank's voting shares were distributed on the basis of economic weight as measured by GDP converted at market rates (60 %) and at purchasing power parity exchange rates (40 %). In order to allow for an increase of at least 3 % in the voting share of DTCs, a further provision was

Table 6.1 Voting power in the IMF (after implementation of reforms agreed in 2010)

Country	IMF voting share
United States	16.5
Japan	6.1
China	6.1
Germany	5.3
France	4.0
United Kingdom	4.0
Italy	3.0
India	2.6
Russian Federation	2.6
Brazil	2.2

Source: IMF (n.d.-d)

added according to which developed countries were only eligible to take up additional shares to reach 90 % of their calculated economic weight. Another 20 % of voting shares were assigned on the basis of past and future contributions to the International Development Agency (World Bank 2010: 6–10).

However, future IDA contributions pledged by member countries were only recognized for developing and transitioning countries that would otherwise have seen their voting share decreased. This provision was therefore no general incentive for the provision of funds to the IDA, but only served to maintain the voting shares of influential developing countries like Russia and Saudi Arabia that might otherwise have vetoed the reform. The remaining 5 % of voting shares were distributed on the basis of the contributions by developing countries to the World Bank's mission – a component that was included to protect the relative voting power of low-income countries (Vestergaard 2011: 37–38).

The aim of an increase of at least 3 % in the voting share of developing countries could only be achieved on the basis of the voluntary forbearance of under-represented countries. The US, Germany, Greece, Portugal and Spain thus refrained from increasing their shares to strengthen the voice of developing countries (World Bank 2010: 7). Moreover, China as the only developing country chose to forego as much as half of its entitlement – reportedly to support a more equitable representation of other developing countries (Vestergaard 2011: 39). As a result of the reform, China's voting share has increased from 2.8 % to 4.4 %, and the country has moved to the number 3 position in the World Bank (see Table 6.2).

6.3.2 *China's Financial Contributions to the Bretton Woods Institutions*

Even though a state's most important source of institutional financial power is its voting share in the IMF and the World Bank, states may increase their power within these institutions by making financial contributions that are unrelated to their quotas. The following sections therefore shed light on China's willingness to

Table 6.2 Voting power in the World Bank (after implementation of reforms agreed in 2010)

Country	IBRD voting share
United States	15.9
Japan	6.8
China	4.4
Germany	4
France	3.8
United Kingdom	3.8
India	2.9
Russian Federation	2.8
Saudi Arabia	2.8
Italy	2.6

Source: World Bank (2010)

provide financial support to the IMF and the World Bank that is not immediately rewarded by an increase in its voting share.

6.3.2.1 Contributions to the IMF

Against the backdrop of the global financial crisis and the ever growing borrowing needs of governments in the developing and the developed world alike, the necessity of an increase of the IMF's financial resources soon became obvious. With many of the IMF's traditional providers of funds struggling to prevent a slump of their domestic economies, Western leaders soon began to demand major financial contributions from countries with big current account surpluses such as China and the Gulf states. China found itself under particular pressure from the US and the UK to boost the IMF's resources and follow the example of Japan and the European Union who had early on pledged to provide financial assistance to the IMF. However, China was rather reluctant to come to the rescue of the developed world and opposed the idea that a country's financial contributions to the IMF should solely be determined on the basis of its foreign exchange reserves.

In an interview with the *Financial Times* (2009), Prime Minister Wen Jiabao argued that "the voting share, the representation, and the say of developing countries" should be strengthened before China increased its financial contribution to the IMF. Moreover, he pointed out that China was still a developing country facing "arduous tasks", implying that it was inappropriate to expect China to rush to the rescue of the developed world. Instead, Wen argued that "running our own affairs well" was China's "biggest contribution to entire mankind." In a similar vein, Vice-Premier Wang Qishan (2009) maintained that "China supports increasing IMF resources on the basis of ensuring safety and reasonable returns." However, he pointed out that "[i]t is neither realistic nor fair to set the scale of contribution simply by the size of foreign exchange reserves", instead arguing that a country's stage of development and particularly its per capita GDP should also be taken into account. Moreover, Wang expressed his hope that "the [IMF's] resources are used mainly to help developing countries seriously affected by the crisis."

In an interview with the *China Daily*, Yu Yongding, then director of the Institute of World Economics and Politics and a former member of the PBOC's Monetary Policy Committee, declared himself against substantial contributions to the IMF, instead arguing that China should only offer symbolic amounts. According to Yu (quoted after You and Fu 2009), China had "many reasons to object" the pressure by developed countries to increase its contributions to the IMF. Apart from ridiculing the idea of "the poor [. . .] rescuing the rich", Yu pointed out that some of the European countries on the IMF's rescue list were known for their "anti-China mentality" and that China therefore had "no reason to help them." Yu argued that the Chinese public would not agree to huge injections of Chinese capital and added that "China's friends in the developing world" had cautioned against such measures. He thus suggested offering direct financial support to African countries suffering from the global financial crisis instead of channeling funds through the IMF.

Despite its reservations, China did not completely withhold its support for the IMF. In August 2009, the PBOC signed a note purchase agreement with the IMF, committing itself to buying IMF bonds of a total principal amount of up to SDR 32 billion (USD 50 billion) (IMF n.d.-c).[12] With provisions amounting to USD 69 billion and USD 66 billion, only the US and Japan provided more substantial amounts of funds than China did. China's contribution became part of the New Arrangements to Borrow (NAB) whose total borrowing capacity was increased from SDR 34 billion to SDR 367.5 billion in the face of the growing borrowing needs resulting from the crisis (see Table 6.3). The NAB can only be activated upon the condition of the agreement of participants representing 85 % of total credit arrangements (IMF 2012c). As its third largest contributor, China could easily arrange coalitions that could block the borrowing facility if that was in its interests.

6.3.2.2 Contributions to the World Bank

Within the World Bank Group, contributions to the International Development Association are the most important channel for provisions of funds that are not necessarily rewarded by an increase in voting shares. Until 1999, China was still a recipient of the IDA's soft loans.[13] Only 8 years later, China made its first contribution to the IDA. The country provided the organization with SDR 17.6 million (IDA15 2008: 62), a move that World Bank President Robert Zoellick (quoted after *gbtimes* 2007) described as "a modest, but significant step"

[12] Even though in the Chinese press it was frequently argued that the purchase of SDR-denominated bonds would contribute to the diversification of its dollar-dominated foreign exchange reserves, the bonds were to be paid for in renminbi.

[13] China does no longer receive funds from the IDA, but continues to borrow from the IBRD.

Table 6.3 Contributions to the NAB

NAB participants	Amount (SDR million)
US	69,074.27
Japan	65,953.20
China	31,217.22
Deutsche Bundesbank	25,370.81
France	18,657.38
UK	18,657.38
Italy	13,578.03
Saudi Arabia	11,126.03
Swiss National Bank	10,905.42
Netherlands	9,043.72
Brazil	8,740.82
India	8,740.82
Russian Federation	8,740.82

Source: IMF (2012c)

underlining China's position as "a stakeholder in the field of development." In the following round of IDA capital replenishment in 2010, China agreed to an early repayment of outstanding IDA credits amounting to USD 1.0 billion. The discount of USD 111 million that China received on these early repayments was passed on by China as a donor contribution to IDA16 (IDA16 2011: 41). The country thus provided SDR 107 million to IDA16, equivalent to a share of 0.5 % of the total (see Table 6.4). Measured against China's foreign exchange reserves that at the end of 2010 amounted to USD 2,847 billion, this contribution does not appear particularly generous.

6.3.3 *China's Representation Among Staff and Management*

In addition to its voting power and its contribution of funds that are unrelated to its quota, a state's representation among the staff and management of the Bretton Woods institutions is an important determinant of its institutional financial power. The following sections therefore shed light on China's representation in the IMF and the World Bank.

6.3.3.1 Representation in the IMF

Since the onset of the global financial crisis in 2007, China's representation in the IMF's professional and managerial staff has strongly improved. While Chinese staff in the institution at the end of 2007 only amounted to 2.1 % of total staff, it had increased to 3.3 % by the end of 2011, while the representation of the US and Canada had decreased from 26.3 % to 22.1 % (IMF 2012a). Moreover, in 2010, the IMF appointed the first Chinese national to a senior official position. Considered

Table 6.4 Contributions to IDA16

Country	Percent of total contributions
United States	12.1
United Kingdom	12
Japan	10.9
Germany	6.5
France	5
Canada	4.1
Spain	3.1
Netherlands	3
Sweden	3
Italy	2.4
Switzerland	2.1
Australia	2.1
Belgium	1.6
Austria	1.6
Norway	1.3
Denmark	1.1
Korea	1
Finland	1
Russia	0.5
China	0.5

Source: IDA16 (2011)

"one of the most prominent financial officials in China" (Dyer 2010), Zhu Min, at the time a Deputy Governor of the PBOC, was made Special Advisor to the Managing Director. Zhu received an M.A. and a Ph.D. in Economics from John Hopkins University, an MPA from Princeton University and a B.A. in Economics from Shanghai's Fudan University. Prior to his service at the PBOC, Zhu was a senior executive at the state-owned Bank of China and spent 6 years working for the World Bank (IMF 2010b; Dyer 2010). Commenting on the appointment, IMF Managing Director Dominique Strauss-Kahn (quoted after IMF 2010b) argued that Zhu would help the IMF "in meeting the challenges facing our global membership in the period ahead, and in strengthening the Fund's understanding of Asia and emerging markets more generally." The appointment was welcomed by the PBOC (quoted after *Xinhua* 2010), which argued that "[w]ith emerging market and developing countries playing an increasing role in the global economy and financial system, it is a good move for the international financial institutions to include more professionals from those economies in their management to reflect the changes in the world economic landscape, and to improve their governance."

The appointment of Zhu Min took place in the context of the IMF's efforts to restore its legitimacy in the Asian region by admitting shortcomings in the Fund's policy responses to the Asian Financial Crisis and asserting its willingness to learn from the region's approach to development. This new attitude was exemplified by Strauss-Kahn (2010), who, speaking at a conference in Korea in 2010, stated that the IMF wanted "to take stock of the last 10 years, and see what has been done correctly and what has not been done correctly" and went on to stress the Fund's willingness "to listen to what Asia has to say – about issues and challenges in this region, but also about the policy priorities for countries in other regions" since "[c]ountries all over the world want to understand how Asia has managed its growth and globalization so successfully."

In July 2011, after the appointment of Christine Lagarde as head of the IMF, a fourth deputy managing director position was created and given to Zhu, a move that was widely interpreted as payback for China's backing of Lagarde (Beattie and Dyer 2011). When the position of the Managing Director had become vacant in May 2011 due to allegations of sexual assault against Strauss-Kahn, China, India, Brazil, Russia and South Africa had issued a joint statement in which they requested the IMF to abandon the informal rule according to which the Managing Director has to be a European, arguing that this convention "undermines the legitimacy of the Fund" and that "[t]he recent financial crisis which erupted in developed countries, underscored the urgency of reforming international financial institutions so as to reflect the growing role of developing countries in the world economy" (*Financial Times* 2011). Despite this statement, Lagarde, who went on a tour to the BRIC countries and Saudi Arabia, vowing that as the IMF's Managing Director, she "would make sure that the diversity of all of its members would be represented at every level" (quoted after Hille 2011), eventually won China's support.

6.3.3.2 Representation in the World Bank

The first Chinese national to be appointed to a senior position in the World Bank was Lin Yifu (also known as Justin Lin), who in 2008 became the World Bank's Chief Economist and Senior Vice President.[14] Lin received his master's degree in Political Economy from Peking University and his Ph.D. in Economics from the University of Chicago. Before joining the World Bank, Lin served as Professor of the China Center for Economic Research (CCER) at Peking University, where his research focused on the role of the state in the Chinese economy and the lessons that can be learned from the success of China's development model. As an economic advisor to the Chinese government, he has had substantial influence on China's 'New Socialist Countryside' policy aimed at raising living standards in rural China (McGregor 2008b). Repeatedly challenging neoliberal economic theory, Lin (2011: 16) has argued that

> China's and other East Asian economies' experiences provide a golden opportunity for rethinking the fundamental issues of the roles of the state, market, and other institutions in a developing country's process of development and transition to catch up with the industrialized nations.

[14] Data on the distribution of professional and managerial World Bank staff by nationality are only available for internal use. According to the Annual Report 2011 that provides information on the distribution of World Bank staff by region, staff from East Asia and Oceania amounted to 14 % of total staff (World Bank 2011: 26).

Announced 1 month after China made its first contribution to the International Development Association, Lin's appointment can be considered a reward for China's perceived willingness to support the World Bank in its fight against global poverty. However, Lin's appointment also needs to be seen in light of the Bank's attempts to integrate the development experiences of countries that achieved economic success without adhering to the tenets of the Washington Consensus into its policy prescriptions. This willingness to "democratize and demystify development economics" (Zoellick 2010) was exemplified in a speech held by President Zoellick in September 2010 in which he argued that with emerging markets playing an ever more important role in the global economy, there was a growing need to pay attention to their development models. He pointed out that a "new multi-polar economy requires multi-polar knowledge", and that the "right policies may differ across phases of development". Moreover, he highlighted the fact that "[t]he success of China and others has raised questions on the role of the state", thus displaying an interest in the political economy of the developmental state.

6.3.4 *A Beijing Consensus?*

Against the backdrop of the ongoing power shift in the Bretton Woods institutions, the question of how China's increasing institutional financial power will affect the policies of the IMF and the World Bank arises. The following sections therefore shed light on the policies that China has been promoting both within the Bretton Woods institutions and in the context of its bilateral development assistance.

6.3.4.1 A Beijing Consensus in the IMF?

Against the backdrop of China's frustration with the IMF's lecturing of developing countries not willing to follow the economic path prescribed by the Washington Consensus, the global financial crisis provided Beijing with a welcome opportunity to draw attention to the shortcomings of the financial systems of developed countries and the risks they pose to the world economy. Already before the outbreak of the crisis, China had been trying to deflect the focus of the IMF's surveillance on exchange rates. At the Spring Meeting of the International Monetary and Financial Committee (IMFC) in 2007, PBOC Deputy Governor Hu Xiaolian (2007: 3) argued that

> [g]iven the limitations of various exchange rate analytical tools, it is well known that the concept of exchange rate misalignment is subject to theoretical weakness, their estimates highly unreliable, and therefore [can] not serve as criteria or premises for surveillance.

Despite Beijing's resistance, the Fund introduced new currency surveillance rules in 2007 that put a country's balance of payments position at the heart of surveillance and allow it to determine if a country manipulates its exchange rate in an effort to boost exports (IMF 2007). These new rules, considered by Beijing "as a U.S. ploy to enlist the fund in its campaign for a stronger yuan" (Wheatley 2009a), have been at the center of China's criticism of IMF policies since the outbreak of the crisis. PBOC Governor Zhou Xiaochuan (2010a: 4) delivered a particularly outspoken criticism at the IMF's Spring Meeting in 2010, claiming that

> [t]he current global financial crisis, which is primarily the result of the inappropriate financial sector in developed countries, has impacted global trade, employment, and income in an unprecedented manner, and the unsustainability (sic) of developed countries' fiscal policies has become the primary risk that threatens global financial stability. In recent years, the focus of Fund surveillance has been inappropriate. The hastily introduced *2007 Decision* contains many flaws, and cannot meet the demands on Fund surveillance posed by global economic and financial development. The Fund should face this reality, resolve the problems in its surveillance as quickly as possible, amend the *2007 Decision*, adjust its surveillance focus, improve modalities, and strengthen surveillance over developed countries, mature financial markets, and cross-border capital flows, in order to avoid a recurrence of the crisis.

Instead of focusing on exchange rates, China has called on the Fund to strengthen the surveillance of the macroeconomic policies of the countries that issue the major reserve currencies in light of the fact that "the continuation of extremely low interest rates and unconventional monetary policies by major reserve currency issuers have created stark challenges for emerging market countries in the conduct of monetary policy" (Zhou 2010b: 1). Moreover, Beijing has repeatedly urged the Fund "to play a key role" (Yi 2011: 5) in reforming the international monetary system by conducting studies on the management of cross-border capital flows and global liquidity and exploring the benefits of a diversification of reserve currencies in general and the extension of the role of the IMF's Special Drawing Rights in particular. Against this backdrop, it can be considered at least a partial success that the IMF in 2010 adopted a more positive stance on the role of capital controls, arguing that "[f]or both macroeconomic and prudential reasons, [. . .] there may be circumstances in which capital controls are a legitimate component of the policy response to surges in capital inflows" (Ostry et al. 2010: 15).[15] Last but not least, China has called on the IMF to provide more resources to developing countries in order to improve their growth potential (Yi 2009: 1).

6.3.4.2 A Beijing Consensus in the World Bank?

China has repeatedly called on the World Bank to respect the country-specifics as well as the country-ownership of development and has urged the Bank to "take stock of the development experiences of the past decades, [. . .] and provide tailored policy advice for developing countries at different development stages" (Xie 2009:

[15] The authors argue that the use of capital controls is justified "if the economy is operating near potential, if the level of reserves is adequate, if the exchange rate is not undervalued, and if the flows are likely to be transitory" (Ostry et al. 2010: 5).

1). However, in order to gain a clearer understanding of China's approach to development assistance and hence the policies that China may want the World Bank to adopt, it is more instructive to shed light on China's bilateral development assistance than on its official statements in multilateral institutions.

China has in recent years emerged as one of the world's leading donor countries, lending more to other developing countries than the World Bank in the period from 2009 to 2010 (Dyer et al. 2011). In its official development assistance, Beijing has taken an approach that does not share many similarities with the Washington Consensus. In its attempts to guarantee its energy security and forge closer economic ties with the developing world, China provides loans that come with no strings attached instead of demanding painful restructuring measures. Unsurprisingly, China's development assistance is highly welcomed by recipient countries. Moreover, especially in Africa, China is increasingly considered a model for development that, with its stress on authoritarian rule and state control over the economy, offers an attractive alternative to the Washington Consensus. "China's model is telling us you can be successful without following the Western example," the Deputy Prime Minister of Zimbabwe (quoted after Wonacott 2011) recently argued, adding that "China is my favorite country." In a similar vein, Senegal's president, Abdoulaye Wade (2008), pointed out that "China's approach to our needs is simply better adapted than the slow and sometimes patronising post-colonial approach of European investors, donor organisations and non-governmental organisations. In fact, the Chinese model for stimulating rapid economic development has much to teach Africa."

Already in 2004, the idea of a 'Beijing Consensus' as a challenge to the Washington Consensus was launched by the American journalist Joshua Cooper Ramo (2004).[16] More recently, the global financial crisis with its revelations of the weaknesses of Western financial systems further reinforced the growing sense that the time has come for China to provide the developing world with a new economic model. This mood was well captured in a report prepared for the U.S.-China Economic and Security Review Commission, in which the authors claim that

> the fallout from the GFC [global financial crisis] has, especially in the eyes of many in the developing world, bolstered the credibility of China's economic development model, and fed a growing sense that while the 20th Century was the American Century, the 21st Century might just be China's (Olson and Prestowitz 2011: 5).

However, the very idea of a Beijing Consensus or a 'China model' has so far been decisively dismissed by Chinese policymakers. In a press conference at the end of the 2011 session of the National People's Congress, Prime Minister Wen Jiabao (quoted after Jian 2011) made this point very clear when he argued that

---

[16] According to Ramo, the key elements of the Beijing Consensus are innovation, sustainability and equality and self-determination. However, as Scott Kennedy (2010: 461) has pointed out, Ramo's idea of a Beijing Consensus is "a misguided and inaccurate summary of China's actual reform experience." For more illuminating analyses of China's development experiences and the question of their replicability see Huang (2011) and Naughton (2010).

"[w]e are still probing in our reforms and construction, and never regard our development as a model." Liu Guijin, China's special representative on African affairs, similarly emphasized that China was not interested in providing the world with a new development model to follow. In the words of Liu (quoted after Wonacott 2011), "China doesn't want to export our ideology, our governance, our model. We don't regard it as a mature model."

6.4 Financial Repression and Institutional Financial Power

Against the backdrop of a power shift in the world economy, China has in recent years successfully pushed for an increase in its voting share in the IMF and the World Bank. In their efforts to maintain their relevance and re-establish their legitimacy, both institutions have appointed Chinese nationals with close ties to the Chinese government to senior management positions and have tried to increase the number of Chinese nationals among the organizations' staff. China's institutional financial power is therefore clearly on the rise. However, China has been extremely hesitant in the provision of funds not immediately rewarded by an increase in voting shares and has thereby missed the chance to further increase its institutional financial power at a time when the Bretton Woods institutions are in urgent need of alternative sources of funding.

In the case of the IMF, this hesitancy can be partly explained by the fact that the idea of China coming to the rescue of indebted countries in the developed world is very unpopular among China's public. Yet the more important reason for China's unwillingness to provide funding that does not come in the form of quotas is the fact that the benefits that China could gain from a more powerful position in the IMF and the World Bank are rather limited. Institutional financial power allows a country to further its economic interests or achieve foreign policy objectives by influencing the provision of credit via international financial institutions and the conditions that come attached with it. However, these objectives can also be pursued by the exercise of a country's relational financial power. With its strong creditor position and its high degree of control over the investment of the country's funds, the Chinese party-state is therefore not as dependent on the acquisition of institutional financial power as a neoliberal state that has significantly less relational financial power at its disposal. This point was already made by Wade (1996: 36), who in his analysis of Japan's quest for a more powerful position in the World Bank argued that while Japan could use its "strong domestic infrastructural power" to achieve its goals on the global stage, the US had to rely on its dominance of international institutions to "augment its own external reach".

Yet despite the fact that Japan also wielded considerable relational financial power, the country was much more determined to increase its power in the Bretton Woods institutions than China currently is – a difference that may be explained by the fact that Japan was eager to use the IMF and the World Bank to promote its ideas on economic development and establish itself as an ideological leader providing the developing world with an alternative to the US variety of capitalism. China, on the other hand, is still keeping a rather low profile and has not yet developed ambitions for ideological leadership – a circumstance that may be explained by the fact that China's leaders are too concerned with maintaining growth and stability in a country that on account of its low per-capita GDP still has to be considered a developing country. Besides, it can be assumed that China's leaders are well aware of the fact that the country's attractiveness as a donor country would be diminished if they pushed the Bretton Woods institutions into adopting China's policy of providing credit that comes with no strings attached.

Nevertheless, against the backdrop of a crisis that revealed the shortcomings of the Western model of capitalism as well as the emergence of alternative sources of funds available to the developing world, the World Bank in particular has shown itself willing to learn from China's development experience. Even though China has not been pushing as hard for policy changes as Japan was in the 1980s, the Bank has shown a much more accommodating stance towards Beijing. The IMF, on the other hand, has so far only yielded to China's influence insofar as it has adopted a more positive attitude towards capital controls, yet has refrained from severely contemplating a radical reform of the international financial system.

Chapter 7
Conclusion

The aim of this book has been to bring the model of the developmental state into the study of financial power, thus explaining how systems of financial repression influence the ability of states to acquire power in international finance. Based on an analysis of the political economies of the financial systems of the Japanese and the Chinese developmental state, it has explained why the developmental state's system of financial repression is a hindrance to the acquisition of most types of structural financial power while it allows for the development of the power to maintain current account surpluses. At the same time, it has explicated why the political economy of the developmental state is highly conducive to the acquisition of relational financial power, thus making the development of institutional financial power largely dispensable.

This book has shown that the political economy of the developmental state inhibits the acquisition of structural financial power since its system of financial repression is not compatible with the development of financial markets capable of attracting international investors on a significant scale. China's financial system is dominated by a banking sector that is characterized by administratively controlled interest rates and a high degree of state-ownership, thus allowing the authorities to channel capital in a way that supports the state-owned sector of the economy and facilitates the implementation of industrial policy. State-ownership of the most important financial institutions and an administered cap on deposit rates do not only guarantee low funding costs for SOEs and low borrowing costs for the government, but also ensure low sterilization costs that have enabled the party-state to prevent a significant appreciation of the domestic currency in the face of massive current account surpluses and allowed it to acquire an enormous amount of foreign exchange reserves.

Within the framework of such a system of financial repression, there is no room for the development of capital markets that would result in an outflow of funds from the banking sector. China's policymakers have thus ensured that the country's bond markets are heavily dominated by securities issued by the government and quasi-governmental agencies whose interest rates can be set artificially low since state-owned banks are mandated to buy them. For this reason, China's bond markets play

S. Heep, *China in Global Finance*, Global Power Shift,

DOI 10.1007/978-3-319-02466-0_7,

no role in the pricing of risk and are thus hardly attractive to international investors. Similarly, China's equity markets mainly serve as capital-raising avenues for the state-owned sector of the economy. Driven by policy decisions of the government instead of economic fundamentals, they lack the potential to attract foreign investors who do not wish to play speculative games.

Just as the Chinese financial system, the financial system of the Japanese developmental state was geared to facilitate the conduct of industrial policy through control over the country's financial resources. However, while the Chinese party-state maintains its control over the allocation of credit through its continuous ownership of the country's most important financial institutions, the Japanese state's control resulted from the dependence of the country's commercial banks on the Bank of Japan for the provision of funds. In contrast with China's system of financial control, Japan's system of administrative guidance thus relied on a continuous shortage of capital creating a dependency relationship between the banks and the state's financial authorities. For this reason, Japan's financial system became subject to significant liberalization pressures in the face of growing financial resources, while the Chinese financial system has proven sustainable in the face of a continuous accumulation of funds.

Just as the developmental state's system of financial repression is not compatible with the development of financial markets with significant international pulling power, it also prevents the acquisition of structural financial power through the establishment of a domestic currency as an international store of value since this aspect of currency internationalization requires internationally attractive financial markets. This incompatibility between financial repression and currency internationalization explains the attitude of Japan's policymakers towards the internationalization of the yen. Fearing that it would undermine the authorities' control over the allocation of credit, jeopardize the country's monetary autonomy and threaten its export-led growth model, they were highly opposed to the prospect of currency internationalization and only started to promote the yen's internationalization when the country's economic decline had already severely diminished the attractiveness of its currency.

Even though China's policymakers should be expected to try and prevent a global role of the renminbi on the very same grounds, a long-standing tradition of policy experimentation and strong nationalistic feelings have encouraged China's authorities to embark on a strategy of promoting the renminbi's function as an international medium of exchange within a system of strict capital controls that allows them to mitigate the risks of monetary policy constraints and currency overvaluation. Yet even if China's policy experiment succeeds, the renminbi's establishment as an international medium of exchange will not significantly bolster China's structural financial power since the latter almost exclusively derives from a currency's role as an international store of value.

While systems of financial repression are a hindrance to the acquisition of most aspects of structural financial power, they are highly conducive to the power to maintain current account surpluses, an aspect of structural financial power that has been neglected in the literature due to its focus on neoliberal political economies.

China's system of financial repression has thus allowed the party-state to withstand currency appreciation pressures by containing the costs of monetary sterilization in the face of massive current account surpluses. Moreover, the political economy of the developmental state is also highly conducive to the acquisition of relational financial power. With their systems of financial repression geared to facilitate rapid economic growth through comprehensive industrial development at the expense of consumption, developmental states frequently embark on export-led growth strategies resulting in significant current account surpluses that turn them into net creditors. China's financial system has even allowed the party-state to accumulate surpluses in the form of foreign exchange reserves without losing control over the monetary impact of reserve accumulation. In the case of China, the state's control over the country's capital outflows is thus significantly higher than it was in the case of Japan whose surpluses were managed by the country's commercial banks. However, as far as their vulnerability to their major debtor is concerned, both China and Japan have suffered from the structural power of the US that has forced the countries to lend in the debtor's currency and thus entrapped them in the dollar block.

Highly conducive to the acquisition of relational financial power, systems of financial repression tend to render the development of institutional financial power largely dispensable since the exercise of both relational and institutional financial power may be directed at the same objectives. Due to their strong creditor positions, developmental states are thus not as dependent on the acquisition of institutional financial power as neoliberal states whose relational financial power tends to be much more limited since they frequently run current account deficits and only muster a very limited degree of control over their domestic financial systems. The fact that institutional financial power may be substituted with relational financial power explains why China has been extremely hesitant in the provision of funds not immediately rewarded by an increase in voting shares at a time when the Bretton Woods institutions are in urgent need of alternative sources of funding. Despite its considerable relational financial power, Japan, on the other hand, was more determined to increase its influence in the IMF and the World Bank since it was eager to establish itself as an ideological leader providing the developing world with an alternative to the US variety of capitalism.

While Japan eventually discarded its system of financial repression, we can only speculate about the path that the Chinese developmental state will take in the future. With China's system of financial repression ultimately serving to maintain the CCP's tight grip over the country's economic and political system, voluntary change is unlikely since it would result in a radical change of China's political economy that would harm the vested interests of many of the most influential players. On the other hand, ostensibly low-key reforms introduced by liberal-minded reformers in the financial bureaucracy may eventually result in a radical change of the financial system unforeseen by China's senior leaders. Even more importantly, China's political economy could become subject to pressures that would make the liberalization of its financial system inevitable. In the face of the recent slowdown in export growth, the sustainability of the country's growth model has already become highly doubtful. In order to maintain sufficiently high growth rates and thus to sustain the regime's legitimacy, China's leaders might eventually be compelled to walk the talk and embark on a consumption-led growth strategy that is not compatible with the current system of financial repression. However, while it would be futile to try and predict the course of China's financial development, we can be sure that a liberalization of China's financial system would eventually result in a radical restructuring of China's political economy. A China with significant structural financial power at its disposal might therefore well be considered much less of a threat in the western world than today's China with its substantial relational financial power.

Interviews

Number	Interviewee affiliation	Date
1	Foreign Research Firm	Nov 2008
2	Chinese Research Institute	Nov 2008
3	Foreign Newspaper	Nov 2008
4	Foreign Embassy	Dec 2008
5	Foreign Business Association	Dec 2008
6	Foreign Research Firm	Dec 2008
7	International Financial Institution	Dec 2008
8	Foreign Bank	Dec 2008
9	Foreign Delegation	Dec 2008
10	Foreign Development Project	Dec 2008
11	Foreign Bank	Dec 2008
12	Foreign Embassy	Dec 2008
13	Chinese Newspaper	Dec 2008
14	Foreign Development Agency	Dec 2008
15	Chinese Newspaper (13)	Dec 2008
16	Chinese Bank	Dec 2008
17	Chinese Fund Management Company	Jan 2009
18	Chinese Newspaper	Jan 2009
19	Chinese Research Institute	Jan 2009
20	Chinese Government Agency	Jan 2009
21	Chinese Research Institute (2)	Jan 2009
22	Chinese Fund Management Company	Jan 2009
23	Chinese Bank	Jan 2009
24	Chinese Bank	Jan 2009
25	International Financial Institution (7)	Jan 2009
26	Chinese Bank (23)	Jan 2009
27	Foreign Research Firm (1)	Jan 2009
28	Foreign Newspaper (3)	Feb 2009
29	Foreign Bank	Feb 2009
30	Chinese Investment Fund	Feb 2009
31	Foreign Business Association	Feb 2009

(continued)

S. Heep, *China in Global Finance*, Global Power Shift,
DOI 10.1007/978-3-319-02466-0,

Number	Interviewee affiliation	Date
32	Chinese Newspaper (13,15)	Feb 2009
33	Foreign Delegation	Feb 2009
34	International Organization	Feb 2009
35	Foreign Bank	Feb 2009
36	Foreign Embassy	Feb 2009
37	Foreign Research Firm (6)	Feb 2009
38	Chinese Fund Management Com. (17)	Mar 2009
39	Chinese Academic Institution	Mar 2009
40	Foreign Newspaper (3, 28)	Mar 2009
41	Foreign Delegation (7)	Mar 2009
42	Foreign Bank	Nov 2010
43	Chinese Newspaper (13, 15, 32)	Nov 2010
44	Foreign Delegation (33, 41)	Nov 2010
45	Chinese Research Institute (2, 21)	Nov 2010

Notes: All interviews were conducted in Beijing. Numbers in brackets indicate identical interviewees

References

ABC. (2013). *Annual report 2012*. Beijing: Agricultural Bank of China. http://www.abchina.com/en/about-us/annual-report/2012/default.htm. Accessed 13 Aug 2013.

Aizenman, J., & Lee, J. (2006). *Financial versus monetary mercantilism: Long-run view of large international reserves hoarding* (IMF Working Paper, WP/06/280). Washington, DC: International Monetary Fund. http://www.imf.org/external/pubs/ft/wp/2006/wp06280.pdf. Accessed 30 July 2012.

Allen, F., Qian, J., & Qian, M. (2005). Law, finance, and economic growth in China. *Journal of Financial Economics, 77*(1), 57–116.

Allen, F., Qian, J., Zhang, C., & Zhao, M. (2012). *China's financial system: Opportunities and challenges* (NBER Working Paper, No. 17828). Cambridge, MA: National Bureau of Economic Research. http://www.iadb.org/intal/intalcdi/PE/2012/09844.pdf. Accessed 9 Aug 2013.

Anderlini, J. (2007a, August 20). Beijing moves to open up markets. *Financial Times*. http://www.ft.com/intl/cms/s/0/f724fcee-4f48-11dc-b485-0000779fd2ac.html#axzz1mNUQl8NC. Accessed 30 July 2012.

Anderlini, J. (2007b, June 14). China's corporate bonds come of age. *Financial Times*. http://www.ft.com/intl/cms/s/0/4804b954-1a9e-11dc-8bf0-000b5df10621.html#axzz2br7opStd. Accessed 14 Aug 2013.

Anderlini, J. (2008a, September 11). Beijing uses forex reserves to target Taiwan. *Financial Times*. http://www.ft.com/intl/cms/s/0/22fe798e-802c-11dd-99a9-000077b07658.html#axzz1NRx1V89R. Accessed 30 July 2012.

Anderlini, J. (2008b, September 11). Beijing's shadowy fund for buying assets. *Financial Times*. http://www.ft.com/intl/cms/s/0/cf2e1a1a-801e-11dd-99a9-000077b07658.html#axzz226d5oS3o. Accessed 30 July 2012.

Anderlini, J. (2008c, March 7). China signals it could ease share curbs. *Financial Times*. http://www.ft.com/intl/cms/s/0/13e65160-eba8-11dc-9493-0000779fd2ac.html#axzz1mNUQl8NC. Accessed 30 July 2012.

Anderlini, J. (2009, July 21). China to deploy foreign reserves. *Financial Times*. http://www.ft.com/intl/cms/s/0/b576ec86-761e-11de-9e59-00144feabdc0.html#axzz1NRx1V89R. Accessed 30 July 2012.

Anderlini, J. (2011a, January 11). China moves warily on easing controls. *Financial Times*. http://www.ft.com/intl/cms/s/0/8cd7010a-1da5-11e0-aa88-00144feab49a.html#axzz1NRx1V89R. Accessed 30 July 2012.

Anderlini, J. (2011b, January 10). Chinese city allows personal investing abroad. *Financial Times*. http://www.ft.com/intl/cms/s/0/b43f72f2-1ce4-11e0-8c86-00144feab49a.html#axzz1v8osjof8. Accessed 30 July 2012.

S. Heep, *China in Global Finance*, Global Power Shift,
DOI 10.1007/978-3-319-02466-0,

Anderlini, J., & Blas, J. (2009, April 24). China reveals big rise in gold reserves. *Financial Times*. http://www.ft.com/intl/cms/s/0/1d23f80c-30aa-11de-bc38-00144feabdc0.html#axzz226d5oS3o. Accessed 30 July 2012.

Anderlini, J., & Hook, L. (2013, July 19). China takes step to financial reform. *Financial Times*. http://www.ft.com/intl/cms/s/0/3a289af0-f06a-11e2-b28d-00144feabdc0.html#axzz2br7opStd. Accessed 13 Aug 2013.

Anderlini, J., & Milne, R. (2011, October 27). China could play key role in EU rescue. *Financial Times*. http://www.ft.com/intl/cms/s/0/7505d210-00ba-11e1-8590-00144feabdc0.html#axzz226d5oS3o. Accessed 30 July 2012.

Anderlini, J., Song, J., & Whipp, L. (2010, August 18). S Korean treasuries sought by China. *Financial Times*. http://www.ft.com/intl/cms/s/0/3752e7a0-aad0-11df-80f9-00144feabdc0.html #axzz1NRx1V89R. Accessed 30 July 2012.

Andrews, D. (Ed.). (2006a). *International monetary power*. Ithaca: Cornell University Press.

Andrews, D. (2006b). Monetary power and monetary statecraft. In D. Andrews (Ed.), *International monetary power* (pp. 7–28). Ithaca: Cornell University Press.

Areddy, J., & Ng, M. (2010, January 4). China will tax some share sales. *Wall Street Journal*. http://online.wsj.com/article/SB10001424052748704162104574629841340038348.html. Accessed 30 July 2012.

Ayyagai, M., Demirgüc-Kunt, A., & Maksimovic, V. (2008). *Formal versus informal finance: Evidence from China* (Policy Research Working Paper, No. 4465). Washington, DC: World Bank. http://elibrary.worldbank.org/docserver/download/4465.pdf?expires=1343652701&id=id&accname=guest&checksum=3BEAD6321348B1A16879B448761CC503. Accessed 30 July 2012.

Ba, S. (2007). Guojia waihui touzi gongsi mianlin liu da tiaozhan [Sovereign wealth fund faces six great challenges]. *Dongshi, 11*, 30–31.

Baek, S.-W. (2005). Does China follow 'the East Asian development model'? *Journal of Contemporary Asia, 35*(4), 485–498.

Barboza, D. (2013, July 4). China to test free trade zone in Shanghai as part of economic overhaul. *New York Times*. http://www.nytimes.com/2013/07/05/business/global/zone-to-test-renminbi-as-currency-for-trading.html?_r=0. Accessed 18 Aug 2013.

Batista, P. N. (2010, September 23). Europe must make way for a modern IMF. *Financial Times*. http://www.ft.com/intl/cms/s/0/8b57a684-c744-11df-aeb1-00144feab49a.html#axzz226d5oS3o. Accessed 30 July 2012.

Beattie, A. (2010, November 10). IMF reform: Change in voting may be more symbol than substance. *Financial Times*. http://www.ft.com/intl/cms/s/0/588e33f4-eb88-11df-bbb5-00144feab49a.html #axzz226d5oS3o. Accessed 30 July 2012.

Beattie, A., & Dyer, G. (2011, July 13). China given key IMF role under Lagarde. *Financial Times*. http://www.ft.com/intl/cms/s/0/4f3f558a-acd0-11e0-9623-00144feabdc0.html#axzz2aXXsvrII. Accessed 30 July 2012.

Beeson, M. (2009). Developmental states in East Asia: A comparison of Japanese and Chinese experiences. *Asian Perspective, 33*(2), 5–39.

Belton, C. (2009, February 17). China lends Russia $25bn for 20 years of oil. *Financial Times*. http://www.ft.com/intl/cms/s/0/4987b5e4-fd2b-11dd-a103-000077b07658.html#axzz1NRx1V89R. Accessed 30 July 2012.

Bergsten, F. (2009, April 9). Beijing's currency idea needs to be taken seriously. *Financial Times*. http://www.ft.com/intl/cms/s/0/96ca4a02-249e-11de-9a01-00144feabdc0.html#axzz1NRx1V89R. Accessed 30 July 2012.

BOC. (2013). *Annual report 2012*. Beijing: Bank of China. http://pic.bankofchina.com/bocappd/report/201303/P020130326573887576644.pdf. Accessed 13 Aug 2013.

Bottelier, P. (2004). *China's emerging domestic debt markets* (Working Paper, No. 202). Stanford: Stanford Center for International Development. http://www.stanford.edu/group/siepr/cgi-bin/siepr/?q=system/files/shared/pubs/papers/pdf/SCID202.pdf. Accessed 30 July 2012.

Bottelier, P. (2009). International monetary reform and the future of the renminbi. *China Brief, 9*(11). Washington DC: Jamestown Foundation. http://www.jamestown.org/single/?no_cache=1&tx_ttnews[tt_news]=35039. Accessed 30 July 2012.

Breslin, S. (1996). China: Developmental state or dysfunctional development? *Third World Quarterly, 17*(4), 689–706.

Brown, K. (2011, February 15). Rising Chinese wages pose relocation risk. *Financial Times*. http://www.ft.com/intl/cms/s/0/52449d1c-3926-11e0-97ca-00144feabdc0.html. Accessed 30 July 2012.

CBRC. (2013). *2012 Nianbao (Annual report 2012)*. Beijing: China Banking Regulatory Commission. http://www.cbrc.gov.cn/chinese/home/docView/18492CCBDD04435A8BFAB3FF6F2CA51C.html. Accessed 13 Aug 2013.

CCB. (2013). *Annual report 2012*. Beijing: China Construction Bank. http://www.ccb.com/en/newinvestor/upload/20130424_1366773142/e00939_AR.pdf. Accessed 13 Aug 2013.

CDB. (2008). *Annual report 2007*. Beijing: China Development Bank. http://www.cdb.com.cn/english/NewsInfo.asp?NewsId=2905. Accessed 30 July 2012.

Chang, Q., & Li, Q. (2007). Woguo waihui chubei touzi de zhanlüexing mubiao jiqi shishi [The strategic objective of the investment of our national foreign exchange reserves and its realization]. *Guoji jingmao tansuo, 23*(7), 72–75.

Chen, X., Liu, W., Wang, J., Zhang, X., Guan, T., Ding, Z., Sun, T., & Pan, H. (2009). Renminbi jiesuan zhengtu [The journey of renminbi settlement]. *Caijing, 5*. http://magazine.caijing.com.cn/2009-05-11/110163631.html. Accessed 30 July 2012.

Chin, G., & Helleiner, E. (2008). China as a creditor: A rising financial power? *Journal of International Affairs, 62*(1), 87–102.

China Bond. (n.d.). *Monthly statistics: Bond issue volume*. Beijing: China Central Depository and Clearing Co. Ltd. http://www.chinabond.com.cn/jsp/include/CB_EN/marketdata/month_stat.jsp?BBND=2012&BBYF=12&sPageType=2&id=317791. Accessed 14 Aug 2013.

Chinn, M., & Frankel, J. (2005). *Will the euro eventually surpass the dollar as leading international reserve currency?* (NBER Working Paper, No. 11510). Cambridge, MA: National Bureau of Economic Research. http://www.nber.org/papers/w11510.pdf?new_window=1. Accessed 30 July 2012.

CIC. (2009). *Annual report 2008*. Beijing: China Investment Corporation. http://www.china-inv.cn/cicen/include/resources/CIC_2008_annualreport_en.pdf. Accessed 30 July 2012.

CIC. (2012). *Annual report 2011*. Beijing: China Investment Corporation. http://www.china-inv.cn/cicen/include/resources/CIC_2011_annualreport_en.pdf. Accessed 17 Aug 2013.

CIC. (2013). *Annual report 2012*. Beijing: China Investment Corporation. http://www.china-inv.cn/cicen/include/resources/CIC_2012_annualreport_en.pdf. Accessed 17 Aug 2013.

Clark, I. (1996). *Should the IMF become more adaptive* (IMF Working Paper, WP/96/17). Washington, DC: International Monetary Fund.

Cohen, B. (1971). *The future of sterling as an international currency*. London: McMillan.

Cohen, B. (1977). *Organizing the world's money: The political economy of international monetary relations*. New York: Basic Books.

Cohen, B. (2001). International finance. In W. Carlsnaes, T. Risse, & B. Simmons (Eds.), *Handbook of international relations* (pp. 429–447). London: Sage.

Cohen, B. (2004). *The future of money*. Princeton: Princeton University Press.

Cohen, B. (2006). The macrofoundations of monetary power. In D. Andrews (Ed.), *International monetary power* (pp. 31–50). Ithaca: Cornell University Press.

Cookson, R. (2009, September 8). Renminbi bond marks first for China. *Financial Times*. http://www.ft.com/intl/cms/s/0/e142ebac-9c8f-11de-ab58-00144feabdc0.html#axzz2nSEbCw60. Accessed 30 July 2012.

Cookson, R. (2010a, October 19). ADB issues landmark renminbi bond. *Financial Times*. http://www.ft.com/intl/cms/s/0/5ca536cc-db7a-11df-ae99-00144feabdc0.html#axzz226d5oS3o. Accessed 30 July 2012.

Cookson, R. (2010b, July 2). Beijing plans route back for offshore funds. *Financial Times*. http://www.ft.com/intl/cms/s/0/7702fc92-8572-11df-aa2e-00144feabdc0.html. Accessed 30 July 2012.

Cookson, R. (2010c, July 28). China revs up renminbi expansion. *Financial Times*. http://www.ft.com/intl/cms/s/0/2ff1d6ea-9a65-11df-87fd-00144feab49a.html. Accessed 30 July 2012.

Dean, J., Areddy, J., & Ng, S. (2009, January 29). Chinese premier blames recession on U.S. actions. *Wall Street Journal*. http://online.wsj.com/article/SB123318934318826787.html. Accessed 30 July 2012.

Dobson, W., & Masson, P. (2009). Will the renminbi become a world currency. *China Economic Review, 20*(1), 124–135.

Dooley, M., Folkerts-Landau, D., & Garber, P. (2003). *An essay on the revived Bretton Woods system* (NBER Working Paper, No. 9971). Cambridge, MA: National Bureau of Economic Research. http://www.nber.org/papers/w9971.pdf?new_window=1. Accessed 30 July 2012.

Drezner, D. (2009). Bad debts: Assessing China's financial influence in great power politics. *International Security, 34*(2), 7–45.

Dyer, G. (2009, October 19). Global insight: Springing China's forex trap. *Financial Times*. http://www.ft.com/intl/cms/s/0/b9383574-bcc2-11de-a7ec-00144feab49a.html#axzz1NRx1V89R. Accessed 30 July 2012.

Dyer, G. (2010, February 24). Chinese official named as top IMF adviser. *Financial Times*. http://www.ft.com/intl/cms/s/0/45147e76-216e-11df-830e-00144feab49a.html#axzz226d5oS3o. Accessed 30 July 2012.

Dyer, G., & Beattie, A. (2009, March 13). Wen calls for US fiscal guarantees. *Financial Times*. http://www.ft.com/intl/cms/s/0/c2770bf0-1002-11de-a8ae-0000779fd2ac.html#axzz1NRx1V89R. Accessed 30 July 2012.

Dyer, G., Cookson, R., & Brown, K. (2010, September 19). Small steps to help reshape renminbi. *Financial Times*. http://www.ft.com/intl/cms/s/0/d38bebfc-c408-11df-b827-00144feab49a.html#axzz226d5oS3o. Accessed 30 July 2012.

Dyer, G., Anderlini, J., & Sender, H. (2011, January 17). China's lending hits new heights. *Financial Times*. http://www.ft.com/intl/cms/s/0/488c60f4-2281-11e0-b6a2-00144feab49a.html. Accessed 30 July 2012.

Eaton, S., & Zhang, M. (2010). A principal-agent analysis of China's sovereign wealth system: Byzantine by design. *Review of International Political Economy, 17*(3), 481–506.

Eccleston, B. (1986). The state, finance and industry in Japan. In A. Cox (Ed.), *State, finance and industry: A comparative analysis of post-war trends in six advanced industrial economies* (pp. 60–79). Brighton: Wheatsheaf Books.

Economist. (2011, September 24). Becoming number one: China's economy could overtake America's within a decade. In *Special report: The world economy* (p. 6).

Emmott, B. (1989). *The sun also sets: The limits to Japan's economic power*. New York: Random House.

Fang, N. (2007). Zhongguo touzi gongsi qihang [The CIC starts its journey]. *Zhongguo duiwai maoyi, 10*, 16–26.

Feng, H. (2006). How the people's bank is shaping China's financial sector. *Central Banking, 17*(1), 35–41.

Financial Times. (2009, February 2). Transcript of interview with Wen Jiabao. http://www.ft.com/intl/cms/s/0/795d2bca-f0fe-11dd-8790-0000779fd2ac.html#axzz1NRx1V89R. Accessed 31 July 2009.

Financial Times. (2011, May 24). Statement from BRIC IMF directors. http://www.ft.com/intl/cms/s/0/e7e6c20c-8645-11e0-9e2c-00144feabdc0.html#axzz226d5oS3o. Accessed 30 July 2012.

Fleming, M. (1962). Domestic financial policies under fixed and floating exchange rates. *Staff Papers – International Monetary Fund, 9*(3), 369–380.

Frankel, J. (1984). *The yen/dollar agreement: Liberalizing Japanese capital markets*. Washington, DC: Institute for International Economics.

Frankel, J. (2009). *New estimation of China's exchange rate regime* (NBER Working Paper, No. 14700). Cambridge, MA: National Bureau of Economic Research. http://www.nber.org/papers/w14700.pdf?new_window=1. Accessed 30 July 2012.

Fung, H.-G., Liu, Q., & Kao, E. (2007). China's outward direct and portfolio investments. *China & World Economy, 15*(6), 53–68.

Garber, P. (2011). *What drives CNH market equilibrium?* New York: Council on Foreign Relations. http://www.cfr.org/china/drives-cnh-market-equilibrium/p26292. Accessed 30 July 2012.

Garnham, P. (2009, June 26). China repeats criticism of dollar dominance. *Financial Times*. http://www.ft.com/intl/cms/s/0/f2236be4-6239-11de-b1c9-00144feabdc0.html. Accessed 30 July 2012.

Garnham, P. (2010, September 27). Reserves: All eyes turn to China's foreign money mountain. *Financial Times*. http://www.ft.com/intl/cms/s/0/66ae77ca-c9c6-11df-b3d6-00144feab49a,s01=1.html#axzz1NRx1V89R. Accessed 30 July 2012.

gbtimes. (2007, December 19). World Bank welcomes China's contribution to IDA: Zoellick. http://gbtimes.com/news/world-bank-welcomes-chinas-contribution-ida-zoellick. Accessed 30 July 2012.

Gerschenkron, A. (1962). *Economic backwardness in historical perspective: A book of essays*. Cambridge, MA: Harvard University Press.

Gilpin, R. (1987). *The political economy of international relations*. Princeton: Princeton University Press.

Green, R., & Torgerson, T. (2007). *Are high foreign exchange reserves in emerging markets a blessing or a burden?* (Occasional Paper, No. 6). Washington, DC: Department of the Treasury – Office of International Affairs. http://www.bestmindsinc.com/documents/DollarReserves.EmergingMarkets.USTreasury.2007.pdf. Accessed 30 July 2012.

Grimes, W. (2003). Internationalization as insulation: Dilemmas of the yen. In U. Schaede & W. Grimes (Eds.), *Japan's managed globalization: Adapting to the twenty-first century* (pp. 47–76). New York: M.E. Sharpe.

Guo, F. (2007a). Lou Jiwei de kaiju [The beginning of Lou Jiwei's match]. *Xiaokang, 9*, 59–61.

Guo, F. (2007b, October 8). Zhongtou gongsi zujian licheng [The course of the CIC's establishment]. *Zhongguo zhengquan bao*. http://news.xinhuanet.com/newscenter/2007-10/08/content_6842589.htm. Accessed 30 July 2012.

Guzzini, S. (1993). Structural power: The limits of neorealist power analysis. *International Organization, 47*(3), 443–478.

He, F., & Zhang, M. (2007). Zhongguo de waihui touzi gongsi hui chongji guoji jinrong shichang ma? [Will the Chinese Sovereign wealth fund seriously affect international financial markets?]. *Guoji jingji pinglun, 5–6*, 20–22.

Heep, S. (2008). Chinas Neuer Staatsfonds: Organisation, Finanzierung und Investitionsstrategie der China Investment Corporation [China's new sovereign wealth fund: Organization, financing and investment strategy of the China investment corporation]. *Asien, 108*, 51–66.

Heep, S., & Hilpert, H. G. (2009). Chinas währungspolitische Offensive [China's monetary offensive]. (SWP-Aktuell, No. 65) Berlin: Stiftung Wissenschaft und Politik. http://www.swp-berlin.org/fileadmin/contents/products/aktuell/2009A65_hlp_hep_ks.pdf. Accessed 30 July 2012.

Heep, S. (2009a). The China Investment Corporation. In D. Pong (Ed.), *Encyclopedia of modern China* (p. 76). Farmington Hills: Charles Scribner's Sons.

Heep, S. (2009b). The State Administration of Foreign Exchange. In D. Pong (Ed.), *Encyclopedia of modern China* (p. 75). Farmington Hills: Charles Scribner's Sons.

Heilmann, S. (2004). *Das politische System der Volksrepublik China [The political system of the People's Republic of China]* (2nd ed.). Wiesbaden: Verlag für Sozialwissenschaften.

Heilmann, S. (2008). Policy experimentation in China's economic rise. *Studies in Comparative International Development, 43*(1), 1–26.

Heilmann, S. (2009). Maximum tinkering under uncertainty: Unorthodox lessons from China. *Modern China, 35*(4), 450–462.

Heilmann, S. (2011a). Experience first, laws later: Experimentation and breakthroughs in the restructuring of China's state sector. In J. Oi (Ed.), *Going private in China: The politics of corporate restructuring and system reform* (pp. 95–118). Stanford: Shorenstein Center.

Heilmann, S. (2011b). Making plans for markets: Policies for the long term in China. *Harvard Asia Quarterly, 13*(2), 33–40.

Heilmann, S., & Gottwald, J.-C. (2002). *Der chinesische Aktienmarkt* [The Chinese equity market]. Hamburg: Institut für Asienkunde.

Heilmann, S., & Kirchberger, S. (2000). *The Chinese nomenklatura in transition: A study based on internal cadre statistics of the Central Organization Department of the Chinese Communist Party* (China Analysis, No. 1). Trier: Chinapolitik.

Heilmann, S., & Perry, E. (Eds.). (2011). *Mao's invisible hand: The political foundations of adaptive governance in China*. Harvard: Harvard University Asia Center.

Helleiner, E. (1989). Money and influence: Japanese power in the international monetary and financial system. *Millennium – Journal of International Studies, 18*(3), 343–358.

Helleiner, E. (1992). Japan and the changing global financial order. *International Journal, 47*(2), 420–444.

Helleiner, E. (2000). Still an extraordinary power, but for how much longer? The United States in world finance. In T. Lawton, J. Rosenau, & A. Verdun (Eds.), *Strange power: Shaping the parameters of international relations and international political economy* (pp. 229–247). Aldershot: Ashgate.

Helleiner, E. (2003). *The making of national money*. Ithaca: Cornell University Press.

Helleiner, E. (2006). Below the state: Micro-level monetary power. In D. Andrews (Ed.), *International monetary power* (pp. 72–90). Ithaca: Cornell University Press.

Helleiner, E. (2008). Political determinants of international currencies: What future for the US dollar? *Review of International Political Economy, 13*(3), 354–378.

Helleiner, E. (2009). The geopolitics of sovereign wealth funds: An introduction. *Geopolitics, 14* (2), 300–304.

Helleiner, E., & Kirshner, J. (Eds.). (2009). *The future of the dollar*. Ithaca: Cornell University Press.

Helleiner, E., & Momani, B. (2007). *Slipping into obscurity? Crisis and reform at the IMF* (CIGI Working Paper, No. 16). Waterloo: Centre for International Governance Innovation.

Hille, K. (2011, June 9). Lagarde 'confident' about IMF job. *Financial Times*. http://www.ft.com/intl/cms/s/0/9963c75c-9251-11e0-9e00-00144feab49a.html#axzz226d5oS3o. Accessed 30 July 2012.

Hilpert, H. G. (1998). Die Internationalisierung des Yen: Aufstieg zur Reservewährung? [The internationalization of the yen: Rising to reserve currency status?]. In A. Ernst & P. Pörtner (Eds.), *Die Rolle des Geldes in Japans Gesellschaft, Wirtschaft und Politik* [The role of money in Japan's society, economy and politics] (Vol. 286, pp. 147–160). Hamburg: Mitteilungen des Instituts für Asienkunde.

HKMA. (2013, March). *Half-yearly monetary and financial stability report*. Hong Kong: Hong Kong Monetary Authority. http://www.hkma.gov.hk/media/eng/publication-and-research/quarterly-bulletin/qb201303/E_Half-yearly.pdf. Accessed 16 Aug 2013.

Hu, X. (2007, April 14). *Statement given at the fifteenth meeting of the International Monetary and Financial Committee*, Washington, DC. http://www.imf.org/external/spring/2007/imfc/statement/eng/chn.pdf. Accessed 30 July 2012.

Huang, Y. (2011). Rethinking the Beijing consensus. *Asia Policy, 11*, 1–26.

ICBC. (2013). *Annual report 2012*. Beijing: Industrial and Commercial Bank of China. http://www.icbc-ltd.com/SiteCollectionDocuments/ICBC/Resources/ICBCLTD/%E4%B8%8B%E8%BD%BD/2013/2012AnnualReport.pdf. Accessed 13 Aug 2013.

IDA15. (2008, February 28). *IDA: The platform for achieving results at the country level*. Washington, DC: International Development Association. http://siteresources.worldbank.org/IDA/Resources/Seminar%20PDFs/73449-1172525976405/FinalreportMarch2008.pdf. Accessed 30 July 2012.

IDA16. (2011, March 18). *Delivering development results*. Washington, DC: International Development Association. http://siteresources.worldbank.org/IDA/Resources/IDA16_Report-English-Final.pdf. Accessed 30 July 2012.

IMF. (2000). *Debt-and reserve-related indicators of external vulnerability*. Washington, DC: International Monetary Fund. http://www.imf.org/external/np/pdr/debtres/debtres.pdf. Accessed 30 July 2012.

IMF. (2004). *Guidelines for foreign exchange reserve management*. Washington, DC: International Monetary Fund. http://www.bcentral.cl/eng/financial-operations/pdf/Guidelines%20for%20Foreign%20Exchange%20Management%20FMI%202004.pdf. Accessed 30 July 2012.

IMF. (2006, August 31). *Report of the executive board to the board of governors: Quota and voice reform in the International Monetary Fund*. Washington, DC: International Monetary Fund. http://www.imf.org/external/np/pp/eng/2006/083106.pdf. Accessed 30 July 2012.

IMF. (2007, June 21). *IMF executive board adopts new decision on bilateral surveillance over members' policies*. Washington, DC: International Monetary Fund. http://www.imf.org/external/np/sec/pn/2007/pn0769.htm. Accessed 30 July 2012.

IMF. (2008). *Reform of IMF quotas and voice: Responding to changes in the global economy*. Washington, DC: International Monetary Fund. http://www.imf.org/external/np/exr/ib/2008/040108.htm. Accessed 30 July 2012.

IMF. (2010a, November 5). *IMF board approves far-reaching governance reforms*. Washington, DC: International Monetary Fund. http://www.imf.org/external/pubs/ft/survey/so/2010/NEW110510B.htm. Accessed 30 July 2012.

IMF. (2010b, February 24). *IMF managing director Dominique Strauss-Kahn names China's Zhu Min as special advisor*. Washington, DC: International Monetary Fund. http://www.imf.org/external/np/sec/pr/2010/pr1058.htm. Accessed 30 July 2012.

IMF. (2012a). *Annual report 2012: Distribution of IMF professional and managerial staff by nationality*. Washington, DC: International Monetary Fund. http://www.imf.org/external/pubs/ft/ar/2012/eng/pdf/webtable51.pdf. Accessed 17 Aug 2012.

IMF. (2012b, March 30). *IMF quotas*. Washington, DC: International Monetary Fund. http://www.imf.org/external/np/exr/facts/quotas.htm. Accessed 30 July 2012.

IMF. (2012c, March 30). *IMF standing borrowing arrangements*. Washington, DC: International Monetary Fund. http://www.imf.org/external/np/exr/facts/gabnab.htm. Accessed 30 July 2012.

IMF. (2013, August 1). *IMF multi-country report*. Washington, DC: International Monetary Fund. http://www.imf.org/external/np/pp/eng/2013/062013a.pdf. Accessed 15 Aug 2013.

IMF. (n.d.-a). *Country representation*. Washington, DC: International Monetary Fund. http://www.imf.org/external/about/govrep.htm. Accessed 30 July 2012.

IMF. (n.d.-b). *Governance structure*. Washington, DC: International Monetary Fund. http://www.imf.org/external/about/govstruct.htm. Accessed 30 July 2012.

IMF. (n.d.-c). *Note purchase agreement between the People's Bank of China and the International Monetary Fund*. Washington, DC: International Monetary Fund. http://www.imf.org/external/np/pp/eng/2009/090209.pdf. Accessed 30 July 2012.

IMF. (n.d.-d). *Quota and voting shares before and after implementation of reforms agreed in 2008 and 2010*. Washington, DC: International Monetary Fund. http://www.imf.org/external/np/sec/pr/2011/pdfs/quota_tbl.pdf. Accessed 30 July 2012.

Itoh, M. (1990). *The world economic crisis and Japanese capitalism*. New York: St. Martin's Press.

Jen, S., & St-Arnaud, C. (2007, July 13). EM currencies: Excess official reserves. In *Global economic forum*. New York: Morgan Stanley. http://www.morganstanley.com/views/gef/archive/2007/20070713-Fri.html#anchorff15cb43-419e-11de-a1b3-c771ef8db296. Accessed 30 July 2012.

Jian, J. (2011, September 14). The myth of the 'China model' in Africa. *Asia Times*. http://www.atimes.com/atimes/china/mi14ad01.html. Accessed 30 July 2012.

Jiao, J. (2007, December). Dui yunyong waihui chubei sheli guojia touzi gongsi de sikao [Reflections on the use of foreign exchange reserves for the establishment of a national investment company]. *Qiyejia tiandi*, 103–104.

Johnson, C. (1982). *MITI and the Japanese miracle: The growth of industrial policy, 1925–1975*. Stanford: Stanford University Press.

Johnson, C. (1987). Political institutions and economic performance: The government-business relationship in Japan, South Korea, and Taiwan. In F. Deyo (Ed.), *The political economy of the new Asian industrialism* (pp. 136–164). Ithaca: Cornell University Press.

Kahler, M. (1990). The United States and the International Monetary Fund: Declining influence or declining interest? In M. Karns & K. Mingst (Eds.), *The United States and multilateral institutions: Patterns of changing instrumentality and influence* (pp. 91–114). Boston: Unwin Hyman.

Kapur, D., Lewis, J., & Webb, R. (1997). *The World Bank: Its first half century* (Vol. 1). Washington, DC: Brookings Institution Press.

Katada, S. (2002). Japan and Asian monetary regionalisation: Cultivating a new regional leadership after the Asian financial crisis. *Geopolitics, 7*(1), 85–112.

Katada, S. (2008). From a supporter to a challenger? Japan's currency leadership in dollar-denominated East Asia. *Review of International Political Economy, 15*(3), 399–417.

Katsuhiro, S. (2007). Global governance, Japan and the World Bank. In G. Hook & H. Dobson (Eds.), *Global governance and Japan: The institutional architecture* (pp. 110–125). London: Routledge.

Kennedy, S. (2010). The myth of the Beijing consensus. *Journal of Contemporary China, 19*(65), 461–477.

Kennedy, S. (2011). Overcoming our Middle Kingdom complex: Finding China's place in comparative politics. In S. Kennedy (Ed.), *Beyond the Middle Kingdom: Comparative perspectives on China's capitalist transformation* (pp. 3–21). Stanford: Stanford University Press.

Keohane, R. (1980). The theory of hegemonic stability and changes in international economic regimes. 1967–1977. In O. Holsti, R. Siverson, & A. George (Eds.), *Change in the international system* (pp. 131–162). Boulder: Westview Press.

Kirshner, J. (1995). *Currency and coercion: The political economy of international monetary power*. Princeton: Princeton University Press.

Kirshner, J. (2006). Currency and coercion in the twenty-first century. In D. Andrews (Ed.), *International monetary power* (pp. 139–161). Ithaca: Cornell University Press.

Kirshner, J. (2008). Dollar primacy and American power: What's at stake? *Review of International Political Economy, 15*(3), 418–438.

Konyn, M. (2012, January 15). Renminbi investment scheme will benefit Chinese fund managers. *Financial Times*. http://www.ft.com/intl/cms/s/0/8b54f10e-3ac1-11e1-a756-00144feabdc0.html#axzz226d5oS3o. Accessed 30 July 2012.

Kroeber, A. (2009a, May 27). Don't believe the renminbi hype. Financial Times. http://www.ft.com/intl/cms/s/0/06c4c5ae-4a55-11de-8e7e-00144feabdc0.html#axzz1v8osjof8. Accessed 30 July 2012.

Kroeber, A. (2009b, June 24). China's accelerating financial reform. *Financial Times*. http://www.ft.com/intl/cms/s/0/8fe40a72-6056-11de-a09b-00144feabdc0.html#axzz1v8osjof8. Accessed 30 July 2012.

Kroeber, A. (2011). Developmental dreams: Policy and reality in China's economic reforms. In S. Kennedy (Ed.), *Beyond the Middle Kingdom: Comparative perspectives on China's capitalist transformation* (pp. 44–65). Stanford: Stanford University Press.

Kunieda, Y. (1995). The internationalization of the yen: A decade since the Yen-Dollar Committee. *Tokyo Financial Review, 21*(6), 1–10.

Lardy, N. (2008). *Financial repression in China* (Policy Brief, PB08-8). Washington, DC: Peterson Institute for International Economics. http://www.iie.com/publications/pb/pb08-8.pdf. Accessed 30 July 2012.

Lardy, N., & Douglass, P. (2011). *Capital account liberalization and the role of the renminbi* (Working Paper, WP 11-6). Washington, DC: Peterson Institute for International Economics. http://www.iie.com/publications/wp/wp11-6.pdf. Accessed 30 July 2012.

Laurence, H. (2001). *Money rules: The new politics of finance in Britain and Japan*. Ithaca: Cornell University Press.

Leyshon, A. (1994). Under pressure: Finance, geo-economic competition and the rise and fall of Japan's postwar growth economy. In S. Corbridge, N. Thrift, & R. Martin (Eds.), *Money, power and space* (pp. 116–145). Oxford: Blackwell.

Li, B. (2007). Shixi zhongguo zhuquan caifu jijin [Analyzing China's sovereign wealth fund]. *Shanghai jinrong, 10*, 53–55.

Lieberthal, K., & Oksenberg, M. (1988). *Policy making in China: Leaders, structures, and processes*. Princeton: Princeton University Press.

Lin, J. Y. (2011, March 23). *China and the global economy*. Remarks at the 20th anniversary of the University of Science and Technology. Hong Kong: University of Science and Technology.

http://siteresources.worldbank.org/DEC/Resources/UST-Justin-Lin-Hongkong.pdf. Accessed 30 July 2012.

Lipscy, P. (2003). Japan's Asian monetary fund proposal. *Stanford Journal of East Asian Affairs, 3* (1), 93–104.

Liu, D. (2009, May 14). Yu Yongding tan renminbi guojihua lujing [Yu Yongding talks about the internationalization of the renminbi]. *Caijing*. http://www.caijing.com.cn/2009-05-14/110166092.html. Accessed 30 July 2012.

Ma, Y. (2011, January 24). Wenzhou's overseas investment trial halted. *Caixin*. http://english.caixin.com/2011-01-24/100220616.html. Accessed 30 July 2012.

Ma, G., & McCauley, R. (2007). *Do China's capital controls still bind? Implications for monetary autonomy and capital liberalisation* (BIS Working Paper, No. 233). Basel: Bank for International Settlements. http://www.bis.org/publ/work233.pdf. Accessed 30 July 2012.

Ma, G., & Zhou, H. (2009). *China's evolving external wealth and rising creditor position* (BIS Working Paper, No. 286). Basel: Bank for International Settlements. http://www.bis.org/publ/work286.pdf. Accessed 30 July 2012.

McCauley, R. (2011). *Internationalizing the renminbi and China's financial development model*. New York: Council on Foreign Relations. http://www.cfr.org/china/renminbi-internationalization-chinas-financial-development-Fmodel/p26290. Accessed 30 July 2012.

McGregor, R. (2007, September 13). China fund may broaden mandate. *Financial Times*. http://www.ft.com/intl/cms/s/0/1dacb784-61ba-11dc-bdf6-0000779fd2ac.html#axzz1NRx1V89R. Accessed 30 July 2012.

McGregor, R. (2008a, February 1). Beijing starts to pay for forex 'sterilisation'. *Financial Times*. http://www.ft.com/intl/cms/s/0/0b83f086-d01e-11dc-9309-0000779fd2ac.html#axzz1NRx1V89R. Accessed 30 July 2012.

McGregor, R. (2008b, January 22). World Bank appointment to strengthen Beijing ties. *Financial Times*. http://www.ft.com/intl/cms/s/0/60ae594a-c88d-11dc-94a6-0000779fd2ac.html#axzz226d5oS3o. Accessed 30 July 2012.

McGregor, R. (2011, January 16). Hu questions future role of US dollar. *Financial Times*. http://www.ft.com/intl/cms/s/0/ae01a8f6-21b7-11e0-9e3b-00144feab49a.html#axzz2nSEbCw60. Accessed 30 July 2012.

McGregor, R., & Mitchell, T. (2007, November 4). China puts Hong Kong share plan on ice. *Financial Times*. http://www.ft.com/intl/cms/s/0/4b3556dc-8b01-11dc-95f7-0000779fd2ac.html#axzz1mNUQl8NC. Accessed 30 July 2012.

McGuinness, P. (2009). An overview and assessment of the reform of the non-tradable shares of Chinese state-owned enterprise A-share issuers. *Journal of Financial Regulation and Compliance, 17*(1), 41–56.

McGuire, P., & von Peter, G. (2009, March). *The US dollar shortage in global banking*. In *BIS quarterly review* (pp. 47–63). Basel: Bank for International Settlements. http://www.bis.org/publ/qtrpdf/r_qt0903f.pdf. Accessed 30 July 2012.

McKinnon, R. (1973). *Money and capital in economic development*. Washington, DC: Brookings Institution.

MOFCOM. (2013, January 30). *Brief statistics on China's import & export in December 2012*. Beijing: Ministry of Commerce. http://english.mofcom.gov.cn/article/statistic/BriefStatistics/201301/20130100017291.shtml. Accessed 18 Aug 2013.

Mohanty, M. S., & Turner, P. (2006, September). Foreign exchange reserve accumulation in emerging markets: What are the domestic implications. In *BIS quarterly review* (pp. 39–52). Basel: Bank for International Settlements. http://www.bis.org/repofficepubl/arpresearch200609.01.pdf. Accessed 30 July 2012.

Moran, M. (1991). *The politics of the financial services revolution: The USA, UK and Japan*. London: McMillan.

Mundell, R. (1963). Capital mobility and stabilization policy under fixed and flexible exchange rates. *Canadian Journal of Economic and Political Science, 29*(4), 475–485.

Murphy, T. (1996). *The weight of the yen: How denial imperils America's future and ruins an alliance*. New York: Norton & Company.

Murphy, M., & Yuan, W. J. (2009). *Is China ready to challenge the dollar? Internationalization of the renminbi and its implications for the United States*. Washington, DC: Center for Strategic and International Studies. http://csis.org/files/publication/091007_Murphy_IsChinaReady_Web.pdf. Accessed 30 July 2012.

NAFMII. (n.d.). *Guidelines on medium-term notes business of non-financial enterprises in the interbank bond market*. Beijing: National Association of Financial Market Institutional Investors. http://www.nafmii.org.cn/english/lawsandregulations/selfregulatory_e/201205/t20120530_15427. html. Accessed 9 Aug 2013.

Nakamoto, M., & Cookson, R. (2010, July 8). China in record Japan Sovereign debt buy. *Financial Times*. http://www.ft.com/intl/cms/s/0/8c861c30-8a5d-11df-bd2e-00144feab49a.html#axzz1NRx1V89R. Accessed 30 July 2012.

Nathan, A. (2003). Authoritarian resilience. *Journal of Democracy, 14*(1), 6–17.

Naughton, B. (2007). *The Chinese economy: Transitions and growth*. Cambridge, MA: MIT Press.

Naughton, B. (2010). China's distinctive system: Can it be a model for others? *Journal of Contemporary China, 19*(65), 437–460.

Nee, V., Opper, S., & Wong, S. (2007). Developmental state and corporate governance in China. *Management and Organization Review, 3*(1), 19–53.

Noble, J. (2011, June 20). Is China picking euro debt over US treasuries? *Financial Times*. http://blogs.ft.com/beyond-brics/2011/06/20/is-china-picking-euro-debt-over-us-treasuries/#axzz228My7mGk. Accessed 30 July 2012.

Oakley, D., & Anderlini, J. (2010, May 27). China eyes cut in euro exposure. *Financial Times*. http://www.ft.com/intl/cms/s/0/f23dcd92-6925-11df-aa7e-00144feab49a.html#axzz2nSEbCw60. Accessed 30 July 2012.

OECD. (2005). *Economic survey of China*. Paris: Organisation for Economic Co-operation and Development.

OECF. (1998). Issues related to the World Bank's approach to structural adjustment: A proposal from a major partner. In K. Ohno & I. Ohno (Eds.), *Japanese views on economic development: Diverse paths to the market* (pp. 61–69). London: Routledge.

Ogata, S. (1989). Shifting power relations in multilateral development banks. *Journal of International Studies, 22*, 1–20.

Olson, S., & Prestowitz, C. (2011). *The evolving role of China in international institutions*. Report prepared for the U.S.–China Economic and Security Review Commission. Washington, DC: Economic Strategy Institute. http://www.uscc.gov/researchpapers/2011/TheEvolvingRoleofChinainInternationalInstitutions.pdf. Accessed 30 July 2012.

Ostry, J., Gosh, A., Habermeier, K., Chamon, M., Qureshi, M., & Reinhard, D. (2010). *Capital inflows: The role of controls* (IMF Staff Position Note, SPN/10/04). Washington, DC: International Monetary Fund. http://www.imf.org/external/pubs/ft/spn/2010/spn1004.pdf. Accessed 30 July 2012.

Park, D. H (2007). *Beyond liquidity: New uses for developing Asia's foreign exchange reserves* (ERD Working Paper, No. 109). Manila: Asian Development Bank. http://www.adb.org/sites/default/files/pub/2007/WP109.pdf. Accessed 30 July 2012.

Parker, G., Dinmore, G., Guha, K., & Lau, J. (2009, July 9). China attacks dollar's dominance. *Financial Times*. http://www.ft.com/intl/cms/s/0/81f3125a-6cae-11de-af56-00144feabdc0.html. Accessed 30 July 2012.

PBOC. (2005, June 6). *People's Bank of China promulgated the administrative rules for short-term financing bills*. Beijing: People's Bank of China. http://www.pbc.gov.cn/publish/english/955/2000/20002/20002_.html. Accessed 9 Aug 2013.

PBOC. (2010a, March 25). *Highlights of China's monetary policy in 2009*. Beijing: People's Bank of China. http://www.pbc.gov.cn/publish/english/955/2010/20100521104245630314035/20100521104245630314035_.html. Accessed 31 July 2012.

PBOC. (2010b, February 11). *Zhongguo huobi zhengce zhexing baogao: Er ling yi jiu ling nian disi jidu* [Report on the implementation of Chinese monetary policy: Fourth quarter of 2009]. Beijing: People's Bank of China. http://www.pbc.gov.cn/publish/zhengcehuobisi/897/2010/20100318182635079140734/20100318182635079140734_.html. Accessed 30 July 2012.
PBOC. (2011a, February 1). *Highlights of China's monetary policy in 2010*. Beijing: People's Bank of China. http://www.pbc.gov.cn:8080/publish/english/955/2011/20110321085259259966571/20110321085259259966571_.html. Accessed 31 July 2012.
PBOC. (2011b, January 30). *Zhongguo huobi zhengce zhexing baogao: Er ling yi ling nian disi jidu* [Report on the implementation of Chinese monetary policy: Fourth quarter of 2010]. Beijing: People's Bank of China. http://www.pbc.gov.cn/publish/zhengcehuobisi/3078/2011/20110130192348658678312/20110130192348658678312_.html. Accessed 30 July 2012.
PBOC. (2011c). *2010 nian guoji jinrong shichang baogao* [2010 report on international financial markets]. Shanghai: People's Bank of China. http://www.pbc.gov.cn/publish/goutongjiaoliu/524/2011/20110325153152445488612/20110325153152445488612_.html. Accessed 30 July 2012.
PBOC. (2012a, February 28). *Highlights of China's monetary policy in 2011*. Beijing: People's Bank of China. http://www.pbc.gov.cn/publish/english/955/2012/20120319093132597913401/20120319093132597913401_.html. Accessed 31 July 2012.
PBOC. (2012b, February 15). *Zhongguo huobi zhengce zhexing baogao: Er ling yi yi nian disi jidu* [Report on the implementation of Chinese monetary policy: Fourth quarter of 2011]. Beijing: People's Bank of China. http://www.pbc.gov.cn/publish/zhengcehuobisi/3679/2012/20120215170702347457349/20120215170702347457349_.html. Accessed 30 July 2012.
PBOC. (2013a, February 25). *Highlights of China's monetary policy in 2012*. Beijing: People's Bank of China. http://www.pbc.gov.cn/publish/english/955/2013/20130314105541578282714/20130314105541578282714_.html. Accessed 13 Aug 2013.
PBOC. (2013b, February 6). *Zhongguo huobi zhengce zhexing baogao: Er ling yi er nian disi jidu* [Report on the implementation of Chinese monetary policy: Fourth quarter of 2012]. Beijing: People's Bank of China. http://www.pbc.gov.cn/publish/bangongting/82/2013/20130206184942484447083/20130206184942484447083_.html. Accessed 15 Aug 2013.
PBOC. (2013c). *Zhongguo jinrong wending baogao 2013* [China financial stability report 2013]. Beijing: People's Bank of China. http://www.pbc.gov.cn/image_public/UserFiles/goutongjiaoliu/upload/File/%E4%B8%AD%E5%9B%BD%E9%87%91%E8%9E%8D%E7%A8%B3%E5%AE%9A%E6%8A%A5%E5%91%8A2013.pdf. Accessed 13 Aug 2013.
PBOC. (n.d.-a). *Sources and uses of credit funds by financial institutions by sector in 2012*. Beijing: People's Bank of China. http://www.pbc.gov.cn/publish/html/2012s03a.htm. Accessed 18 Aug 2013.
PBOC. (n.d.-b). *Sources and uses of credit funds by financial institutions by sector in 2011*. Beijing: People's Bank of China. http://www.pbc.gov.cn/publish/html/2011s03a.htm. Accessed 18 Aug 2013.
PBOC. (n.d.-c). *Sources and uses of credit funds by financial institutions by sector in 2010*. Beijing: People's Bank of China. http://www.pbc.gov.cn/publish/html/2010s03a.htm. Accessed 31 July 2012.
PBOC. (n.d.-d). *Sources and uses of credit funds by financial institutions by sector in 2009*. Beijing: People's Bank of China. http://www.pbc.gov.cn/publish/html/2009s03a.htm. Accessed 31 July 2012.
PBOC. (n.d.-e). *Sources and uses of credit funds by financial institutions by sector in 2008*. Beijing: People's Bank of China. http://www.pbc.gov.cn/publish/html/2008S03a.htm. Accessed 18 Aug 2013.
PBOC. (n.d.-f). *Sources and uses of credit funds by financial institutions by sector in 2007*. Beijing: People's Bank of China. http://www.pbc.gov.cn/publish/html/2007S03a.htm. Accessed 18 Aug 2013.
Pei, M. (2008). *China's trapped transition: The limits of developmental autocracy*. Harvard: Harvard University Press.

Peng, L. (2011, August 17). Zhou Xiaochuan: qiye fugang fa renzhai guimo cengzhi 500 yi [Zhou Xiaochuan: Worth of renminbi bonds that corporations are allowed to issue in Hong Kong increases to CNY 50 billion]. *Xinlang Caijing*. http://finance.sina.com.cn/g/20110817/134410331562.shtml. Accessed 30 July 2012.

People's Daily. (2008, November 7). Agricultural Bank of China receives 130 bln yuan capital injection. http://english.people.com.cn/90001/90776/90884/6529061.html. Accessed 30 July 2012.

People's Daily. (2013, May 9). China's Central Bank resumes bill issuance to drain liquidity. http://english.people.com.cn/90778/8238877.html. Accessed 14 Aug 2013.

Pilling, D. (2010, August 25). Long March to renminbi convertibility. *Financial Times*. http://www.ft.com/intl/cms/s/0/f815ca7e-b08a-11df-8c04-00144feabdc0.html#axzz1NRx1V89R. Accessed 30 July 2012.

Prasad, E., & Wei, S.-J. (2005). *The Chinese approach to capital inflows: Patterns and possible explanations* (IMF Working Paper, WP/05/79). Washington, DC: International Monetary Fund. http://www.imf.org/external/pubs/ft/wp/2005/wp0579.pdf. Accessed 30 July 2012.

Prasad, E., Rumbaugh, T., & Wang, Q. (2006). Putting the cart before the horse? Capital account liberalization and exchange rate flexibility in China. In IMF, *China and India learning from each other: Reforms and policies for sustained growth* (pp. 181–199). Washington, DC: International Monetary Fund.

Rabinovitch, S. (2011, August 17). China issues $3.1bn of bonds in Hong Kong. *Financial Times*. http://www.ft.com/intl/cms/s/0/90ff79e6-c8c3-11e0-a2c8-00144feabdc0.html#axzz226d5oS3o. Accessed 30 July 2012.

Ramo, J. C. (2004). *The Beijing consensus*. London: Central Books.

Rapkin, D., & Strand, J. (1997). The U.S. and Japan in the Bretton Woods institutions: Sharing or contesting leadership? *International Journal, 52*(2), 265–296.

Reuters. (2013, July 12). China to increase QFII-quota, expand RQFII to London, Singapore – CSRC. http://www.reuters.com/article/2013/07/12/china-qfii-idUSL4N0FI20O20130712. Accessed 15 Aug 2013.

Rosenbluth, F. M. C. (1989). *Financial politics in contemporary Japan*. Ithaca: Cornell University Press.

SAFE. (2012a, July 30). *Balance of payments of China*. Beijing: State Administration of Foreign Exchange. http://www.safe.gov.cn/wps/portal/!ut/p/c5/04_SB8K8xLLM9MSSzPy8xBz9CP0os3gPZxdnX293QwP30FAnA8_AEBc3C1NjIxMjU6B8JG75YGMKdLubGRDQHQ5yLX7b8ciDzQfJG-AAjgb6fh75uan6BbmhEQaZAekAc9mgLQ!!/dl3/d3/L2dJQSEvUUt3QS9ZQnZ3LzZfSENEQ01LRzEwT085RTBJNkE1U1NDRzNMTDQ!/?WCM_GLOBAL_CONTEXT=/wps/wcm/connect/safe_web_store/state+administration+of+foreign+exchange/data+and+statistics/balance+of+payments/03119b804c296bc0a405af4393d9cc2e. Accessed 18 Aug 2013.

SAFE. (2012b, August 7). *China's foreign exchange reserves*. Beijing: State Administration of Foreign Exchange. http://www.safe.gov.cn/wps/portal/!ut/p/c5/04_SB8K8xLLM9MSSzPy8xBz9CP0os3gPZxdnX293QwP30FAnA8_AEBc3C1NjIxMjA6B8JE55dzMDArrDQfbhVhFsjFcebD5I3gAHcDTQ9_PIz03VL8iNMMgMSFcEAP5jfwo!/dl3/d3/L2dJQSEvUUt3QS9ZQnZ3LzZfSENEQ01LRzEwT085RTBJNkE1U1NDRzNMTDQ!/?WCM_GLOBAL_CONTEXT=/wps/wcm/connect/safe_web_store/state+administration+of+foreign+exchange/data+and+statistics/forex+reserves/bb4353804c420bf6aa0aaefd3fd7c3dc. Accessed 18 Aug 2013.

SAFE. (2012c, June 19). *2001–2011 nian waizhai zongti qingkuang* [Overall situation of China's external debt]. Beijing: State Administration of Foreign Exchange. http://www.safe.gov.cn/wps/portal/!ut/p/c5/hc1BC4IwHAXwTxR7wzXncZu5_ZcZJpR5EQ8RQmqH6POndAuq944_Ho81bO7YPftr9-insbuxmjWyFUClDNdQWZ6A1jpVPBEmr-TsZ9lap72Ic0AJB5Aw-8LbkoOiP-vT8idbb1O72zoOl1kD0tUxypzgAdGHK0EWRKHchOD5IY3f_ut_cXyJBiv8NFzYfajR00q_AE0Uwho!/dl3/d3/L2dJQSEvUUt3QS9ZQnZ3LzZfSENEQ01LRzEwODRJQzBJSU pRRUpKSDEySTI!/?WCM_GLOBAL_CONTEXT=/wps/wcm/connect/safe_web_store/safe_web/tjsj/node_tjsj_wzsj/node_tjsj_wzsj2_store/fa3bb0804af059fd9eb59f8299a02c57. Accessed 18 Aug 2013.

SAFE. (2013a, April 3). *Balance of payments 2012*. Beijing: State Administration of Foreign Exchange. http://www.safe.gov.cn/wps/portal/!ut/p/c5/04_SB8K8xLLM9MSSzPy8xBz9CP0os3gPZxdnX293QwP30FAnA8_AEBc3C1NjIxMjU6B8JG75YGMKdLubGRDQHQ5yLX7b8ciDzQfJG-AAjgb6fh75uan6BbmhEQaZAekAc9mgLQ!!/dl3/d3/L2dJQSEvUUt3QS9ZQnZ3LzZfSENEQ01LRzEwT085RTBJNkE1U1NDRzNMTDQ!/?WCM_GLOBAL_CONTEXT=/wps/wcm/connect/safe_web_store/state+administration+of+foreign+exchange/data+and+statistics/balance+of+payments/ebc0bb004f1fd6b5b323ffb346e93bc7. Accessed 18 Aug 2013.

SAFE. (2013b, July 1). *China's international investment position*. Beijing: State Administration of Foreign Exchange. http://www.safe.gov.cn/wps/portal/english/Data/Investment. Accessed 16 Aug 2013.

SAFE. (2013c, March 14). *Zhongguo waihui chubei 2012 nian* [China's foreign exchange reserves in 2012]. Beijing: State Administration of Foreign Exchange. http://www.safe.gov.cn/wps/portal/!ut/p/c5/hc2xDoIwGATgJzK9SoEytsW2PyIGSRRZCIMxJAIOxucX4mai3o1fLscaNnfsnv21e_TT2N1YzZqoFUAlNVeQNk9AoUolT4QOw3j2c9Qap7yIc0AKB5DQ-8KbkoOCP-vT8he13qRmt3UczhoNUtUxsE7wwK4_XAoyIMrKTZZ5fkjjt__6XxxfosAKPw0Xdh9q9LRSL5COXLU!/dl3/d3/L2dJQSEvUUt3QS9ZQnZ3LzZfSENEQ01LRzEwODRJQzBJSUpRRUpKSDEySTI!/?WCM_GLOBAL_CONTEXT=/wps/wcm/connect/safe_web_store/safe_web/tjsj/node_tjsj_whcb/node_tjsj_whcbs_store/945bd3004ee234cb821acf67bbb2cc48. Accessed 18 Aug 2013.

Schlichting, S. (2008). *Internationalising China's financial markets*. Houndmills: Palgrave Macmillan.

Sender, H. (2008a, June 10). China's SAFE to invest $2.5bn in TPG fund. *Financial Times*. http://www.ft.com/intl/cms/s/0/d793921e-3714-11dd-bc1c-0000779fd2ac.html#axzz226d5oS3o. Accessed 30 July 2012.

Sender, H. (2008b, February 8). CIC close to fund deal with JC flowers. *Financial Times*. http://www.ft.com/intl/cms/s/0/aeaf55dc-d5b1-11dc-8b56-0000779fd2ac.html. Accessed 30 July 2012.

Setser, B. (2008). *Sovereign wealth and sovereign power: The strategic consequences of American indebtedness*. New York: Council on Foreign Relations. http://www.cfr.org/economics/sovereign-wealth-sovereign-power/p17074. Accessed 30 July 2012.

Setser, B., & Pandey, A. (2009). *China's $1.7 trillion bet: China's external portfolio and dollar reserves*. New York: Council on Foreign Relations. http://www.cfr.org/content/publications/attachments/CGS_WorkingPaper_6_China.pdf. Accessed 30 July 2012.

Shaw, E. (1973). *Financial deepening in economic development*. New York: Oxford University Press.

Shih, V. (2007). *Factions and finance in China: Elite conflict and inflation*. Cambridge: Cambridge University Press.

Shih, V. (2009). Tools of survival: Sovereign wealth funds in Singapore and China. *Geopolitics, 14*(2), 328–344.

Shirk, S. (1993). *The political logic of reform in China*. Berkeley: University of California Press.

Sina. (n.d.). *Chao zhuquan chubei huobi zhongjie meiyuan bawang?* [Will a supra-national reserve currency end the dollar's hegemony?]. Beijing: Sina. http://survey.news.sina.com.cn/voteresult.php?pid=31974. Accessed 31 July 2012.

State Council. (2004, February 2). Guowuyuan guanyu tuijin ziben shichang gaige fazhan de jiutiao yijian [The state council's nine suggestions on moving forward the reform, opening and development of the capital markets]. *Renmin Ribao*. http://www.people.com.cn/GB/jingji/1037/2314920.html. Accessed 9 Aug 2013.

State Council. (2009, April 14). *Guowuyuan guanyu tuijin shanghai jiakuai fazhan xiandai fuwuye he xianjin zhizaoye jianshe guoji jinrong zhongxin he guoji hangyun zhongxin de yijian* [The State Council's opinion on the promotion of Shanghai's accelerated development of a modern service industry and an advanced manufacturing center, the construction of an International Financial Center and an International Shipping Center] (Document No. 19). Beijing: State Council. http://www.gov.cn/zwgk/2009-04/29/content_1299428.htm. Accessed 30 July 2012.

Stern, N., & Ferreira, F. (1997). The World Bank as 'intellectual actor'. In D. Kapur, J. Lewis, & R. Webb (Eds.), *The World Bank: Its first half century* (Vol. 2, pp. 523–609). Washington, DC: Brookings Institution Press.

Strange, S. (1971). *Sterling and British policy: A political study of an international currency in decline*. London: Oxford University Press.

Strange, S. (1973). IMF: Monetary managers. In R. Cox & H. Jacobson (Eds.), *The anatomy of influence: Decision making in international organization* (pp. 263–297). New Haven: Yale University Press.

Strange, S. (1982). Still an extraordinary power: America's role in a global monetary system. In R. Lombra & W. Witte (Eds.), *The political economy of international and domestic monetary relations* (pp. 73–93). Ames: Iowa State University Press.

Strange, S. (1986). *Casino capitalism*. Oxford: Blackwell.

Strange, S. (1988). *States and markets*. London: Pinter Publishers.

Strange, S. (1990). Finance, information and power. *Review of International Studies, 16*(3), 259–274.

Strauss-Kahn, D. (2010, July 12). *Asia and the global economy: Leading the way forward in the 21st century*, Opening remarks at the Asia 21 conference, Daejeon. http://www.imf.org/external/np/speeches/2010/071210.htm. Accessed 31 July 2012.

Stumm, M. (2011, March 4). World Bank: More responsibility for developing countries. Development and Cooperation. http://www.dandc.eu/en/article/how-voice-reform-came-about-world-bank. Accessed 31 July 2012.

Subacchi, P. (2010). *One currency, two systems: China's renminbi strategy* (Chatham House Briefing Paper). London: Chatham House. http://www.chathamhouse.org/sites/default/files/public/Research/International%20Economics/bp1010renminbi.pdf. Accessed 31 July 2012.

Takagi, S. (2011). Internationalising the yen, 1984–2003: Unfinished agenda or mission impossible?. In *Currency internationalisation: Lessons from the global financial crisis and prospects for the future in Asia and the Pacific* (BIS Paper, No. 61, pp. 75–85). Basel: Bank for International Settlements. http://www.bis.org/publ/bppdf/bispap61.pdf. Accessed 31 July 2012.

Tavlas, G. (1991). *On the international use of currencies: The case of the Deutsche mark* (Princeton Essays in International Finance, No. 181). Princeton: Princeton University. http://www.princeton.edu/~ies/IES_Essays/E181.pdf. Accessed 31 July 2012.

Terry, E. (2000). How Asia got rich: World Bank vs. Japanese industrial policy. *The Japanese Economy, 28*(2), 76–96.

TIC. (n.d.). Foreign portfolio holdings of US securities. Washington, DC: Department of the Treasury – Treasury International Capital System. http://www.treasury.gov/resource-center/data-chart-center/tic/Documents/shlhistdat.html. Accessed 18 Aug 2013.

Tsai, K., & Cook, S. (2005). Developmental dilemmas in China: Socialist transition and late liberalization. In S. Pekkanen & K. Tsai (Eds.), *Japan and China in the world political economy* (pp. 45–66). London: Routledge.

UN. (2003). *Monterrey consensus on financing for development*. New York: United Nations. http://www.un.org/esa/ffd/monterrey/MonterreyConsensus.pdf. Accessed 31 July 2012.

US Treasury. (2012, December 31). *Monthly statement of the public debt of the United States*, Washington, DC: Department of the Treasury. http://www.treasurydirect.gov/govt/reports/pd/mspd/2012/opds122012.pdf. Accessed 18 Aug 2013.

Vestergaard, J. (2011). *The World Bank and the emerging world order: Adjusting to multipolarity at the second decimal point* (DIIS Report). Copenhagen: Danish Institute for International Studies. http://www.diis.dk/graphics/publications/reports2011/rp2011-05-world-bank-voice-reform_web.pdf. Accessed 31 July 2012.

Wade, R. (1996). Japan, the World Bank, and the art of paradigm maintenance: The East Asian miracle in political perspective. *New Left Review, 217*, 3–35.

Wade, A. (2008, January 23). Time for the west to practise what it preaches. *Financial Times*. http://www.ft.com/intl/cms/s/0/5d347f88-c897-11dc-94a6-0000779fd2ac.html#axzz226d5oS3o. Accessed 31 July 2012.

Walter, A. (2006). Domestic sources of international monetary leadership. In D. Andrews (Ed.), *International monetary power* (pp. 51–71). Ithaca: Cornell University Press.

Walter, C., & Howie, F. (2003). *Privatizing China: The stock markets and their role in corporate reform*. Singapore: Wiley.

Walter, C., & Howie, F. (2011). *Red capitalism: The fragile financial foundation of China's extraordinary rise*. Singapore: Wiley.

Wang, J. (2007a). Zhongguo touzi gongsi 'fuchu shuimian' [The CIC emerges from the water]. *Liaowang, 41*, 61.

Wang, X. (2007b). China as a net creditor: An indication of strength or weaknesses? *China & World Economy, 15*(6), 22–36.

Wang, Q. (2009, March 27). G20 must look beyond the needs of the top 20. *The Times*. http://www.timesonline.co.uk/tol/comment/columnists/guest_contributors/article5982824.ece. Accessed 31 July 2012.

Wheatley, A. (2009a, February 9). China wants IMF to be tougher with rich states. *Reuters*. http://www.reuters.com/article/2009/02/09/g20-china-idUSPEK17709220090209. Accessed 31 July 2012.

Wheatley, J. (2009b, February 19). Brazil to supply oil to China for loans. *Financial Times*. http://www.ft.com/intl/cms/s/0/65f2d5b8-fedb-11dd-b19a-000077b07658.html. Accessed 31 July 2012.

White, G. (1988). State and market in China's socialist industrialisation. In G. White (Ed.), *Developmental states in East Asia* (pp. 153–192). Houndmills: MacMillan Press.

White, G., & Wade, R. (1988). Developmental states and markets in East Asia: An introduction. In G. White (Ed.), *Developmental states in East Asia* (pp. 1–29). Houndmills: MacMillan Press.

Williamson, J. (1990). What Washington means by policy reform. In J. Williamson (Ed.), *Latin American adjustment: How much has happened?* (pp. 7–20). Washington, DC: Institute for International Economics.

Wilson, J., & Anderlini, J. (2011, August 11). China's Safe now a main Munich Re shareholder. *Financial Times*. http://www.ft.com/intl/cms/s/0/e17eb524-c41f-11e0-b302-00144feabdc0.html#axzz226d5oS3o. Accessed 31 July 2012.

Wonacott, P. (2011, September 2). In Africa, U.S. watches China's rise. *Wall Street Journal*. http://online.wsj.com/article/SB10001424053111903392904576510271838147248.html. Accessed 31 July 2012.

Woo-Cumings, M. (1999). Introduction: Chalmers Johnson and the politics of nationalism and development. In M. Woo-Cumings (Ed.), *The developmental state* (pp. 1–31). Ithaca: Cornell University Press.

Woods, N. (2003a). The International Monetary Fund and World Bank. In M. Hawkesworth & M. Kogan (Eds.), *Encyclopedia of government and politics* (2nd ed., Vol. 2, pp. 953–968). London: Routledge.

Woods, N. (2003b). The United States and the international financial institutions: Power and influence within the World Bank and the IMF. In R. Foot, N. MacFarlane, & M. Mastanduno (Eds.), *US hegemony and international organizations* (pp. 93–114). Oxford: Oxford University Press.

World Bank. (1993). *The East Asian miracle: Economic growth and public policy*. Oxford: Oxford University Press.

World Bank. (2010, April 19). *World Bank group voice reform: Enhancing voice and participation of developing and transition countries in 2010 and beyond*. Paper prepared for the Development Committee meeting. Washington, DC: World Bank. http://siteresources.worldbank.org/DEVCOMMINT/Documentation/22553921/DC2010-006%28E%29Voice.pdf. Accessed 31 July 2012.

World Bank. (2011). *Annual report 2011*. Washington, DC: World Bank. http://siteresources.worldbank.org/EXTANNREP2011/Resources/8070616-1315496634380/WBAR11_YearInReview.pdf. Accessed 31 July 2012.

World Bank. (n.d.-a). *Boards of directors*. Washington, DC: World Bank. http://web.worldbank.org/WBSITE/EXTERNAL/EXTABOUTUS/ORGANIZATION/BODEXT/0,,pagePK:64020055~theSitePK:278036,00.html. Accessed 31 July 2012.

World Bank. (n.d.-b). *Boards of governors*. Washington, DC: World Bank. http://web.worldbank.org/WBSITE/EXTERNAL/EXTABOUTUS/0,,contentMDK:20873632~menuPK:8336903~pagePK:51123644~piPK:329829~theSitePK:29708,00.html. Accessed 31 July 2012.

World Bank. (n.d.-c). *How IBRD is financed*. Washington, DC: World Bank. http://web.worldbank.org/WBSITE/EXTERNAL/EXTABOUTUS/EXTIBRD/0,,contentMDK:21116541~menuPK:3126976~pagePK:64168445~piPK:64168309~theSitePK:3046012,00.html. Accessed 31 July 2012.

World Bank. (n.d.-d). *IDA replenishments*. Washington, DC: World Bank. http://web.worldbank.org/WBSITE/EXTERNAL/EXTABOUTUS/IDA/0,,contentMDK:21021125~menuPK:2842661~pagePK:51236175~piPK:437394~theSitePK:73154,00.html. Accessed 31 July 2012.

Xie, X. (2009, October 5). *Statement given at the eightieth meeting of the Development Committee*, Istanbul. http://web.worldbank.org/WBSITE/EXTERNAL/DEVCOMMEXT/0,,pagePK:64000837~piPK:64001152~theSitePK:277473~contentMDK:22632840,00.html. Accessed 31 July 2012.

Xinhua. (2006, March 16). *Zhonghua renmin gongheguo guomin jingji he shehui fazhan di shiyi ge wunian guihua gangyao* [Eleventh five-year plan for the development of the National Economy and Society of the People's Republic of China]. Beijing: Xinhua. http://www.gov.cn/ztzl/2006-03/16/content_228841.htm. Accessed 31 July 2012.

Xinhua. (2010, November 9). IMF chief names Chinese banker as his special advisor. http://www.china.org.cn/business/2010-11/09/content_21305745.htm. Accessed 31 July 2012.

Xinhua. (2012, June 28). China to issue 23 bln yuan sovereign bonds in Hong Kong. http://news.xinhuanet.com/english/china/2012-06/28/c_131681301.htm. Accessed 15 Aug 2013.

Xu, M. (2009). Building the Shanghai International Financial Centre: Strategic target, challenges and opportunities. In S. Young, D. Choi, J. Seade, & S. Shirai (Eds.), *Competition among financial centres in Asia-Pacific: Prospects, benefits, risks and policy challenges* (pp. 231–244). Singapore: Institute of Southeast Asian Studies.

Ye, G. (2012, January 8). HK approves first set of RQFII funds. *Financial Times*. http://www.ft.com/intl/cms/s/0/9aa4d2f8-3852-11e1-9d07-00144feabdc0.html#axzz1v8osjof8. Accessed 31 July 2012.

Yi, G. (2009, October 4). *Statement at the twentieth meeting of the International Monetary and Financial Committee*, Istanbul. http://www.imf.org/external/am/2009/imfc/statement/eng/chn.pdf. Accessed 31 July 2012.

Yi, G. (2011, April 16). *Statement given at the twenty-third meeting of the International Monetary and Financial Committee*, Washington, DC. http://www.imf.org/external/spring/2011/imfc/statement/eng/chn.pdf. Accessed 31 July 2012

Yiu, E. (2013, July 19). Investors want more details on Qianhai. *South China Morning Post*. http://www.scmp.com/business/china-business/article/1285700/investors-want-more-details-qianhai. Accessed 15 Aug 2013.

You, N., & Fu, J. (2009, March 17). Inject less money to IMF, China cautioned. *China Daily*. http://www.chinadaily.com.cn/bizchina/2009-03/17/content_7585135.htm. Accessed 31 July 2012.

Yu, Y. (2008, December 7). *Meiguo guozhai yu xiongmao zhaiquan* [US treasuries and panda bonds] (Policy Brief, No. 08083). Beijing: Research Center for International Finance.

Yu, J. (2013, January 23). Investors wary of new QDII prospects. *South China Morning Post*. http://www.scmp.com/business/money/markets-investing/article/1132555/investors-wary-new-qdii-prospects. Accessed 15 Aug 2013.

Yu, Y., & Gao, H. (2011). The internationalization of the renminbi. In Y.-W. Cheung & G. Ma (Eds.), *Asia and China in the global economy* (pp. 191–217). Hackensack: World Scientific.

Yuan, Z. (2009, February 27). Renminbi guojihua 'anzhan' [The dark war of the renminbi's internationalization]. *Jingji guancha bao*. http://www.eeo.com.cn/eeo/jjgcb/2009/03/02/130670.shtml. Accessed 31 July 2012.

Zhang, M. (2008, September 11). Shei lai zhuzi zhongguo yanghang? [Who will recapitalize China's Central Bank?]. *Financial Times Chinese*. http://www.ftchinese.com/story/001021882. Accessed 31 July 2012.

Zhang, M. (2009a). *Quanqiu jinrong weiji xia de zhongguo guoji jinrong xin zhanlüe* [The new Chinese international financial strategy in the international financial crisis] (Policy Brief, No. 09028). Beijing: Research Center for International Finance. Accessed 16 Apr 2009.

Zhang, T. (2009b, February 14). Zonghe guoli jueding renminbi guojihua [Comprehensive power decides the renminbi's internationalization]. *Zhengquan ribao*. http://news.xinhuanet.com/fortune/2009-02/14/content_10817296.htm. Accessed 31 July 2012.

Zhang, M., & He, F. (2009). China's sovereign wealth fund: Weakness and challenges. *China & World Economy, 17*(1), 101–116.

Zhang, H., & Li, T (2009, May 20). Ha Jiming: renminbi guojihua 'yi li wei zhu' [Ha Jiming: Giving priority to construction in the renminbi's internationalization]. *Caijing*. http://www.caijing.com.cn/2009-05-20/110169001.html. Accessed 31 July 2012.

Zheng, F. (2011, November 29). Chouzi 36 yi yuan: Baogang xianggang dianxin zhai faxing wanbi [CNY 3.6 bn raised: Baogang's Hong Kong dim sum bond issuance completed]. *Caixin Wang*. http://finance.caixin.com/2011-11-29/100332357.html. Accessed 31 July 2012.

Zhong, F. (2007). Chuanghuizhe ying you qi hui [Foreign exchange reserves should remain in the hands of their creators]. *Zhongguo qiyejia*, *19*, 32.

Zhongguo qiyejia wang. (2010, June 26). Xie Guozhong PK Li Daokui: renminbi guojihua zhi zheng [Xie Guozhong versus Li Daokui: The struggle to internationalize the renminbi]. http://finance.jrj.com.cn/people/2010/06/2610117673928.shtml. Accessed 31 July 2012.

Zhou, X. (2006). China's corporate bond market development: Lessons learned. In BIS, *Developing corporate bond markets in Asia*. Proceedings of a BIS/PBC seminar held in Kunming on 17–18 November 2005 (BIS Papers, No. 26, pp. 7–10). Basel: Bank for International Settlements. http://www.bis.org/arp/conf_0602.pdf. Accessed 9 Aug 2013.

Zhou, X. (2009, March 23). *Reform the international monetary system*. Beijing: People's Bank of China. http://www.pbc.gov.cn/publish/english/956/2009/20091229104425550619706/20091229104425550619706_.html. Accessed 31 July 2012.

Zhou, X. (2010a, April 24). *Statement given at the twenty-first meeting of the International Monetary and Financial Committee*, Washington, DC. http://www.imf.org/external/spring/2010/imfc/statement/eng/chn.pdf. Accessed 31 July 2012.

Zhou, X. (2010b, October 9). *Statement given at the twenty-second meeting of the International Monetary and Financial Committee*, Washington, DC. http://www.imf.org/external/am/2010/imfc/statement/eng/chn.pdf. Accessed 31 July 2010.

Zhu, C., & Lin, D. (2008, February 28). China needs sovereign pension fund – Govt scholar. *Reuters*. http://www.reuters.com/article/2008/02/28/china-pension-overseas-idUSHKG10968120080228. Accessed 31 July 2012.

Zoellick, R. (2010, September 29). *Democratizing development economics*. Washington, DC: Georgetown University. http://web.worldbank.org/WBSITE/EXTERNAL/NEWS/0,,contentMDK:22716997~pagePK:34370~piPK:42770~theSitePK:4607,00.html. Accessed 31 July 2012.

Zysman, J. (1983). *Governments, markets, and growth: Financial systems and the politics of industrial change*. Ithaca: Cornell University Press.

Printed by Printforce, the Netherlands